Education Research on Trial

Education research is a scientific field in crisis. The foundation of the current crisis is a long-time perception that too much of the work of educational researchers fails to meet minimum standards of scientific rigor. This perception constitutes the "bad reputation" from which the field of education research suffers. Long-simmering scientific doubts became a full-blown crisis, however, when critics—mostly critics from outside the field—recently launched charges that education research has failed to provide a solid evidence base for the improvement of educational practice, in part because educational researchers have been preoccupied with the wrong questions and in part because much of their research has been based on the wrong research methods. We see, then, that the crisis of confidence in the quality of education research goes hand in hand with a crisis of confidence in the quality of American education. The solution to both sets of shortcomings, critics maintain, is to pose different research questions and address them with more "rigorous" scientific methods. The charges about the shortcomings of education research and the proposed means of improving it are the subject of this book.

Pamela Barnhouse Walters is the James H. Rudy Professor of Sociology and Director of the Center for Education and Society at Indiana University.

Annette Lareau is the Stanley I. Sheerr Term Professor in the Department of Sociology at the University of Pennsylvania.

Sheri H. Ranis is Senior Research Officer in the U.S. Programs/Education Division of the Bill & Melinda Gates Foundation.

Education Research on Trial

Policy Reform and the
Call for Scientific Rigor

Edited by
Pamela Barnhouse Walters
Annette Lareau
Sheri H. Ranis

NEW YORK AND LONDON

First published 2009
by Routledge
270 Madison Ave, New York, NY 10016

Simultaneously published in the UK
by Routledge
2 Park Square, Milton Park, Abingdon, Oxon OX14 4RN

Routledge is an imprint of the Taylor & Francis Group, an informa business

© 2009 Taylor & Francis

Typeset in Minion by
Keystroke, 28 High Street, Tettenhall, Wolverhampton
Printed and bound in the United States of America on acid-free paper by
Edwards Brothers, Inc.

All rights reserved. No part of this book may be reprinted or reproduced or utilized in any form or by any electronic, mechanical, or other means, now known or hereafter invented, including photocopying and recording, or in any information storage or retrieval system, without permission in writing from the publishers.

Trademark Notice: Product or corporate names may be trademarks or registered trademarks, and are used only for identification and explanation without intent to infringe.

Library of Congress Cataloging in Publication Data
Education research on trial : policy reform and the call for scientific rigor / Pamela Barnhouse Walters, Annette Lareau, Sheri H. Ranis, editors. — 1st ed.
p. cm.
Includes bibliographical references and index.
1. Education–Research–United States. I. Walters, Pamela Barnhouse.
II. Lareau, Annette. III. Ranis, Sheri H.
LB1028.25.U6E34 2008
370.72073–dc22
2008031611

ISBN10: 0-415-98988-4 (hbk)
ISBN10: 0-415-98989-2 (pbk)
ISBN10: 0-203-92868-7 (ebk)

ISBN13: 978-0-415-98988-6 (hbk)
ISBN13: 978-0-415-98989-3 (pbk)
ISBN13: 978-0-203-92868-4 (ebk)

Contents

Acknowledgments	ix
Introduction PAMELA BARNHOUSE WALTERS AND ANNETTE LAREAU	1
PART I The Politics of Knowledge	15

1 The Politics of Science: Battles for Scientific Authority in the Field of Education Research 17
PAMELA BARNHOUSE WALTERS

   Walters argues that the current debates about the quality of education research and the best ways to improve it do not turn only on issues of the scientific merits of competing positions. The debates are part of the political and social struggles among groups of scientific experts and between policymakers and scientific experts over who gets to decide what counts as science and to claim scientific legitimacy within the research field.

2 A History of Efforts to Improve the Quality of Federal Education Research: From Gardner's Task Force to the Institute of Education Sciences 51
MARIS A. VINOVSKIS

   Vinovskis shows that the current critique of the quality of education research is related in important ways to recurring dissatisfaction on the part of federal lawmakers and bureaucrats with the decisions and priorities of the federal agencies that provide the bulk of federal funding for education research.

PART II Seeking Rigor; Finding Rigor   81

3   Assessing Quality in Educational Journals   83
BARBARA SCHNEIDER

Schneider addresses the question of whether the quality of education research is as bad as its critics charge by comparing the scientific standards and processes in place at major education journals with the standards and processes in place in journals in other fields generally considered to be more scientific. She finds the education journals to be comparably rigorous.

4   Can Non-randomized Studies Provide Evidence of Causal Effects? A Case Study Using the Regression Discontinuity Design   105
LARRY V. HEDGES AND JENNIFER HANIS-MARTIN

While in sympathy with the call to make education research more rigorous, Hedges and Hanis-Martin show that randomized controlled trials are not the only way to rigorously assess causal relationships about education. They illustrate the usefulness of regression discontinuity models for assessing causality in conditions in which random assignment is not possible.

5   Blending Quality and Utility: Lessons Learned from the Education Research Debates   125
SHERI H. RANIS

Ranis shows that the debates about the *quality* of education research have been propelled by and conflated with debates about the *utility* of education research in ways often unacknowledged. She demonstrates that research utility became a "resonant problematic" that provided a powerful justification for the movement to improve the quality of education research.

PART III Toward a More Comprehensive Understanding of Science and Policy   143

6   Narrow Questions, Narrow Answers: The Limited Value of Randomized Controlled Trials for Education Research   145
ANNETTE LAREAU

Lareau argues that the education sciences movement has misapplied the medical model to education research. She suggests there is a need for more attention to a broader array of questions about meaning, process, and interactional dynamics and greater attention to issues of implementation.

7 A Quixotic Quest? Philosophical Issues in Assessing the Quality of Education Research 163
D. C. PHILLIPS

Phillips demonstrates that the current drive to establish a single model of scientific research in education takes an overly-simplistic view of the nature of "science," in the process ignoring the complexities inherent in studying the intrinsically social and cultural dynamics of schooling. He calls the search for a single model of scientific research a "quixotic quest."

8 Education Research That Matters: Influence, Scientific Rigor, and Policymaking 197
PAMELA BARNHOUSE WALTERS AND ANNETTE LAREAU

Walters and Lareau identify the studies and lines of research that have been highly influential within the scholarly community of educational researchers as well as the studies that have had a substantial impact on educational policy and practice. They show that broadly-framed inquiries generally have the most lasting impact on both scholarship and on policy and practice, and that it takes a special set of political and social conditions for even "good" research to shape educational policy and practice.

Appendices

The selections in the appendices are portions of much longer federal documents that constitute key elements of the recent federal reforms to improve education research. The first three are the key definitions of "scientific" research that were written into federal legislation, and the last is a succinct statement of the view by federal lawmakers and bureaucrats of the problem that needs to be solved.

Appendix A The Definition of "Scientifically Based Research" in the No Child Left Behind Act of 2001 221
Appendix B The Definitions of "Scientifically Based Research" in the Education Sciences Reform Act of 2002 223
Appendix C Mission and Functions of the Institute of Education Sciences, as Detailed in the Education Sciences Reform Act of 2002 225

Appendix D Selection from Request for Proposals for Predoctoral
            Interdisciplinary Research Training Programs in the
            Education Sciences, Issued by the Institute of Education
            Sciences in 2004   227

Notes on Contributors   231

Index   235

Acknowledgments

This book seeks to show the importance of the political and institutional context in shaping ideas. In a play within a play, our own ideas were developed in a particular context. A number of different individuals and institutions played a key role in helping this book come forth. In 2000, Craig Calhoun, the President of the Social Science Research Council, and Ellen Condliffe Lagemann, at that time the President of the National Academy of Education, decided that the SSRC and the NAE should join forces to establish a study committee on education research. At their invitation, Pamela Barnhouse Walters and Larry V. Hedges agreed to co-chair the committee, and an outstanding group of scholars drawn from schools of education and social science disciplines were recruited to serve as members of the committee. The Spencer Foundation provided the committee with an initial planning grant and with later funds to support its efforts, and the committee's work was supported by the talented program staff of the SSRC, including, notably, Sheri H. Ranis. We are grateful to the SSRC and to the Spencer Foundation for the provision of financial and institutional support.

With that support, a group of researchers from diverse fields met regularly over a 4-year period to take stock of the state of education research, with particular attention to issues of the quality of the research produced. Some of those voices from around the table are represented here: in addition to the co-chairs, committee members who are contributors to this volume include Maris Vinovskis and Annette Lareau. In the course of the many conversations, we learned a great deal from a number of scholars whose voices are not represented in this book: Carol Weiss, Robert Levine, Michael Cole, Harris Cooper, Helen Ladd, James Farr, Lowell Hargens, Carol Greenhouse, and Robert Boruch.

Although it is unlikely that all of these scholars would agree with all that we have written here, they have enriched our thinking. In addition, a number of scholars came to meet with the committee, including David Labaree, Margaret Eisenhart, Jane Junn, Henry Small, Lisa Towne, and Denis C. Phillips. Their presentations were also valuable. Finally, we acknowledge the special debt we owe to Larry Hedges, who, with Pamela Barnhouse Walters, co-chaired the committee and who played a critical role in the development of this book.

The Center for Advanced Study in the Behavioral Sciences offered a wonderful intellectual home for 2005–2006 for Pamela Barnhouse Walters and Annette Lareau to make this book a reality. We are grateful to Douglas McAdam for his pivotal role in bringing us to the Center, to Claude Steele, Cynthia Brandt, and Linda Jack for their support during our fellowship year, and to the other fellows in the 2005–2006 class for the rich intellectual environment they provided which helped this book take shape. Walters is also grateful for a 2007–2008 resident fellowship from the Spencer Foundation, which provided support for the completion of the manuscript and a warm intellectual environment in which to discuss the field of education research.

Closer to home, Indiana University and the University of Maryland (Lareau's former university) have provided institutional support for Walters and Lareau, respectively. Rebecca Holtz provided valuable editorial assistance. Any errors are the responsibility of the co-editors, and the positions and/or viewpoints they express herein are their own and not necessarily those of their employers or employing institutions.

Introduction

PAMELA BARNHOUSE WALTERS AND ANNETTE LAREAU

When the smoke and dust had settled, it became clear that the field of education research had been hit by a major earthquake. Roughly between 1995 and 2002, numerous reports citing scientific deficiencies in education research or suggesting that it was a field in need of rehabilitation were issued.[1] Critics of education research charged that the designs on which much of the research is based are inferior, the quality of the data typically collected is shoddy, and the results of most studies are not to be believed or trusted. To make matters worse, critics charged, the poor quality of education research rendered it useless as a scientific guide to policymakers' and practitioners' decisions about how to improve education in the United States. Consider, for example, the argument expressed in a recent U.S. Department of Education document that the education research community has not produced a "solid research base" to guide policymakers' decisions, resulting in those decisions often being "guided by personal experience, folk wisdom, and ideology."[2]

The critiques gained momentum and legitimacy from each other, and led to a series of efforts to remedy the scientific deficiencies identified by those reports. Between 1999 and 2002 a series of federal laws were passed that put in place new definitions of "scientifically based research" or "scientific validity" in education research.[3] Those in the vanguard of these legislative efforts to rehabilitate the field of education research proposed a new "gold standard" for rigorous research: the randomized controlled trial. They also placed high priority on research that would be relevant or useful to educators in the field. The implications of these remedies are still unfolding but, at least potentially, they stand to significantly change core aspects of the field of education research: what counts for legitimate knowledge, what research is funded, the standards for training of young scholars, and the studies taken into account in policy formation.

What caused this earthquake? Many saw it as a long-overdue awakening of the education research community to the problem of the low quality of research in education. Others saw it as a move that was itself deficient on scientific grounds, especially because it underestimated and misunderstood the importance of research methods other than randomized controlled trials. Regardless of position on the legitimacy of the accusations about the poor quality of education research or the means proposed to move the field to stronger scientific ground, however, few in the education research community remained untouched by the controversies. The scathing reports were widely read by educational researchers and widely discussed in the field's professional journals, as were the ensuing calls for new standards of scientific rigor to be adopted by educational researchers. As well they should. Because new federal guidelines about what constituted good methods for education research were backed up by the considerable federal funding the agencies in question provided, the new "gold standard" had great significance.

But, as some authors suggest in this book, this major earthquake was not just a methodological war waged between scientists, to be decided principally on the basis of the scientific merits of the competing arguments. Instead, the fissures and shifts in the grounds for research had sources other than the technical weaknesses of research. Indeed, as this perspective suggests, if one looks carefully, one sees that the fissures and fault lines revealed much about the social and political underpinnings of scientific norms about education research and the allegedly scientific-neutral controversies about them. Moreover, the critiques of education research and attempts to rehabilitate it have been echoed, albeit in different ways, in other related scientific fields similarly devoted to social welfare or health. Hence the case of the scientific controversies about education research is illuminating for many research fields.

The long-term critique of the quality of education research—the charge that it is shoddy and weak—and the recent call for the greater use of "scientific methods" constitute an important example of a scientific movement, an example we call the education sciences movement. This movement provides an important and useful opportunity to consider the conditions under which fields of scientific research are subject to critique and subject to attempts to remake them. "Progress" and "improvement" in the practice of science are often understood to proceed as a gradual change in the norms of a scientific community. Sources of change in scientific norms are important to understand because they shape and regulate the work of every member of the research community in question. For example, they constitute a taken-for-granted consensus about the general problems that warrant scientists' attention, the specific questions that should be asked, and the methods that are most appropriate when addressing those questions. That typical process of gradual change in scientific norms is, however, occasionally punctuated by an intense period of questioning, a crisis of confidence about the previously taken-for-granted norms that had governed the practice of science within the community. Scientific controversies bring to the fore the tacit, often unstated, scientific-technical assumptions of a field as well as render more visible the factors that maintain them or, in some situations, transform them. Thus periods of challenge provide opportunities for studying the foundation of the routine practice of science as well as the factors that produce significant challenges to those rules and standards and the process by which new scientific rules and standards get put in place.

Alongside the scientific questions raised by the critique of the field of education research, the purpose of this book is to examine the social and political conditions that gave rise to or fueled the critique, to review the debate over what should be done to improve education research, and to reflect on the new research infrastructure that has been developed to support greater use of randomized controlled trials in education research. By reflecting on the conditions under which such calls for scientific rigor occur, the limits and possibilities of various strategies for promoting better research methods, and the social, philosophical, and political underpinnings of the scientific enterprise, we address important and long-term issues about the conduct of "science" that transcend the specifics of the crisis in education research. The issues we address are germane to many other scientific fields, especially those that bridge basic and applied research, such as medicine, agriculture, criminal justice, and social welfare. Thus the lessons about the genesis of the debates about how to improve the field of education, the role of rigorous education research in those attempts at improvement, and the debates over the best methods for education research are of interest in other applied fields as well.

Indeed, these other fields are often held up as exemplars for education of "evidence-based fields" in which practices have been transformed as a result of experimental research that identified more effective interventions. Medicine is the most-cited exemplar, based on the argument that medical practice was transformed when double-blind trials led to the identification and later wide adoption of effective new drug therapies for the treatment of illness. The hope is that bringing the same tradition of experimental research on the effectiveness of interventions, treatments, and programs to education will lead to significant improvements in the quality of American education and thus significant advances in achievement on the part of American students (see, e.g., Committee on a Feasibility Study 1999).

Before we discuss the major issues that will be addressed in this volume, let us review briefly the major developments that constitute the education sciences movement. There are many ways in which randomized controlled trials have come to be seen as a legitimate, often the only legitimate, approach to doing research on education.

Federal lawmakers and bureaucrats have long expressed concern with the quality of the education research that has been supported with funding from the federal government. A particularly persistent criticism has been its failure to provide good evidence to policymakers and practitioners. This has led to and is reflected in a series of attempts to reorganize the main federal agency responsible for the bulk of federal funding for education research, which before 1979 was the U.S. Department of Health, Education, and Welfare and after 1979 was the U.S. Department of Education. As historian Maris Vinovskis describes in Chapter 2, federal policymakers have been particularly unhappy with the research office within the U.S. Department of Education, the Office of Educational Research and Improvement. Originally established in 1979, when the U.S. Department of Education was created, it was reorganized in 1985 and again in 1994 in an attempt to improve the quality of the research it funded and to better disseminate the findings of that research to "customers"—especially practitioners in state and local education agencies throughout the country. The most recent transformation of that same office occurred in 2002, when it was abolished and replaced with the Institute of Education Sciences (IES), a new research arm intended to transform education into an evidence-based field. As we shall see, many of the steps taken to establish randomized controlled trials as the new gold standard for education research originate from the IES.

Alongside brewing discontent among federal bureaucrats and lawmakers about the poor performance of the federal agency charged with oversight of much of the nation's research on education was a brewing discontent within the education research community itself about the poor quality of education research. A telling early reflection of that discontent was the publication in 1993 of an article by Carl Kaestle titled "The Awful Reputation of Education Research." Although reporting primarily the "low regard" in which education research was held by policymakers and practitioners, the article also named a key concern held within the education research community about its "awful reputation" within the community of university scholars and scientists. That is, educational researchers were held in low regard by their peers in other academic units within the university.

The education research community took a series of steps that constituted, in essence, attempts at self-assessment about the quality and scientific integrity of education research. Important milestones here include the constitution in 1995 of a study group by the National Academy of Education, a scientific society that includes those widely acknowledged as the leading scholars of education, to find ways to improve education research (see Viadero 1996). Published in 1999 as *Issues in Education Research* (Lagemann and Shulman, eds.), the report endorsed a new model of research for the education research community that "focused explicitly on solving current problems of [educational] practice" (Viadero 1999a). This stance represented an incorporation by a group of leaders within the education research community of the call from the policymaker community to make education research more useful to them and to practitioners.

In the meantime, the National Research Council (NRC) of the National Academy of Sciences had constituted a study group to identify new priorities for education research. In 1999 the study group released its report, titled *Improving Student Learning: A Strategic Plan for Education Research and Its Utilization*, in which it outlined the need to make research more useful. It called for a focused agenda for education research and more sustained attention to the identification of solutions to educational problems, but stopped far short of endorsing particular research methods to do so (see Olson 1999). It was, however, a call from yet another quarter to focus education research more directly on the questions of greatest interest to policymakers and practitioners. At the same time as the NRC panel was going about its work, the Office of Educational Research and Improvement tasked its advisory board, the National Educational Research Policy and Priorities Board (NERPPB), to evaluate its research operations. In its report, also released in 1999, the NERPPB recommended that funding be focused on fewer priority areas, that more resources be devoted to education research, that a more rigorous scientific review process be put in place, and that more research be focused on solving the real-world problems educators confront in the classroom (Viadero 1999b). There was a call for, in effect, greater scientific rigor for education research (again, absent the call for a particular method to achieve that end), combined with the now-frequent call for education research to be more explicitly focused on educational policy and practice.

The first step, in which this concern to make research more useful to policymakers and practitioners was fully merged with a prescriptive attempt to identify the scientific methods to improve the quality of the research, was the passage of a landmark piece of federal legislation in 1999, the Reading Excellence Act. The act provided a definition of scientifically-based research that applied to *reading* research. The definition was fairly broad—it used terms such as "empirical methods" and "rigorous data analyses"—and did not name a particular method or set of methods that qualified as "scientific" or "rigorous."[4] Its importance for purposes of the present discussion is largely that it set a precedent for subsequent action to define through legislation the meaning of scientifically-based research that applied to all of education research, not just research on reading.

The Reading Excellence Act was followed by a piece of proposed (but unpassed) legislation sometimes referred to as the "original Castle bill" that would have reorganized the U.S. Department of Education and, along the way, set a new—and quite narrow—standard (from the perspective of most in the scientific community) about what constitutes scientific research in education more broadly. To try to inform the legislative process and inject into it an understanding of "science" from scientists' vantage point, the NRC convened a panel to define what constitutes scientific quality in education research, funded by NERPPB (see Eisenhart and Towne 2003). The volume that resulted from that panel's deliberations was not released until 2002, but parts of it were circulated in prepublication form in 2001, in time to influence some of the key legislative developments (described below).

The next legislative step, and one that garnered far more attention than the Reading Excellence Act, was the 2001 passage of the No Child Left Behind (NCLB) Act. Initially widely celebrated, NCLB quickly became a hotly-contested piece of legislation as many schools and school districts found themselves subject to strong disincentives for failure to meet strict new standards for student performance. What is obscured by the public's overwhelming attention to charges that NCLB's yardsticks for student performance are unreasonable are the enormous changes that NCLB instituted in the conduct of education research. The definition of "scientifically based research" that became law with the passage of NCLB uses a language of "experimental and quasi-experimental designs" and explicitly establishes a preference for "random-assignment experiments." In effect, NCLB gave the federal government an unusual degree of authority for setting standards for what constitutes good science and an unusual degree of control over the conduct of "science." In short order, randomized controlled trials became the "gold standard" for education research, the hallmark of "rigorous" science.

NCLB's reach into the practice of research came through a back door: The bill regulated funding for educational programs but stipulated that only those instructional reforms that are "grounded in scientifically-based research" could receive federal dollars. That is, the bill gave the federal government the authority to regulate the decisions of educational practitioners at the state and local level, requiring that they adopt for classroom use only those educational programs, treatments, and interventions that had been proven effective for the purpose of advancing student achievement, largely on the basis of randomized controlled trials.

In 2002 the National Academy of Sciences released its report *Scientific Research in Education* (Shavelson and Towne 2002). Although the definitions of and guidelines for "scientific research" contained in the report are far broader than the definitions contained in the NCLB legislation, it generated an enormous controversy within the education research community.[5] As Eisenhart and Towne (2003) note, many educational researchers were deeply troubled that certain methods of research were labeled "nonscientific" even as their contribution to knowledge about education was noted. These issues were heatedly debated in packed sessions at the American Educational Research Association annual meetings in the spring of 2002 and again in 2003, and an entire 2002 special issue of *Educational Researcher* was devoted to discussion of scientific research in education (Jacob and White 2002).

The legislative drive to make education research more scientifically based was reinforced in an additional piece of legislation passed in 2002, the Education Sciences Reform Act (ESRA), which laid out a set of criteria for what counts as scientifically-based research in education. Again, high priority was placed on "random assignment experiments," which the legislation identified as the only designs adequate for purposes of making "claims of causal relationships." This time the limitations applied directly to the research community: those scholars whose proposed studies were based on random-assignment methods would receive the highest priority for funding.[6]

Through its regulation of the ways in which classroom practices must be supported with the findings of "rigorous" research and its regulation of the kinds of research that have highest priority for funding, these developments have been highly consequential for the kinds of investigations and studies that can be mounted about education. And the implications extend far beyond the research that receives federal funds: The new research priorities established by the federal government set a national tone for what kinds of research should be seen as legitimate. All in all, the government's unequivocal embrace of randomized controlled trials is highly consequential, whether for better or worse.[7]

Many in the education research community responded loudly and critically to these developments.[8] In the period since NCLB and the ESRA were passed and the education sciences movement was decisively launched, backed by the power of the federal purse, a number of people have raised concerns about the attack on education research and, especially, the promotion of randomized controlled trials as the method of choice for the education research community. In addition to the previously-noted 2002 special issue of *Educational Researcher* devoted to a discussion of Scientific research in education, there have been three other special issues of education journals devoted to the debate over scientific research in education: *Qualitative Inquiry* in 2004, *Educational Theory* in 2005, and the *Teachers College Record* in 2005. Further, in response to the heated debates over the quality of education research and over federal attempts to set scientific standards for the field, in 2006 the professional society that represents the vast and diverse community of educational researchers, the American Educational Research Association (AERA), issued its own position on standards for reporting empirical research.[9]

Too often, however, those who have engaged in this debate have accepted the terms offered (implicitly) by the critics: that research is a technical and neutral enterprise and that the solution to the problem of insufficiently-clear research findings includes better tools to measure educational outcomes and better designs for assessing the impact of educational interventions on those outcomes. For example, some critics assert that the promoters of randomized controlled trials do not properly understand what constitutes "science" or that they fail to acknowledge the difficulty of assessing complex social processes with random-assignment methods (see, e.g., Erickson and Gutierrez 2002; Berliner 2002). Many critics of the education sciences argue that a full causal analysis of processes in education must augment randomized controlled trials with qualitative research (see, e.g., Maxwell 2004; Erickson 2005; Howe 2004; Ryan and Hood 2004). Still others have embraced the call for more rigorous quantitative research while at the same time arguing that additional methods can be considered "rigorous" and can yield valid findings about causal relationships, especially regression discontinuity methods (see, e.g., Schneider et al. 2007).

The contributors to this volume represent a range of viewpoints about whether the field of education research is scientifically wanting and, if so, what should be done to improve it. Despite important differences among the contributors, they show in various ways that the existing debates have overly focused on the charges that education research is deficient on technical-neutral grounds and disagree with the position that a single methodological "gold standard" exists that, if widely adopted, will improve the quality of education research. Some chapters in this volume sketch the historical, political, and social underpinnings of the current scientific controversies about education research. Some critically assess the charges that the main problem with the field of education research is that most studies are insufficiently rigorous. Some agree that education research needs to become more scientifically rigorous while nonetheless providing important correctives to either the problem diagnosis or the recommended remedy offered by proponents of randomized controlled trials. Some argue that the conception of science and scientific inquiry on which the current debates are premised is overly narrow and simplistic, failing to take into account the social and cultural complexities of schools and schooling. Taken together, their contributions shed new light on the reasons why education research is currently considered to be in trouble and help us to better understand the limits as well as the possibilities of proposed new standards for scientific rigor.

The Themes of This Book

The adoption of new research standards at the federal level in the U.S. Department of Education is highly consequential for the education research community as well as the community of education policymakers and practitioners. The chapters in this volume provide new perspectives on the recent methodological debates about whether and how to make education research more scientific and rigorous. The chapters are organized into three parts, each one corresponding to different aspects of the debate over the quality of education research and what can and should be done to improve it.

Part I provides two analyses of the historical backdrop to the current debates, both of which highlight the shifting political nature of knowledge and show that standards of knowledge are always constructed historically. Sociologist Pamela Barnhouse Walters shows that the very effort to introduce scientific rigor into education research can be fruitfully conceived as a social movement. Long-standing attempts by the education research community to establish the field as scientifically authoritative precipitated a crisis of legitimacy in education research that, in turn, made possible federal lawmakers' and bureaucrats' success in establishing *for* the scientific community new standards for scientific rigor. Those efforts by "non-scientists" to establish scientific standards for a scientific community also depended on an alliance between a group of acknowledged scientific experts, lawmakers, and bureaucrats. Walters' chapter thus provides a critical assessment of the supposed technical neutrality of the terms of the current debate.

As historian Maris Vinovskis shows in his chapter, federal legislators and bureaucrats have not historically held a consistent set of expectations about what they want from the education research community. Vinovskis' analysis of recurring federal efforts dating to the early 1960s to transform the key federal agencies charged with funding and monitoring the quality of education research reveals that federal legislators have changed their minds, early and often, about what they wanted from education research. Further, he offers a useful discussion of the political roadblocks that interfered with past efforts and the policy legacies of earlier reforms of the federal education bureaucracy with which those who currently wish to rehabilitate education research must contend. Taken together, Walters and Vinovskis remind us that the recent calls for "rigor" took place in a particular historical and political context and were shaped by prior historical developments both within the federal government and within the education research community. Their attention to the historically- and politically-contingent nature of knowledge suggests that the overwhelming focus in the current methodological controversies on "scientific merit" is misplaced, since it fails to acknowledge the politics of science.

The chapters in Part II address head-on the merits of the charge that education research fails to meet commonly-accepted standards of scientific rigor or the merits of the assertion that randomized controlled trials are the only scientifically-legitimate means of establishing causality in education. Despite important differences among them, the authors of each chapter share a concern with the problem diagnosis of education as a particularly low-quality field or a concern with the way that recent efforts to improve the quality of education research have been implemented. Sociologist Barbara Schneider directly addresses the question of whether the field of education research deserves its bad reputation by considering whether the scientific controls in place in the major journals of the field compare favorably with prevailing scientific norms. Journals are important not only because they are the main way in which research findings are disseminated; they are also the main venue for vetting and evaluating scientific research in a field. Her comparison of journals in education to journals in other fields shows, importantly, that education journals do not differ markedly from journals in fields such as psychology and sociology in many standardly-accepted markers of scientific rigor, including selectivity, the peer review process, and the selection of editors. Educational psychologists Larry V. Hedges and Jennifer Hanis-Martin provide an analysis of an extant postdoctoral fellowship program for education scholars using a regression discontinuity design. Their study demonstrates the utility of an alternative to randomized controlled trials under conditions when it is not possible to conduct random assignment. They thus make the case that approaches other than randomized controlled trials can be considered "rigorous" and "scientific." Sheri Ranis, a researcher who currently serves on the funding side of education research, examines how the debates about the quality of education research have been propelled by a largely-unacknowledged set of assumptions that "good" research is research that is useful to educational policymakers and practitioners. The conflation of quality issues with utility issues has clouded the debates about the range of appropriate methods for education research, but at the same time is providing a compelling justification for the field to pursue applied research endeavors. Ranis shows that the utility arguments have privileged some research questions over others and have refocused the field's attention on the identification and testing of proposed solutions to educational problems seen as particularly pressing.

The chapters in Part III constitute, in effect, a call for a more comprehensive understanding of science and its scope, as well as its connection to policy and practice. Sociologist Annette Lareau's chapter demonstrates that our studies of "what works" have to take into account the social and political context in which students and schools are embedded, a process that requires a range of methodological approaches. Above all, our ability to design policies and practices that work with (rather than against) existing institutional arrangements requires a sophisticated understanding of those institutional arrangements, a process that cannot be studied via random assignment. She suggests that a diversity of styles of research is necessary to address the broad range of questions and topics that matter in education, and that random-assignment experiments do not easily travel beyond the laboratory to real-world educational settings.

The chapter by philosopher Denis C. Phillips shows that the issues that need to be confronted when thinking about quality and rigor are neither simple nor clear. By highlighting an important set of epistemological and philosophical foundations to the education research enterprise, Phillips shows that the intrinsic social and cultural nature of educational activity irrevocably alters the kinds of knowledge that can be collected, particularly in contrast to the physical sciences. He also suggests that there are complexities in the judging of research that sometimes are ignored, especially by those who have diagnosed education research as suffering from ill health. For Phillips, the focus on rigor, the call for research to have more of a practical impact, and the emphasis on causation are a "quixotic quest." He calls on researchers to "resist" the lure of a single model and offers a thoughtful reflection on important challenges in the effort to improve education research.

The final chapter, by sociologists Annette Lareau and Pamela Barnhouse Walters, turns on its head the recent focus on what is wrong with the field of education research and instead asks what studies and lines of scholarship have done the most to move the field forward, what kinds of research have in the past made the biggest impact on educational policy and practice, and under what conditions can research findings inform policy and practice. They conclude that both the low-quality and low-utility charges have been overstated, and show that research on the policy development process indicates that even under optimal conditions—that is, when "good" research findings are readily available—empirical findings play a much smaller part in policy development than is generally acknowledged by those who are attempting to turn education into an evidence-based field.

Taken as a whole, then, the chapters contained within this book challenge the reader to rethink the recent charges that the field of education research is remiss on purely scientific grounds and the recent call from some quarters for educational researchers to widely adopt randomized controlled trials as *the* method of choice. The analyses contained herein show that one can agree that not all education research is of high quality, and perhaps even agree that the field needs to become more scientifically rigorous, without accepting the problem diagnosis that motivated the recent federal attempts to legislate a particular definition of good science or without accepting the premise that randomized controlled trials are the "gold standard" for education research.

Again, the particular case we explore here—the state of the education research enterprise—is a lens that provides opportunities for reflecting on broader questions about controversies over norms of research in scientific fields more generally. Education research is not the only applied and multidisciplinary field of research in which research findings may, under some conditions, prove useful to practitioners and policymakers. Thus the controversy within the education research community over what constitutes appropriate norms of scientific research, and the difficulty of coming to an agreement over appropriate standards of research, have implications for other contentious fields such as social work, criminology, and health care. The current debate offers important opportunities for reflecting on the definition and meaning of science, on the ways in which science is shaped by politics, on the limitations of political intervention into the practice of science, and of the conditions under which the meaning and definition of science are politically contested. These are issues that transcend the particulars of the current debate over the quality of education research and what should be done to improve it. If the notion of randomized controlled trials as the gold standard for education research disappeared tomorrow, these issues would still be with us.

Notes

1. The reports, which were sponsored by a range of governmental and non-governmental groups, are described in more detail below.
2. The statement appears in a 2004 call for proposals for a new Predoctoral Interdisciplinary Research Training Program in the Education Sciences. See http://www.ed.gov/offices/OESE/REA/overview.html. Retrieved December 21 2007. The relevant selection is included in Appendix D to this volume.
3. See the Appendices for relevant selections from these legislative acts.
4. See http://www.ed.gov/offices/OESE/REA/overview.html. Retrieved December 27, 2007.
5. See the executive summary of *Scientific Research in Education* for a summary statement of the scientific principles that the National Academy of Sciences panel established as a guide for education research. See http://books.nap.edu/catalog/10236.html. Retrieved December 15, 2007.
6. For good summaries of the charges about education research made by many of its critics and important examples of the unfavorable comparisons made between education research and other scholarly fields often considered by its critics to be more "scientific," see Whitehurst (2003) and

the statement about the shortcomings of education research contained in the 2004 IES call for proposals for a new predoctoral training program. The relevant passage is included in Appendix D.
7. For a good working definition of what officially counts for "quality" research in education in the federal environment established by No Child Left Behind and the Education Sciences Reform Act, see the revised 2006 standards for evaluating education research that were developed by the What Works Clearinghouse, a body set up by the IES to rate existing education research according to the newly-established criteria for scientific legitimacy. These standards are meant to inform the consumers of education research about what kinds of studies should be seen as legitimate and trustworthy.
8. The article by Margaret Eisenhart and Lisa Towne, published in 2003 as "Contestation and Change in National Policy on 'Scientifically Based' Education Research" in *Educational Researcher*, provides a helpful discussion of reactions within the education research community to *Scientific Research in Education* (*SRE*) and offers a defense of the positions adopted within that volume. Importantly, they show that *SRE* establishes a broader definition of "scientifically based research" than either NCLB or ESRA.
9. See "Standards for Reporting on Empirical Social Science Research in AERA Publications," adopted June 2006 by the Council of the American Educational Research Association. Retrieved December 20, 2007 (http://www.aera.net/uploadedFiled/opportunities/StandardsforReporting EmpiricalSocialScience_PDF.pdf).

References

Berliner, David C. 2002. "Educational Research: The Hardest Science of All." *Educational Researcher* 31:18–20.
Committee on a Feasibility Study for a Strategic Education Research Program. 1999. *Improving Student Learning: A Strategic Plan for Education Research and Its Utilization.* National Research Council. Washington, DC: National Academy Press.
Educational Researcher. 2002. Theme issue on *Scientific Research in Education.* 31:3–29.
Educational Theory. 2005. The Education Science Question: A Symposium. 55:235–322.
Eisenhart, Margaret and Lisa Towne. 2003. "Contestation and Change in National Policy on 'Scientifically Based' Education Research." *Educational Researcher* 32:31–38.
Erickson, Frederick. 2005. "Arts, Humanities, and Sciences in Educational Research and Social Engineering in Federal Education Policy." *Teachers College Record* 107:4–9.
Erickson, Frederick and Kris Gutierrez. 2002. "Culture, Rigor, and Science in Educational Research." *Educational Researcher* 31:21–24.
Howe, Kenneth R. 2004. "A Critique of Experimentalism." *Qualitative Inquiry* 10:42–61.
Jacob, Evelyn, and C. Stephen White (eds.). 2002. Theme issue on *Scientific Research in Education. Educational Researcher*, 31(8):3–29.
Kaestle, Carl F. 1993. "The Awful Reputation of Education Research." *Educational Researcher* 22:23, 26–31.
Lagemann, Ellen Condliffe and Lee S. Shulman (eds.). 1999. *Issues in Education Research: Problems and Possibilities.* San Francisco, CA: Jossey-Bass.
Maxwell, Joseph A. 2004. "Causal Explanation, Qualitative Research, and Scientific Inquiry in Education." *Educational Researcher* 33:3–11.
National Educational Research Policy and Priorities Board. 1999. *Investing in Learning: A Policy Statement with Recommendations on Research in Education by the National Educational Research Policy and Priorities Board.* Washington, DC: United States Department of Education.
Olson, Lynn. 1999. "NRC Seeks New Agenda for Research." *Education Week* 18(31):1–2.
Qualitative Inquiry. 2004. Symposium on *Scientific Research in Education.* 10:5–129.
Ryan, Katherine E. and Lisa K. Hood. 2004. "Guarding the Castle and Opening the Gates." *Qualitative Inquiry* 10:79–95.
Schneider, Barbara, Martin Carnoy, Jeremy Kilpatrick, William H. Schmidt, and Richard J. Shavelson. 2007. *Estimating Causal Effects Using Experimental and Observational Designs* (a report from the Governing Board of the American Educational Research Association Grants Program). Washington, DC: American Educational Research Association.
Shavelson, Richard J. and Lisa Towne (eds.). 2002. *Scientific Research in Education.* Committee on Scientific Principles for Educational Research, National Research Council. Washington, DC: National Academy Press.

Teachers College Record. 2005. A Symposium on the Implications of the *Scientific Research in Education* Report for Qualitative Inquiry. 107:1–58.

Viadero, Debra. 1996. "A Model Roadway: Research Panel May Follow Highway-Funding Path." *Education Week* 15(40):12.

———. 1999a. "Experts' Panel Seeks New Research Priorities." *Education Week* 18(29):20–21.

———. 1999b. "Panel Suggests Federal Research Priorities." *Education Week* 18(34):5.

Whitehurst, Grover J. (Russ). 2003. "The Institute of Education Sciences: New Wine, New Bottles." Address at the annual meeting of the American Educational Research Association, April. Retrieved December 20, 2007 (http://www.ed.gov/rschstat/research/pubs/ies.pdf).

PART I
The Politics of Knowledge

CHAPTER 1

The Politics of Science: Battles for Scientific Authority in the Field of Education Research

PAMELA BARNHOUSE WALTERS

Scientific controversies are never just about the "science." They are social and political struggles over what counts as science, over the authority and credibility of one set of scientific claims versus another, and over the very nature of scientific knowledge itself (see, e.g., Frickel and Gross 2005; Latour 1987; Fuchs 1992; Shapin 1995). They are struggles that produce winners and losers—perhaps between scientists and non-scientists, perhaps among competing groups of scientists—in which issues of power and control are never far from the surface.

The current debate over scientific research in education is no exception. As the introduction and several other chapters in this volume make clear, since the late 1990s there has been a concerted attempt to remake the field of education research into an endeavor more closely aligned with a certain set of scientific principles. Critics of scholarship about education have charged that much of the research lacks rigor, fails to adhere to widely-accepted principles for the conduct of science, and fails to provide a solid evidence base that can guide real-world decisions that policymakers and practitioners make. In their attempts to turn education into an evidence-based field—like medicine and agriculture—critics of education research have called for far greater use of randomized controlled trials to assess causal relationships about education.

Although concerns about the quality of education research have long preoccupied many within the education research community, the factors that precipitated the current push to "rehabilitate" education research by making it more scientific and the leadership of that effort were located largely outside of the education research community. The precipitating factor was federal legislation that for the first time wrote into law a definition of what constitutes "scientific research" in education—a definition that established randomized controlled trials as the "gold standard." As described in more detail below, these steps by lawmakers led to a reorganization of a federal agency charged with the funding and oversight of education research—the Office of Educational Research and Improvement in the U.S. Department of Education—and put in place new bureaucrats and new bureaucratic authority for institutionalizing this particular model of good science for education research.

The push to establish a new scientific model for education research ignited a firestorm of controversy. While many within the education research community were sympathetic to the charge that too much research on education was of poor quality, and some strongly supported the move to promote randomized controlled trials as the best way to study causal relationships, many educational researchers took strong exception to the definition of "science" that the legislation established and that a number of key federal bureaucrats worked to enforce. Much of this debate has constituted a defense of or attack on other scientific principles that had gained great currency within the education research community in the previous two or three decades—including ethnomethodology, critical theory, postmodernism, and other qualitative and interpretive approaches. The debate often turned on questions about which set of scientific claims were more defensible on technical or epistemological grounds. As such, the debates proceeded largely as if the only matter at stake was the scientific merits of the arguments.

In this chapter I argue that the heretofore overriding focus on the scientific merits of competing definitions of what constitutes "scientific" principles for education research largely misses the fact that above all this is a political struggle over whose claims to scientific legitimacy will prevail. I consider the controversy over the education sciences to be an example of the politics of expertise and expert knowledge, and as such I attend to the political and social struggles and conflicts among sets of actors in different institutional locations, each attempting to gain a monopoly on scientific credibility and authority (see, e.g., Epstein 1996; Fuchs 1993; Harding 1991). As such, this chapter explores those social and political processes that have given rise to the current controversy over what constitutes a legitimate basis for scientific research in education.

How have the dominant views about the best ways to conduct education research become established? Which groups and spokespersons have come to be seen as the most authoritative scientific voices in the debates? As part of answering these questions, I assess how the power base from which the groups and their representatives operate influences the views of the nature of "good" research in education that have come to prevail. I also ask how the power base has influenced which claims and claims makers have emerged as most believable, and which claims makers have gained the power to see their claims institutionalized, whether or not those claims have gained wide acceptance.

Education research is but one example of a scientific field. Scholars who study scientific fields have shown that scientific fields are self-governing. That is, within the social group that constitutes a scientific community—termed an "invisible college" long ago by Diana Crane (1972)—scholarly networks facilitate the process of scientific development, including new understandings of what constitutes good science (Camic and Xie 1994; Friedkin 1998; Griffith and Miller 1970; Long and McGinnis 1985). Particularly important are the shared communication ties and shared scientific understandings among leading scholars *within* the scientific research community; typically, once new approaches to "doing" science emerge within this group, they are diffused to and adopted by rank-and-file scholars throughout the field (Cole and Cole 1973; Collins 1989; Friedkin 1998; Zuckerman 1977).

From this perspective, developments that are often represented as technical-neutral matters of scientific "progress" are better understood as changes in the shared understanding *among the members of a scientific field* about how to best do science. Even those scientific movements that challenge prevailing scientific principles or practices and attempt to replace them with new ones are understood to be propelled from within the field: As described by Frickel and Gross (2005:209), a scientific movement is most likely to succeed when "high-status intellectual actors [inside the field] harbor complaints against what they understand to be the central intellectual tendencies of the day." For the present purposes, two important points follow from this understanding. One, consensus is harder to reach when a scientific field is distributed among multiple institutional locations, as is the field of education research. Although the field's center of gravity is in schools of education, educational researchers can be found in other professional schools, in many traditional disciplines, and outside of universities entirely. These organizational divides act as barriers to strong social ties and interactions among the scientists within the field, thereby creating greater possibilities for dispute about what constitutes good science than is the case in fields that are more organizationally unified. As we shall see, an increasing diversity in institutional locations and allegiances of members of the education research community over the past several decades precipitated a series of methodological and epistemological "wars" within the community and an internal critique on the part of much of the education-research elite over scientific shortcomings within the field.

Two, scientific standards seldom change as a result of efforts on the part of outsiders to the scientific community. This makes the case at hand—the education sciences movement—highly unusual. In this case, although the field was weakened by internal conflicts in the 1990s and earlier, the drive to establish new methodological standards for rigorous research, especially the randomized controlled trial, was spearheaded by lawmakers and federal bureaucrats. A key question this chapter addresses, then, is how did this happen? A crucial part of the answer, I demonstrate, is a resonance between the field-based experimental methods advocated by the lawmakers and bureaucrats and the lab-based experimental methods long esteemed by a core group of elites within the education research community, educational psychologists. This resemblance turned out to be only a surface similarity in important respects, though, and educational psychologists were conspicuously underrepresented among the vanguard of those calling for widespread adoption of the randomized controlled trial for education research. The scientific experts in that vanguard came instead largely from related scientific fields, especially evaluation studies and psychology—fields in which the methods now advanced for education research by lawmakers and bureaucrats had long enjoyed great scientific legitimacy. The degree of success that the education sciences movement has enjoyed is, I argue, the result of the coalition between outside scientific experts, on the one hand, and lawmakers and bureaucrats, on the other—a coalition that, however, gained considerable leverage from the weakening of the education research community through prior internal debates about the quality and rigor of the body of research produced by its members.

More specifically, the argument I present in this chapter is that recent efforts to establish a science of education can best be understood as a confluence of three separate developments that are as much "political" as they are "scientific." The first development is internal to the education research community, especially that sizable part of it located in schools of education. Efforts to put education research on a more scientific footing constitute the latest episode in a long-standing effort within the education research community to establish itself as scientifically authoritative and credible. Early in its history, the education research community derived its legitimacy and scientific authority from an adoption of methods from psychology. In recent years, the appropriateness of a model of "good science" based on psychology has been challenged by some and defended by others. Importantly, in the last few decades elites within the education research community (especially faculty in schools of education) have themselves launched a set of critiques of the poor quality of education research that further weakened the field's scientific legitimacy. I argue that the lack of consensus among educational researchers about what constitutes good research, and the continued low status of education research within the academic community, made it vulnerable to scientific attacks from the outside. Thus the origins of what is best understood as a scientific crisis in the field of education research long predate efforts starting in the late 1990s by lawmakers and bureaucrats to establish a new scientific basis for education research.[1]

The second development was the emergence of a new scientific field that embraced the scientific standards that later came to be held up as the exemplar for education research. The origin of this development was the unprecedented amount of federal funding that flowed to new social programs in the 1960s, including educational programs, which led to calls to systematically evaluate the effects of the efforts. To do so, a new scientific field, evaluation research, was established and thrived. This community had a beachhead in the academy (mostly outside of schools of education) but its center of gravity was in private research firms and government agencies. Many prominent scholars within this community—the majority of whom had university appointments in psychology, statistics/measurement, and sociology —struggled for legitimacy within the academy, a setting in which applied research was held in low regard, but took to task the education research community for a lack of engagement with systematic large-scale evaluations of (expensive) new educational programs and experiments. It was in this context that "random field trials"—the transport of psychologists' traditional experimental methods from the lab to the field—first gained currency.

The third development was an attack on American education that quickly came to include an attack on education research for its lack of utility to policymakers and practitioners. Since the 1980s, policymakers and educational practitioners have turned national attention to a series of presumed failings in American schools, especially at the K-12 level. The critique of American *education* included a critique of education research for failing to provide better guidance for the real-world decisions with which policymakers and practitioners are charged. More specifically, the national crisis of confidence over the quality of American schooling that has unfolded since the 1980s led to increased questioning about what could or should be done to fix the schools and a new critique of education research for failing to provide a firm evidence base for improving educational practice and policy. The attempt to turn education into an evidence-based field, like medicine or agriculture, depended on making education research more consistent with prevailing practices in medical and agricultural research. From this perspective, the education research community had long been preoccupied with "basic" research questions and needed to refocus its attention on questions of what policies, programs, and interventions were most effective. Taking a page from the methods that prevailed in the evaluation of interventions in medicine and agriculture, as well as in the evaluation of large-scale social programs, the policymakers and bureaucrats who spearheaded the calls for education to be transformed into an evidence-based field promoted random field trials as the best means for doing so. And a number of psychologists from the evaluation research community who had long been advocates of experimental methods became their allies in the effort.

In short, questions of scientific legitimacy that had long plagued the field of education research *dovetailed* with the politics of social program evaluation and the politics of educational policymaking to produce in the late 1990s through the early years of the twenty-first century both a sustained multifaceted critique of the quality of education research and the drive to establish randomized controlled trials as the "gold standard" for rigorous research in education. The crisis of scientific legitimacy of education research predated the politics of social program evaluation and educational policymaking *and* opened the door for these two political developments from outside the field of education research to reshape education research.

To fully understand the recent attempts to remake education research, then, one must examine the education research community's century-old quest for scientific authority and legitimacy and for a secure place within the American research university. As I argue below, the quest for scientific credibility and the legitimacy of scholars of education is bound up in important ways with the professional project of schools of education. As schools of education became more and more established within American universities, education scholars located therein gained greater autonomy and control. Their establishment as professional schools apart from traditional disciplines also brought with it a move toward more applied research, a form of science that is relatively low-status in the academy; in this respect, the professionalization project exacerbated the field's problem of scientific legitimacy within the larger community of university-based scholars. The strategy typically adopted in any scientific field's quest for legitimacy (that is, greater status in the eyes of scientists in higher-status fields) is to adopt the methods associated with a higher-prestige field or fields. In the case of education research, the founders of the field turned to psychology, the putatively most "scientific" of the social sciences, as an exemplar for scientific method and hence scientific legitimacy. Thus influential elements of the education research community have long maintained that experimental methods are the *sine qua non* of good (scientific) research, a position that facilitated the imposition from without of its close cousin, the randomized controlled trial, as the most recent "gold standard" for education research. As the discussion in the following section demonstrates, the education research community's struggle for scientific legitimacy within the academy made it vulnerable to recent attempts by outsiders to set a new standard for what constitutes good science.

Within the University: The Institutionalization of Schools of Education and Educational Researchers' Quest for Scientific Legitimacy

The Successful Institutionalization of Schools of Education: 1890s–1950

Debates about what constitutes a true science of education research are not new. The first ones surfaced in the nineteenth century, as education was emerging as a distinct field of study in American higher education and, indeed, as the modern research university was taking shape in the U.S., and these old debates informed and made possible the current ones.

Between the late nineteenth and the early twentieth century, as research universities began to offer courses on education and establish separate departments or schools of "pedagogy," faculty in these new schools or departments were faced with the challenge of establishing their professional legitimacy and credibility. In their quest they "oftentimes took their inspiration from . . . the new and 'scientific' medical educators . . . [by advocating] the academic pursuit of science, and all that it promised" to raise their professional and economic status (Clifford and Guthrie 1988:89–90). More specifically, they called on their colleagues to turn to "scientific methods" to do so. Thus the call for a "science of education" was part and parcel of an attempt to establish legitimacy for the new field and, especially, for the faculty who staffed the schools and departments of pedagogy within universities (Robarts 1968). By the late nineteenth century the experimental methods that were thought to be transforming psychology into an "exact science" were seen as holding out the greatest hope for similarly transforming education into a science (Lagemann 2000; Robarts 1968). By the turn of the century, the field of education research modeled itself on the questions and methods of psychology—particularly behaviorist psychology (Lagemann 2000; Mitchell and Haro 1999; Reuben 2003). Early American education research was a "measurement science" self-consciously modeled after psychology, in which "quantitative measurement became a mark of validity" (Lagemann 1997:7). Nonetheless, the field's scientific standing with the American university remained low.

By the 1920s, professional schools of education had secured a solid institutional base in the research university: Schools or departments of pedagogy could be found in many of the leading American universities (Labaree 2004). Further indications of successful institutionalization as a scientific field were the establishment of both an independent association and a new journal: the American Educational Research Association was founded in 1916 and in 1920 it established the *Journal of Educational Research*. Soon new journals devoted to education research were founded by schools of education at three of the nation's leading universities—Teachers College, Chicago, and Harvard. As Clifford and Guthrie (1988:78) put it, "By founding journals and monograph series, education schools could do what other ambitious departments were doing to build their reputations: stimulate research and ensure a place for the publications of faculty and graduate students." The flip side of growing professional autonomy was increased isolation from most traditional academic disciplines, however, other than psychology (Katz 1966; Lagemann 1997)—that is, increased distance from the established pillars of good science.

Thus increased control over the field of education research exacerbated the field's long-standing problems of legitimacy. Educational researchers' commitment to study practical problems of teaching and learning in American schools marginalized them in the status hierarchy of American universities, in which "basic" research is accorded much higher status than "applied" research (Labaree 2004).

We see, then, that the early years of education scholarship were marked by a quest for professional stature, a drive to establish a single model of scientific research based on the principles of psychology, and a problem of low status that continues to plague the field. The point here is that the struggle over what counted as "science" was bound up with issues of professional status and legitimacy in the larger scholarly and scientific community of the modern university within which education scholars wanted to establish themselves. A further point is that the founders of the new field of education undertook to borrow status from related research fields with greater scientific legitimacy, especially psychology. By the 1920s a scientific approach to education research modeled closely on psychology had become established and schools of education in American universities had become the main locus of that research.

Until theories and methods of research by education faculty diversified dramatically in the 1970s and later, the methods of educational psychology set the unchallenged standards for a science of education (Lagemann 2000). Educational psychologists might suffer from being considered second-class citizens relative to their colleagues in psychology departments, but they were the highest-status and most self-consciously scientific group within schools of education. Nonetheless, the adoption of the methods of psychology as the exemplar for education research did not solve the field's legitimacy crisis. By the mid twentieth century the field was professionally secure but remained scientifically insecure within the university. An increasing focus on the preparation and training of practitioners—a development that had allowed schools of education to grow—only furthered the field's crisis of scientific legitimacy (Labaree 2004).

The Challenges of Success: Expansion, Diversification, and the Paradigm Wars

In the second half of the twentieth century, schools of education experienced further professional success that, ironically, again did little to bolster the field's scientific legitimacy. Indeed, this period witnessed the "paradigm wars" that significantly broadened the methodological and theoretical scope of the field of education research while at the same time leaving the field more open to attack from a particular scientific vantage point. As we shall see later, in significant ways the education sciences movement of the late 1990s and later can be seen as an attempt to rewrite the outcome of the paradigm wars of the 1970s and 1980s.

Growth in the size of schools of education in the 1960s and later, made possible by rapidly-growing enrollments in teacher education programs, required a rapid increase in faculty positions. To fill the newly-available lines, increasingly schools of education hired faculty with training in the disciplines. Many of these new faculty brought with them models of research from the humanities and from social sciences other than psychology (Lagemann 1997). Although many in the field celebrated the increased methodological and theoretical diversity, the increased influence within the education research community of a variety of social science and humanities disciplines clearly was a source of intellectual disunity.

The spectacular growth was accomplished, then, by an equally striking increase in internal diversity that undermined the influence of psychology within the field. Not only did faculty devoted to the methods and theories of psychology come to constitute a smaller share of the education research community, they also shrank in absolute size. For example, the annual numbers of doctorates awarded in educational psychology—the specialty area on which the field of education research had staked its claim to scientific status early in the twentieth century—and its close cousin, statistics and measurement, declined after the 1970s (Hoffer et al. 2003). Speaking in sheer numerical terms, then, after the 1970s the center of gravity in schools of education radically shifted away from their early-twentieth-century anchor in psychological theory and methods, the subfields in which the enterprise's claims to scientific legitimacy had been previously based.

Thus between the 1950s and the 1980s the field of education research—at least that substantial part of it located within the research university—was transformed from a research community allied primarily with psychology and devoted "almost exclusively to issues of tests and measurement" (Jackson 1990:7) to a sprawling community wrought with internal divisions. Methodologically, qualitative methods gained a new standing; researchers who relied on quantitative methods in general or experimental methods in particular could no longer enjoy an uncontested claim to the scientific high road, as long-held norms of "normal science" were challenged on epistemological grounds (see, e.g., Lather 2004a, 2004b; Lincoln and Cannella 2004). In the eyes of some, the conflicts among different camps of education scholars became "paradigm wars" by the 1980s (Gage 1989). Some of the change was due to a renewed influence within schools of education of academic disciplines other than psychology after the 1960s (a development that occurred at the same time as fewer and fewer scholars in the disciplines undertook research on education); thus the intellectual currents in fields such as anthropology, sociology, philosophy, and history made their way into the work of scholars in schools of education (Lagemann and Shulman 1999; Viadero 1998). As Jackson (1990:7) put it, "terms like *poststructuralism, deconstruction, interpretivists, hermeneuticists, critical theory*, and more" entered the vocabulary of education scholars through an increased borrowing from the social sciences. The victories of those who eschewed the long-standing methods of educational psychology—the creation of what Lincoln and Cannella (2004:176) characterize as a "mature and sophisticated multiparadigmatic social context and the freedom to engage in research using a variety of models and methods"—challenged the near-monopoly that educational psychology and educational psychologists had long enjoyed on the claims of being a science and to scientific legitimacy, respectively.

The paradigm wars did little to bolster the scientific legitimacy of the field of education research. Indeed, in moving it further away from the style of research that bore the greatest similarity to "normal" science (educational psychology), the paradigm wars may have further weakened the field's scientific legitimacy in the eyes of scholars in other fields who considered themselves standard-bearers of good science (typically those in "hard" science fields—the implicit contrast in the eyes of those who characterized education as a "soft" science). Thus the periodic questioning of the quality and scientific rigor of the field witnessed prior to the paradigm wars continued in their aftermath. And educational psychologists and faculty in measurement and statistics remained an influential group within the education research community, one whose claims to scientific authority and credibility were echoed to some degree by the scientific claims made by the proponents of the education sciences in the late 1990s and after.

The Education Research Community Takes Stock

By circa 1990, many leading education scholars embraced the proliferation of methods and approaches to research ushered in by the paradigm wars while at the same time allowing that questions of "rigor" needed to be addressed. Consider, for example, an assessment of the quality of education research undertaken by the National Academy of Education (NAE), a society founded in 1965 to advance high-quality education research and promote its use in policymaking, whose members are considered to be among the leading scholars of education.[2] In the volume that resulted from the assessment undertaken at the behest of the NAE, an elite of the education research community emphasized that there are many forms of high-quality research while also acknowledging that ongoing attempts to monitor research quality were warranted (NAE 1991; see discussion in Lagemann and Shulman 1999). Given the heated nature of the paradigm war that had been waged shortly before this assessment was undertaken, this round of stocktaking was remarkably even-toned: Contributors emphasized the value of a broad range of research styles, if well executed.

These debates took place among members of the scientific community of education scholars, and mostly concerned matters of whether the increasingly-broad range of studies being conducted by educational researchers met the standards for good science that were appropriate to each. This was a within-field scientist-to-scientist discussion in which the principal concern was whether research in the field met commonly-accepted scientific standards; perhaps reflecting the greater legitimacy accorded new styles of research by the paradigm wars, few suggested that particular methods, in and of themselves, could not be rigorous when conducted in an exemplary manner. Further, it was assumed that the primary purpose of research was to advance our understanding of education and learning, not necessarily to inform the decisions of practitioners and policymakers (see Jackson's (1990) presidential address to the membership of the American Educational Research Association (AERA)). The concerns focused primarily on whether members of the education research community who were embracing new methodological approaches were sufficiently well trained for purposes of conducting their own research and for purposes of training graduate students in schools of education.

Not all members of the education research community welcomed the increased paradigmatic diversity of the field in the 1970s and later, however. In the eyes of some, particularly many of those who were most committed to experimental research and the traditions of psychology, the issue was not whether the new forms of research making their way into education were meeting the method-specific standards for the conduct of good science; the issue was the scientific legitimacy of the new forms of research themselves. Writing in 1998, for example, Constas (p. 26) lamented that the qualitative and postmodern turns in education research had moved the field "away from scientifically situated research." This unsettled issue was rekindled by the education sciences movement.

Making Education Research More Useful

Education research was not only weakened by a critique from within the scientific field. In the 1990s a widespread critique of the field was mounted by the policymaker and practitioner community. Policymakers and practitioners criticized educational researchers for not asking questions about the efficacy of educational programs and interventions—that is, for failing to provide answers to the kinds of questions that were most pressing to policymakers and education practitioners (see discussion later in this chapter). This critique was taken to heart by the research community, and substantial commitments were made to make education research more useful. These new understandings on the part of the education research community of the importance of research that would be useful to policymakers and practitioners were consistent with the model of the purposes of education research advanced by the lawmakers and bureaucrats who launched the attempt to turn education into an evidence-based field in the late 1990s and later.

A new commitment to useful research was apparent in the next step the education research community itself took to address concerns about the quality of work in the field. In 1995, after a lengthy debate among its membership, the NAE again established a commission of its members to find ways to improve education research. Ellen Condliffe Lagemann, one of the two co-chairs of the commission, embraced the need to more closely link education research to the improvement of schools: "We think education research is important and can be helpful to practice, if well done" (Viadero 1995b). This comment, and the debate among NAE members it reflected, as well as the work of the commission that it foreshadowed, marked a clear turn in the discussion among the elite of the education research community: Now a commitment to produce "work of high quality" that would "foster improvements in educational policy and practice" was high on their agenda (Lagemann and Shulman 1999:11). It did not displace concerns with the quality of "basic" scientific research, but it placed alongside those concerns an interest in making education research more relevant and useful to those who were responsible for the nation's schools. This new charge to education scholars from the leadership of the education research community to turn greater attention to research that would help improve educational policy and practice opened the door to and legitimated later efforts from the policymaking community to undertake a large-scale rehabilitation of the education research enterprise.

Program Evaluation Gives Rise to a New Scientific Field

Scientific legitimacy can only be conferred by scientists. As we have seen, by the 1990s for the most part elites within the education research community were critical of the quality of education research but hardly united in their views of what should or could be done to improve it and were by no means calling for a particular gold standard of good research methods. Thus the scientists needed to back the drive to rehabilitate education research by means of widespread adoption of randomized controlled trials had to come largely from outside the education research community. Many were found in the related and relatively new field of evaluation research.

The evaluation research community was established following the federal government's funding of a number of very large and expensive social programs in the 1960s and 1970s intended to alleviate poverty, reduce discrimination, and the like. In the wake of these huge outlays of public funds, legislators, bureaucrats, and the public started to call for evidence that they were achieving their objectives. Hence a number of large-scale evaluation studies of a wide range of social programs, some of which were educational programs,[3] were undertaken in the 1960s and 1970s.

The very applied nature of the evaluation studies, however, made them unappealing to discipline-based scholars. The funding available for such studies fueled an explosive growth in an evaluation-research sector located largely outside of universities but influenced by a handful of evaluation-research experts within the academy and the methodological guidance they provided to those who undertook the bulk of the actual studies. This sector, which included but was by no means limited to those interested in the evaluation of educational programs, was well established by the 1970s. Two signs that this new sector was beginning to constitute a professional field with a legitimate "scientific" standing were the founding of a set of journals devoted to evaluation methods and studies, and the establishment of three professional organizations concerned with social experimentation (see Riecken and Boruch 1978).

The research methods promoted by the university-based evaluation-research experts were an adaptation of the experimental methods long established as the standard of good science in psychology and educational psychology. For purposes of evaluating the effects of new (unproven) social programs, random-assignment experimental research was taken out of the psychological (and educational psychological) laboratory and transported to the "field" of real social settings. Psychologists (not educational psychologists) were the ones who did the most to establish experimental methods as the preferred approach for evaluating social experiments. Campbell and Stanley's (1963)[4] *Experimental and Quasi-experimental Designs for Research* became the "bible" for evaluation research. It upheld the use of experimental and control groups as the most scientifically-valid way to assess causal effects of interventions, even as it allowed that other approaches (that yielded less reliable estimates of treatment efficacy) could be used when random assignment of subjects to treatment and control groups was not possible. Cook and Campbell's (1979) book *Quasi-experimentation: Design and Analysis Issues for Field Settings*[5] continued in this tradition: While sanguine about the obstacles to conducting randomized experiments in field settings, it nonetheless advocated them as the most valid approach for assessing causal effects of social experiments. Campbell's influence on debates about the best way to determine whether educational programs have their hoped-for effects would be hard to overestimate.

Besides Campbell, Cook, and Stanley, other psychologists were in the vanguard of the call to use experimental methods in real-world field settings to evaluate social programs. First in collaboration with a medical researcher and later in collaboration with other social scientists, psychologist Robert Boruch also became a leading advocate of the use of randomized field experiments (sometimes called randomized field trials) for social program evaluation (see, e.g., Berk et al. 1985; Boruch, McSweeney, and Soderstrom 1978; Riecken and Boruch 1974).[6] Boruch, Campbell, and Cook reappear in significant ways in the debates starting in the late 1990s about scientific research in education—Cook and Boruch as active participants, with Campbell and his legacy invoked widely by proponents of the education sciences.

In their calls for "rigorous" evaluation of social programs—particularly in welfare, criminal justice, employment policy, and education—these prominent psychologists, along with a handful of sociologists and statisticians, provided the intellectual leadership of the evaluation-research sector in the 1970s and 1980s.[7] Equally importantly, their voices and/or their arguments decisively figured in the renewed calls by the late 1990s for the adoption of randomized controlled trials for studying "causal" relationships in educational programs and settings.

The calls for randomized studies of social programs were heeded to some degree by those responsible for some of the important educational experiments of the 1960s. Notable examples of random field-trial evaluations of 1960s educational programs include evaluations of *Sesame Street*, the Perry Preschool Project, and a small-scale school desegregation project (Cook and Payne 2002). These landmark evaluations, however, were not the product of education faculty; they were undertaken by research firms in the private sector, with federal funds (Rossi and Wright 1984). The *methods* long favored by educational psychologists were transported out of the laboratory and into field settings in these studies, but educational psychologists were not themselves party to the studies. Further, the prominence and impact of this initial spate of random field trials of educational programs notwithstanding, randomized evaluations of educational programs became rare events during the 1970s and 1980s, even as they continued apace in other fields—primarily criminal justice, social welfare, and employment and training (Boruch, de Loya, and Snyder 2002; Cook 1999).

Proponents of experimental methods for the evaluation of social programs, drawn largely from psychology, statistics, medicine, and sociology, were troubled by the lack of random field evaluations of educational programs during the 1970s and later, and continued to call for random field trials to be used to evaluate programs and interventions in education as well as other social service arenas (see, e.g., Berk et al. 1985; Boruch et al. 1983; Cook and Campbell 1979; Rossi and Wright 1984; Riecken and Boruch 1974, 1978). The intellectual leadership provided by university-based scholars (outside of education) notwithstanding, however, most of the random field trials of social programs were conducted by personnel outside of university-based academic departments—in social service agencies or in private research firms. A single firm, Manpower Demonstration Research Corporation (MDRC), alone accounted for over 30 major random assignment evaluations of social programs between 1975 and 2000 (Gueron 2002).

During this same period, the most notable random field trial of an educational program that was attempted was the Tennessee evaluation of the effects of reducing class size, initiated in 1985 (Boruch et al. 2002; Cook and Payne 2002). The experiment itself was conducted by the Tennessee State Department of Education, in consultation with a number of faculty from universities in the state (Boyd-Zacharias 1999). This study enjoyed a high profile, in part because the data were reanalyzed and the findings popularized by prominent statisticians and economists. And the study had a clear impact on public policy: The primary finding that students in smaller classes enjoyed larger achievement gains led to expensive and ambitious efforts to reduce class sizes in Tennessee and elsewhere (most notably, California). Its prominence within both the academic and the public-policy communities gave new impetus to the call for the adoption of random field trials in education.

Two other highly-visible random field evaluations of educational programs took place during the 1990s: a multisite evaluation of Comer's School Development Program, which was a prominent example of the popular "whole-school reform" movement, and the evaluation of school voucher programs, first Milwaukee's publicly-funded program and then a three-site experiment with privately-funded vouchers (Boruch et al. 2002; Cook 1999). As Cook (1999:4) observed, one of the striking things about these studies is that "nearly all were conducted by scholars whose primary organizational affiliation is outside of education. The best-known class size experiment was begun by educators . . . , but popularized by statisticians. . . . The Milwaukee voucher study was done by political scientists . . . and reanalyzed as a randomized experiment by political scientists . . . and economists. . . . The Comer studies were conducted by sociologists and psychologists. . . . [T]he work on school choice programs in Washington, New York and Cleveland is also being done by political scientists." Clearly, by the 1990s the resurgence of interest in randomized field trials in education was the responsibility of academic experts outside of schools of education.

Educational psychologists, the group within schools of education who traditionally were the standard-bearers for experimental methods, were not party to this particular application of them. The experimentalists within the education research community, that is, basically lay low during the 1980s and 1990s. (Indeed, Cook [1999] later argued that they were "lying fallow" and could be reactivated to the cause of random-assignment experimentation.) Their support for experimentalism, especially in the context of the dormant-but-not-settled paradigm wars, was, however, crucial to the success of the education sciences movement after 2000. Nonetheless, the renewed calls in the 1990s for the education research community to become more scientific (by adopting randomized controlled trials) came from without.

Policymakers and Practitioners Mount a Critique of Education Research

At the same time as the psychologists and experimentalists were losing the paradigm wars in education research, the field of education research came under increased scrutiny from stakeholders outside of the research community itself. The chief complaint was the failure of education research to address the needs of educational practitioners and policymakers. Some date the concern about a disconnect between education research, on the one hand, and the needs of policymakers and practitioners, on the other, to a general disappointment that set in in the 1970s with the lack of evidence that the vast spending on educational programs initiated in the War on Poverty of the prior decade had proven effective. Lagemann (1997), for example, argues that the disappointing results of the educational evaluations of the late 1960s and 1970s not only discredited the programs themselves but also led to a critique of education research for its presumed failure to increase the effectiveness of American education. One result was the creation in 1972 of the new National Institute of Education (NIE), intended to provide a more effective knowledge base to inform educational policy and practice (see Chapter 2 for more detail).

The critique of education research through the back door of the critique of the poor quality of American education really picked up steam, however, with the release of *A Nation at Risk* (National Commission on Excellence in Education 1983). The influential report was a blistering attack on the quality of American education. It famously warned, for example, that "the educational foundations of our society are presently being eroded by a rising tide of mediocrity that threatens our very future as a Nation and a people." The concern over the alleged poor showing of American schools quickly came to include a stepped-up attack on the shortcomings of education research for its failure to provide better guidance for educational reform. Whereas the debate within the education research community (especially among those with appointments in universities) about what was wrong with education research was mostly about its rigor and scientific validity, not about whether it asked the wrong questions, the critique of education research from outsiders that gained momentum during the 1980s was about whether it was addressing the kinds of questions that were most pressing to policymakers and practitioners. This critique in effect faulted education research for being too scholarly and overly focused on "basic" science; the corrective was to turn it into a more "applied" field that would help improve American education. Whereas the (academic) psychologists and methodologists who were critical of the direction of the field of education research during the 1970s and 1980s held up the methods of psychology, particularly the randomized experiment, as the exemplar of good science, the critique from policymakers and practitioners held up as exemplars other applied fields, particularly medicine and agriculture, in which applied research had allegedly led to dramatic improvements in health care and food production. The question asked in this context was why can't education research be more like medical and agricultural research?

As Vinovskis recounts in Chapter 2, discontent in the policymaking community with the agency responsible for much of the federally-funded education research led in 1985 to a reorganization of the Department of Education's Office of Educational Research and Improvement (OERI) and elimination of the National Institute of Education. With Chester E. Finn, Jr. at the helm as the newly-appointed Assistant Secretary of Education for Research and Improvement, the new OERI was expected to do a better job than the old agency of ensuring that education research was not only scientifically sound but also useful. In fact, it was the latter charge that took on the greatest force. In 1985, for example, Finn was quoted as saying, "There has been a lot of criticism about the lack of success in translating research findings into forms that policy-makers and practitioners can use" (*New York Times* 1985:9). Part of Finn's mission, as he expressed it the following year, was to "rehabilitate educational research as a worthwhile endeavor" (Fiske 1986:12). In yet another interview, Finn explained that policymakers' chief complaint about education research was "that it's of no use to anyone because it is never in a form people can understand or do anything about," which is why federal lawmakers "don't think it's worth investing in" (Werner 1986:28). In this context, issues about the quality of the stream of research funded by OERI were confused with issues about the quality of research on education in general and conflated with issues about the utility of education research. (For more on the conflation of quality and utility issues, see Chapter 5.)

As part of the effort to rehabilitate education research, Finn led a project to summarize the results of research on effective instructional methods, released as a 66-page booklet entitled "What Works: Research about Teaching and Learning" (Fiske 1986:12). This apparently marked the first systematic effort by the federal agency responsible for education research to systematically review research on "what works" in public education; when federal officials established the What Works Clearinghouse in 2002 for purposes of providing "a central and trusted source of scientific evidence of what works in education,"[8] they were in essence resuming and ramping up an effort begun under the auspices of the "old" OERI. Further, the concerns that led to the 1985 reorganization of OERI demonstrate that the complaint about a disconnect between education research findings and the information of greatest interest to policymakers long predated the critique of education research launched by lawmakers in the late 1990s.

A key element of the charge in the 1980s by policymakers and practitioners that education research was a "soft science," then, was its alleged failure to point the way to significant improvements in American schools and schooling. The 1985 reorganization of OERI did not alleviate their concerns, and the criticisms continued apace. Continued federal lawmaker impatience with the failure of studies funded by OERI to produce findings that clearly led to school improvement (see discussion in Chapter 2) led to yet another round of reorganization of the federal education research bureaucracy. In 1994, OERI was again overhauled. Part of the "Goals 2000: Educate America Act," the reorganization plan called for the creation of a central office designed to ensure "that federally financed education research gets to—and is used by—the nation's schools and educators" (Viadero 1995a:19). Department of Education officials and federal legislators promised that the new OERI would be "customer driven." This meant that federal funds for education research (which were primarily administered by OERI) would henceforth be focused on solving "persistent educational problems" (Viadero 1995a:19).

The criticism implicitly behind this reorganization was of "federally-funded education research," not all education research, but once again the distinction was blurred and perhaps even lost in later rounds of critique of the field. Further, the critique of the field for not asking the right questions (that would be most useful to policymakers and practitioners) fused with the older critique that had come from within the education research community itself for insufficient "quality" and "rigor" of research.

While the critiques of the main federal agency responsible for education research, OERI, gained further momentum during the 1990s, a different kind of education research was gaining a small but significant foothold in a different federal agency, the National Institutes of Health (NIH). Under the direction of G. Reid Lyon, a psychologist, in the 1990s NIH's Child Development and Behavior Branch undertook a number of experimental studies of different methods of reading instruction in an effort to identify the one that was most effective. Perhaps partly as a function of his own background in the psychology lab, Lyon in effect heeded the call of the evaluation-research community to use experimental methods to assess the effectiveness of competing models of social-program intervention. Against the grain of prevailing wisdom on the part of many reading experts, the research Lyon supported suggested that phonics-based instruction was more effective than a whole-language approach. Inspired by the results of what they saw as a systematic, rigorous scientific investigation, federal lawmakers—that is, members of Congress, a group typically not considered to be arbiters of or standard-bearers for "science"—undertook what would turn out to be their first attempt to strengthen the link between education research and educational practice: They wrote into the Reading Excellence Act of 1998 a clause that directed funding only to reading programs using "scientifically based reading research" (Viadero 1999c:2).⁹ The acclaim of NIH's experimental research on reading, then, led to the first federal law calling for "scientifically based research" as a precondition for programmatic funding. The precedent of writing into law a requirement that *reading* research be "scientific" opened the way to an effort on the part of lawmakers to legislate "scientific" research in education much more broadly in the next few years. It also brought lawmakers into efforts begun previously by bureaucrats within the Department of Education to "rehabilitate" education research.

The Education Sciences Take Shape

1999: The Critiques Fuse into a Wholesale Assault on Education Research

In 1999, three groups that each included a number of prominent members of the education research community issued reports on the problems plaguing the field of education research. As discussed previously, a group commissioned by the NAE released an edited volume entitled *Issues in Education Research* (Lagemann and Shulman 1999) that called for, among other things, more fully focusing education research on problems of educational practice (Viadero 1999a:20), and the National Academy of Sciences' Strategic Education Program Panel issued a report that, in part, criticized education in the U.S. for not resting on a strong evidence base (see Olson 1999:1). Underscoring the perceived need to make education research more useful, on the occasion of the release of the latter report the President of the National Academy of Sciences, Bruce Alberts, was quoted as saying, "It is poignantly clear that research has not had the kind of impact on education that is visible in medical practice, space exploration, energy, and many other fields" (Olson 1999:1). Further, the advisory board to the Office of Educational Research and Improvement (the National Educational Research Policy and Priorities Board) released a report calling for "the boundaries between research and practice" (Viadero 1999b:5) to be torn down. The chief complaint about education research that had been mounted by policymakers and practitioners—its lack of utility to them—was reflected, then, in all three reports; in turn, the reports gave an imprimatur of the scientific research community to the policymaker and practitioner call to make education a more evidence-based field and, to that end, to direct the education research community to focus its work on solving current problems of educational policy and practice.

There was another significant development in 1999, this time from the evaluation-research community: the establishment of the Campbell Collaboration. It was formed by an international group of scientists and policymakers who advocated randomized experiments in the "soft sciences," including education.¹⁰ The membership of the Campbell Collaboration was intent on promoting evidence-based social policy in a number of fields, including education, for purposes of helping practitioners and policymakers make good decisions. It took its cue from the Cochrane Collaboration, an organization based in the U.K. that systematically reviews findings from randomized experiments in health care (Viadero 2002b). This group's support for "evidence-based social policy" dovetailed with lawmakers' stepped-up calls for "better" research in education for purposes of informing policymaking. Although few leaders of the education research community in the U.S. were counted among its founding members, the calls for randomized trials issued by this body that included a number of prominent "scientists"[11] gave additional legitimacy to the similar calls coming from policymakers and federal lawmakers. Further, in short order the Campbell Collaboration specifically, as well as the community of scholars outside of education calling for evidence-based social policy more generally, would prove to be invaluable allies in federal bureaucrats' efforts to promote a new vision of scientific research in education over the vociferous objections of a broad swathe of the education research community, including many of its acknowledged elite.

Lawmakers and Bureaucrats Succeed in Setting Standards for Research

Returning to legislative developments, in the span of about two years, between the passage of the Reading Excellence Act in 1998 and the bill proposed but not passed in 2000 to reauthorize the Elementary and Secondary Education Act (ESEA), language about "scientifically based research" in education was placed in several education bills (Viadero and Portner 2000). The bill proposed to reauthorize ESEA in 2000 by Rep. Bob Schaffer (Rep-CO), however, contained the most stringent language: it defined scientific research as "randomized experiments" (Viadero and Portner 2000:10). Also notably in 2000, Rep. Michael Castle (Rep-DE) introduced a bill to reauthorize the Office of Educational Research and Improvement that was intended to improve federal education research. The language of that bill stipulated that federal research funds be limited to the support of "scientifically valid research," and it set out separate "scientifically-based" standards for qualitative and quantitative research (Eisenhart and Towne 2003).

Although neither of the aforementioned bills passed as originally written, they instigated a firestorm of debate within the education research community, between educational researchers and policymakers, and between educational researchers and those calling for evidence-based practice in other fields, about what constituted "scientific" research in education. In the short term a number of professional associations objected to the language proposed by Schaffer that defined scientific research as randomized trials.[12] More importantly for the longer-term legislative and bureaucratic developments, in response to Castle's proposed language the scientific community mobilized to come up with a definition of what constitutes "scientific" research in education that would, they hoped, forestall efforts to write into legislation definitions that were overly narrow. Hence the National Research Council formed a committee to consider the question of what constitutes scientific research in education. Significantly, just as previous policy discussions came to blur the distinction between the quality of all education research versus the quality of OERI-supported education research, the line was starting to be blurred between the methods most appropriate for investigating the effectiveness of social programs or treatments versus the methods that were most appropriate for education research writ large. This blurring, in turn, created possibilities for individuals and groups that were vocal proponents of random experiments for (the relatively limited purposes of) the evaluation of social program effectiveness to use the critique appropriate (from their perspective) for educational evaluations as a blunt-instrument critique of education research as a whole.

The panel that produced the NRC report *Scientific Research in Education* (Shavelson and Towne 2002) consisted of a number of prominent faculty members in schools of education, along with faculty members from other social science and science fields as well as a couple of representatives from the private research sector. Not surprisingly, then, the recommendations they issued about how to define "scientific" research in education were more moderate than the arguments coming from those outsiders to the scientific field who wished to transform education research into an experimental enterprise. The volume endorsed a broad range of methodological approaches and established principles for the conduct of "scientific" research that allowed that a number of approaches besides randomized experiments could be rigorous and scientific.[13] The tempered approach advocated by the panel did not, however, forestall efforts by lawmakers to write into law specific (and narrower) definitions of scientific research in education or efforts by those at the helm in the U.S. Department of Education to align education research more closely with experimental-research traditions.

The efforts begun in the 1990s by political actors to set standards for what constitutes rigorous research methods in education were furthered by the science policies adopted by the administration of President George W. Bush. From the time he took office in 2001, President Bush insisted that decisions in all policy domains, including education, should be based on "sound science" (Brainard 2004). Almost immediately, however, the administration's handling of science policy came under sustained attack from the scientific community: Large numbers of eminent scientists charged that a broad range of the administration's science policies were at odds with established research findings, that the administration was choosing members of scientific panels and advisory committees on political grounds rather than on the basis of scientific expertise, and that President Bush was moving too slowly in filling key scientific posts in the administration (Brainard 2004; Mooney 2005; Weiss 2002). The scientific community's criticisms of Bush administration science policy were made widely known, through editorials and news articles in major newspapers and through editorials in highly-respected general-interest science journals. The journal *Nature*, for example, published an editorial in March 2001 charging that key policy decisions on workplace safety, climate, and the environment ignored what science had to say (*Nature* 2001:499). A few months later an editorial in *Scientific American* charged that the administration's stands on controlling carbon dioxide emissions and on strategic missile defense were at odds with "the scientific consensus" (*Scientific American* 2001:8). An article published in *Science* in 2002 charged that the administration manipulated appointments to scientific advisory panels for political ends (Michaels et al. 2002); similar concerns over the unprecedented degree to which appointments to scientific advisory committees and review panels were based on "tests of political loyalty" rather than objective scientific qualifications were expressed in another article in *Science* a few months later (Kennedy 2003:625).

Criticism of Bush administration political interference with the conduct of science in the field of education was overshadowed by the scientific community's outcry over the administration's policies concerning stem-cell research, global warming, intelligent design, and HIV/AIDS. Nonetheless, the education research community voiced early objections to what it saw as the manipulation of scientific findings to suit administration education policy goals. In October 2002, for example, the American Educational Research Association (AERA) and a number of other education associations sent a letter to Secretary of Education Rod Paige that protested a directive to remove from the Department of Education website a broad range of factual material and research findings that ran counter to educational policies being advanced by the administration (U.S. House of Representatives Committee on Government Reform 2003:14–15).

The direction of Bush administration policy concerning the conduct of education research became apparent within the first year. In the summer of 2001, Grover J. "Russ" Whitehurst, an academic with a long-time faculty appointment in psychology, was named the new Assistant Secretary for Educational Research and Improvement in the U.S. Department of Education. That is, he became the new head of the beleaguered and much-criticized agency responsible for the direction of much of the research on education supported with federal dollars. Like Finn, one of his predecessors in the office, he too was intent on rehabilitating education research. Shortly after his confirmation by the Senate, he recounted a now-familiar litany of complaints about the research OERI had been funding: It was of poor quality, politically suspect, and "too far removed from the real needs of classroom educators and policymakers to make a difference." The education research community needed to be "retooled" to "respond to the practical needs of the field" (Viadero 2001a:38). The initial agenda outlined by Whitehurst, then, took up the criticism of OERI-funded research that had animated the policymaker/practitioner community and extended it to education research more broadly. His own credentials as a respected academic psychologist gave additional legitimacy to the charges against OERI's research portfolio that heretofore had come primarily from non-scientists.[14]

A further important development in 2001 was the founding of the Coalition for Evidence-Based Policy, a "non-partisan, Washington-based group that advocates the use of randomized field trials in evaluating government programs" (Viadero 2004:12). The advisory board consists of a mix of individuals from academia (mostly outside of education),[15] the private-research sector, and think tanks. They hoped to promote research that could do for a range of public-policy fields—notably education, poverty policy, criminal justice, and substance abuse—what random experiments in medicine had done in health care.[16] In short order they too not only provided scientific legitimacy to calls for randomized trials in education emanating from legislators and bureaucrats but also became allies with the Department of Education officials who were trying to make education an evidence-based field through greater use of randomized experiments.

In November 2001 the National Research Council released a prepublication version of *Scientific Research in Education*; the rush to prepublication was intended to obviate the need felt by some lawmakers to regulate the education research community through legislation defining good science. As panel chair Richard Shavelson[17] said, "We certainly hope that our report makes it unnecessary for federal legislators to say what they think science research is" (Viadero 2001b:12). The arguments in *Scientific Research in Education* did not, however, prevent a narrower definition of "scientifically based research" from being written into law with the passage of No Child Left Behind (NCLB) in January 2002. The language in NCLB applied to the research evidence in support of *programs* (interventions) that could be eligible for receiving federal funds—in other words, it applied to the *users* of education research, not to the *producers*—but it was of great significance to the research community nonetheless. The effectiveness of programs eligible for federal funding had to be demonstrated through "experimental or quasi-experimental designs," and the bill expressed a clear preference for "random-assignment experiments" (see Eisenhart and Towne 2003:34–35).

In 2002, Rep. Michael Castle (Rep-DE)—the author of the bill with the proposed language about "scientific" research in education that prompted the National Academy of Sciences to form the panel that issued *Scientific Research in Education*—introduced a bill to abolish OERI and replace it with an "academy of education sciences" (Viadero 2002a). The bill, now known as the Education Sciences Reform Act (HR 3801), passed in October 2002 (Morgan 2002). The replacement of OERI was at that point called the Institute of Education Sciences, and the former head of OERI, "Russ" Whitehurst, was named to a six-year term as its director. Castle hoped the new institute would promote "greater rigor" in education research. He said, "I want quality education research, not fads or anecdotes, to inform educators' decisions on the best way to improve student learning and narrow achievement gaps" (Viadero 2002a:31). Whereas NCLB applied sanctions to the education research community only indirectly (by stipulating that to be eligible for federal funding a program's effectiveness had to have been demonstrated through the set of methods deemed scientific), the ESRA applied directly to the kinds of research for which members of the research community could get federal funding.

Even before OERI was replaced by IES, Whitehurst undertook the first of what would be a series of bold steps intended to transform education research into an experimental field. In August 2002, for example, OERI awarded an $18.5 million contract to the What Works Clearinghouse (WWC) to review and vet extant research for purposes of systematically determining whether there was rigorous scientific evidence to support claims of treatment/program effectiveness (Viadero 2002c; Eisenhart and Towne 2003). Randomized trials were the WWC standard for "rigorous" research. Further, as early as fiscal year 2002 almost three-quarters of the research funded by OERI/IES comprised random-assignment experimental studies (Eisenhart and Towne 2003:34). The preference had been no secret: The document that solicited grant proposals in fiscal 2002 and 2003 "*requires* [emphasis in original] proposed evaluation designs to use random assignment" (Angrist 2004:202).

The particulars of the WWC award are significant in other respects. The principal contractors to whom the award was granted were the Campbell Collaboration, the group composed largely of scientists and private-sector research personnel outside of education who had long promoted random field trials for the assessment of social programs, and the American Institutes for Research, a leading contract research firm. The lead investigator for the Campbell Collaboration was Robert Boruch, a psychologist and statistician (and now faculty member at the University of Pennsylvania with a partial appointment in education) who had written widely on the need for random field trials in program evaluation since the 1970s. The Department of Education, then, in effect bypassed the established scientific leadership of the education research community in this initial effort to institutionalize random-assignment methods within the field. The scientific leadership for the education sciences movement came largely from psychology, with support from a sprinkling of scholars in sociology and economics as well as the fields of measurement and quantitative methods (Schwandt 2005).[18]

The creation of the IES, backed up by two forms of legislative mandates (NCLB and ESRA) to rehabilitate education research under a particular vision of what constitutes good science, institutionalized within the federal bureaucracy a means of retooling the field. With a strong leader at the helm who was prepared to take full advantage of the power of the federal purse to leverage change, random-assignment research on "what works" in education came to the fore in short order. In an interview in December 2002, Whitehurst was quoted as saying, "It's very clear in No Child Left Behind that questions of what works in education will have high priority. Questions of what works link naturally to randomized trials" (Viadero 2002d:32).

Even before the legislative developments of 2001 and 2002, some psychologists/methodologists who were long-standing proponents of experimental research recognized that it might be difficult to persuade established members of the education research community to adopt random-assignment methods. As articulated by Cook (1999:55), many educational researchers "are convinced that anyone pursuing a scientific model of knowledge growth is an out-of-date positivist seeking to resuscitate debates that are rightly dead. So the community sees little value in better connections to recent research design as understood in statistics or psychology." He advocated an "end run" around the education research community, allowing that there was great expertise in experimental research in private research firms and on the part of some "educational faculty who are now lying fallow" (p. 57).

Once constituted as IES, the federal agency responsible for funding education research took even greater steps to, in effect, heed Cook's call. For example, in its call for proposals for new (*very* generously funded) predoctoral training programs for 2004, IES stipulated that support was limited to students in "traditional degree programs" such as psychology, political science, economics, or sociology—that is, doctoral students in schools of education were not eligible. Faculty in schools of education could be involved in the training programs, but only as collaborators with faculty in these other fields with stronger traditions of experimental or quantitative research; the students would receive a certificate in the education sciences and their training would emphasize education research and statistics.[19]

IES took these steps over the vociferous objections of the established education research community. The symposia in several education journals that overwhelmingly objected to the move to establish randomized controlled trials as the "gold standard" for scientific research in education is one key example. Another example is a resolution adopted by the council of the AERA in 2003 opposing the position on random-assignment experimental methods taken by the Department of Education:

> The Council of the AERA reaffirms its commitment to improving the quality of educational research.... A fundamental premise of scientific inquiry is that research questions should guide the selection of inquiry methods. Council recognizes randomized trials among the sound methodologies to be used in the conduct of educational research and commends increased attention to their use as is particularly appropriate to intervention and evaluation studies. However, the council of the association expresses dismay that the Department of Education, through its public statements and programs of funding, is devoting singular attention to this one tool of science, jeopardizing a broader range of problems best addressed through other scientific methods.[20]

This objection, like many of the objections raised by members of the education research community to policymakers' and lawmakers' efforts to make education research more "scientific," is notable for the scientific-technical language it deploys. The disagreement is cast in terms of the scientific validity of competing research methods and models; the explicit charges of manipulation and distortion of science for political purposes that were made loudly and frequently with respect to other Bush administration science policies[21] were largely absent from the education research community's attempts to defend itself from Bush administration initiatives to "rehabilitate" it. In the case of education research, Bush administration officials were able to invoke "good science" to make the case for the changes they wanted to institute. In the case of stem-cell research, global warming, and other contentious science-policy domains, the administration's critics were able to claim that administration science policies were *at odds* with good science and good scientific practice.

How is it that non-scientists—bureaucrats and lawmakers—were better able than the intellectual leadership of the education research community to invoke the norms of good science in support of their arguments about how education research should be conducted? The attempts by bureaucrats and lawmakers to set standards of good research for the education research community, over the widespread objection of the intellectual leadership of the education research community itself that the standard was overly narrow and restrictive (that is, scientifically unsound and indefensible), would likely not have succeeded had the bureaucrats and lawmakers not been able to enlist as allies to their cause other scientists and experts.[22] Those allies were found in professional scientific bodies that drew primarily from fields outside of education research. IES activated some of the previously-identified existing groups in their efforts to institutionalize their new standards for scientific research in education. In 2004, for example, the Coalition for Evidence-Based Policy was hired by the IES to produce a guide to what constitutes "rigorous" evidence of educational-program effectiveness. The guide "maintains that only well-designed randomized, controlled studies provide 'strong' evidence of an intervention's effectiveness," a standard consistent with IES's position that randomized controlled trials are the "gold standard" for rigorous research (Viadero 2004:12). The WWC, under the leadership of the Campbell Collaboration, proceeded with its efforts to evaluate existing research on education, using randomized controlled trials as the primary benchmark for identifying studies that provide good information on the causal effects of educational interventions.[23]

In addition to enlisting as allies existing scientific groups with a membership largely (but not entirely) outside of the education research community, and bypassing the organizations representing or including the scientific elite of the education research community, the Department of Education created new scientific bodies that became allies in its endeavors. Most importantly, the IES created a board to advise it on research policies and priorities, called the National Board for Education Sciences, which met for the first time in 2005. Among its 14 members only six were classified as "researchers."[24] One of those researchers was an educational psychologist retired from a school of education; the others included two economists, a mathematician, a professor of pediatrics, and a psychologist. Among the other members were the Director of the Coalition for Evidence-Based Policy, a foundation president, a business executive, three school administrators, and a former senior advisor to the former Bush-administration Secretary of Education (Viadero 2005). As the former chair of the OERI advisory board, Kenji Hakuta,[25] noted, "This board is clearly chosen to send a message that favors researchers who prefer a narrow definition of scientifically based research" (Viadero 2005:32). Further, the composition of the board shows, once again, that the scientific expertise marshaled in support of randomized controlled trials came almost entirely from outside of the established education research community.[26]

The most recent development in efforts to establish random-assignment experiments as the method of choice for education research was a substantial ($760,000) grant from the IES to establish in 2006 a new scientific society intended to advance "scientifically rigorous studies in education" (Viadero 2006a:1). In a move widely considered to be an attempt to bypass the influence of the AERA, the new society drew its membership from a diverse set of disciplines and soon began planning for professional meetings, to establish a new journal, and to issue a three-volume handbook—all indicators of the constitution of a scientific field (Viadero 2006b). Called the Society for Research on Educational Effectiveness, the group was co-founded by a professor of statistics and social policy and an education professor who was, until 2003, a program director in the Department of Education (Viadero 2006a). By the time of its first meeting, the new society had 250 dues-paying members and a 15-person advisory board. The advisory board included Robert Boruch and Thomas Cook, both long-time advocates of random field trials for program evaluation, and several individuals with backgrounds in psychology, medicine, economics, or statistics, some of whom hold appointments in schools of education.[27]

The movement to establish by legislative and bureaucratic decree a new set of standards for the conduct of scientific research in education has experienced considerable success, even though the definition of "good science" promoted by the advocates of the new science of education research remains contested by broad sections of elite scholars *within* the field of education research.[28] It is beyond the scope of this chapter to speculate on the staying power of the movement, once the administration changes hands and thus the leadership of the Department of Education and the IES may change, but much progress has been made in institutionalizing programs, funding guidelines, and the very definition of rigorous research supported by advocates of the education sciences. For example, through its generous funding of predoctoral and postdoctoral programs the IES has created new cohorts of educational researchers drawn from disciplines and departments outside of education whose scientific and methodological training likely predisposes them to place high priority on randomized controlled trials in their own and others' research. Further, the creation of a new professional society aligned with current IES priorities, complete with annual meetings, a new journal, and the like, is another mark of successful institutionalization of this new model of a good science of education research.

Perhaps most telling, however, is that the established education research community is on the defensive. The détente that had apparently been reached in the paradigm wars has given way to an apparent need to vigorously defend all forms of research that stand outside of the experimental and quasi-experimental tradition. Even as it called for a definition of appropriate scientific methods that embraced a range of approaches far broader than just randomized controlled trials, the NRC volume *Scientific Research in Education* reserved the term "scientific" for quantitative research. In response, qualitative researchers of many stripes repudiated the report (see the introduction to this volume for a discussion of the special issues of journals devoted to a defense of qualitative methods) and expended much effort to, in effect, try to regain the ground they had gained in the paradigm wars: establishing the scientific legitimacy of qualitative and interpretive studies and their necessary role for purposes of answering important questions about educational processes and outcomes. The need to mount such a vigorous defense, though, speaks loudly to the success of the education sciences movement in drawing the boundary around "science" in such a way as to exclude and delegitimize these approaches.

Consider too the relative narrowness of the AERA's most recent attempt to expand beyond the randomized trial the methods that are understood to be scientifically valid in education research. Although in their 2003 statement the Council of the AERA called for a recognition of the usefulness of a very broad range of scientific methods (see prior discussion), in 2007 the AERA issued a "white paper" that largely accepted the superiority of quantitative methods (including, but not limited to, randomized trials) for purposes of studying causal relations (see Schneider et al. 2007).[29] At the time of the report's release, one of its co-authors, Richard Shavelson, was quoted as saying that for purposes of making causal inferences "Randomized-control trials are the gold standard," even as he acknowledged that analyses of large-scale datasets can also be useful (Viadero 2007:12). Given the close association of "science" with the study of "causal effects," the report's stance is yet another indicator of the successful institutionalization of a new and far narrower definition of good science. Again, the range of acceptable methods promoted in this context is considerably narrower than the range recognized as scientifically valid a short decade ago.

Concluding Thoughts

The analysis in this chapter suggests that the current move to reshape education into an evidence-based field and to make education research more rigorous is the most recent episode in a quest for scientific legitimacy for the field of education research that has been under way for more than a century. Although the attempt to establish randomized trials as the new "gold standard" for education research was spearheaded by lawmakers and bureaucrats who stood outside of the education research community, the field's low status and unresolved quest for scientific legitimacy made it vulnerable to attempts from outside the field to retool and transform it. Especially important in this respect were a series of critiques that elites from within the education research community mounted against the field—charges that too much of the research lacked rigor and was "unscientific." By the 1990s the field's scientific legitimacy had been threatened by these internal critiques and by the flowering of new research traditions that, while arguably important and healthy for the field in many respects, displaced from preeminence the exemplar of psychological methods and theories in which the field had long based its claims to scientific legitimacy.

In and of themselves, these developments furthered the crisis of scientific legitimacy within the field and in so doing provided a necessary but not sufficient opening for the education sciences movement, which was essentially an attempt by outsiders to put education research on a putatively sounder scientific basis and to usurp the scientific authority of the research community to do so. The education sciences movement was made possible by two other parallel developments from outside the education research community: a critique of the failings of American *education* that developed in the 1980s and continues apace today, and the establishment of a new scientific field devoted to the use of randomized field trials for the evaluation of new social programs.

The critique of American education included a political critique of the field of education research for failing to provide a strong evidence base to inform educational policy and practice. Both policymakers and educational researchers increasingly talked about the need to make education research more relevant to problems of educational policy and practice. Thus the education research community itself accepted as legitimate an increasing emphasis on applied research within the field. By the 1990s the education research community and the policymaker/practitioner community both called for tighter links between education research, on the one hand, and educational policy and practice, on the other. This greater acceptance of the study of what was later called "what works" in education provided a crucial opening for advocates of randomized trials, because advocates were able to argue that they were the ideal methodological tool for questions of what works in education.

If politicians had been the only group calling for a wholesale transformation of the field of education research, the effort would likely not have gotten much political traction. After all, science is supposed to be divorced from politics. But an alternative set of scientific experts was found whose calls for a new way of doing scientific research in education provided the scientific legitimacy to the attempt to usurp the scientific authority of acknowledged experts within the field. These experts came from the interdisciplinary field of evaluation research, in which few members of the education research community participated, who promoted random field trials for the evaluation of social programs in a broad range of fields. These scholars/experts had their own legitimacy problems within the traditional social science disciplines in the academy, and suffered the stigma of working in an "applied" field. They took their methodological cue from the most "scientific" fields in the social sciences—psychology and statistics—and took education research to task for the lack of widespread adoption of random field trials for purposes of evaluating educational programs.

Once the education research community accepted the importance of the research-policy/practice link, and policymakers ramped up their calls for education to become an evidence-based field, the stage was set for random field trials to be held up as the method to accomplish it in education. The call for random field trials for fairly limited purposes (evaluation of educational interventions) was blurred (at times) into a call for an expansive use of experimental methods to make all of education research more "scientific." But what became, essentially, an attempt by non-scientists—federal bureaucrats and lawmakers—to dictate scientific standards to an unwilling, unreceptive scientific community could not have succeeded if it had not been able to enlist a set of authoritative expert scientific voices from elsewhere. Expert advocates of randomized trials were found in the field of evaluation research —predominantly "scientists" with backgrounds (if not current appointments) in psychology and/or statistics. Educational psychologists, the long-time standard-bearers of "scientific" research methods within the education research community, were largely absent from this group's ranks. Without the backing of this group of acknowledged experts, lawmakers and bureaucrats could not have managed to pull off what amounted to an end run around the education research community.

Notes

1 The starting point for recent developments is often seen as the passage of the Reading Excellence Act in 1999—see, e.g., Eisenhart and Towne (2003).
2 The NAE consists of a maximum of 150 members at any one time who are elected on the basis of their scholarly and research achievements. As such, the NAE membership constitutes an elite within the education research community. Within the larger university-based community of scientists and scholars, however, NAE members—especially the majority of whom hold or are retired from appointments in schools of education—cannot escape what Carl Kaestle (1993) famously termed the "awful reputation" of education research.
3 Indeed, the 1965 provision requiring the evaluation of Title I of the Elementary and Secondary Education Act was an early impetus to the development of the evaluation-research sector (Lagemann 1997:12).
4 Donald Campbell was on the psychology faculty at Northwestern University; Julian Stanley was on the psychology faculty at Johns Hopkins University.
5 At the time of its publication, Thomas D. Cook was a colleague of Campbell's in psychology at Northwestern University.
6 At the time of these writings, Boruch was a colleague of Cook's and Campbell's in the psychology department at Northwestern University.
7 To note just a couple, sociologists Peter Rossi and Richard Berk wrote widely about the use of experimental methods for the evaluation of social interventions (e.g., Berk 1981; Rossi and Freeman 1982) or used them in studies of the effects of criminal-justice programs (e.g., Rauma and Berk 1982; Rossi, Berk, and Lenihan 1980). Significantly, his prominence within the evaluation-research sector notwithstanding, Berk (1981) lamented the low regard in which evaluation research was held in the academy and the difficulty of publishing evaluation studies in top journals in the social sciences. This again illustrates a divergence between what constituted scientific legitimacy in the scholarly community versus the community of users of evaluation

research findings, especially policymakers and practitioners. For a discussion of how the long-standing tension between the applied nature of professional fields versus the focus on basic research that is more characteristic of the traditional disciplines plays out in education research, see Mitchell and Haro (1999).

8 July 1, 2004 Institute of Education Sciences news release. Retrieved February 18, 2005 (http://www.ed.gov/news/pressreleases/2004/07/07012004.html).

9 Importantly, the language about "scientifically based research" was developed after staff of the House Education and Workforce Committee consulted widely with university-based researchers, primarily cognitive psychologists (Eisenhart and Towne 2003). Hence it was based on a shared understanding of what constitutes good science as commonly practiced in psychology labs.

10 Note that the group is named in honor and memory of Donald T. Campbell, the co-author of the "bible" of experimental methods for social research.

11 I find significant the language used here: they are described as "scientists" rather than "researchers" or "scholars."

12 Most prominently, the American Educational Research Association, the Consortium of Social Science Associations, and the Federation of Behavioral, Psychological, and Cognitive Sciences. See Viadero and Portner (2000).

13 Nonetheless, the authors of the report adopted a more limited definition of "scientific research" than the definitions promoted by many who were perceived to be on the winning side in the education research paradigm wars. *Scientific Research in Education* thus unleashed a fierce debate within the education research community, undertaken primarily in education association conferences and special issues of education journals, between those advocating a more limited definition of scientific research that was seen by detractors as unduly privileging quantitative methods (although not only randomized experiments) versus those who objected to the report's classification of now-well-established forms of education research, such as interpretivism, postmodernism, critical theory, and some forms of qualitative research, as useful for some purposes but "unscientific" (see Eisenhart and Towne 2003).

14 Note also that Whitehurst's efforts and policies were supported by G. Reid Lyon, whose program at the National Institutes of Health had been responsible for the influential series of random experiments on the effectiveness of various reading programs. This lent the scientific authority of the NIH, as well as the scientific authority of the program Lyon directed, to criticisms of education research as it had been practiced.

15 The exception is Robert Boruch, who holds an appointment in the Graduate School of Education at the University of Pennsylvania. See http://coexgov.securesites.net/index.php?keyword=a432fbc71d7564&PHPSESSID=6db8acad28256db34f39da32e0cc5cfc. Retrieved November 16, 2007. Boruch is by training a psychologist and methodologist, however, who for most of his career held an appointment in a psychology department. He was also one of the early members of the interdisciplinary community calling for the increased use of randomized field trials for purposes of social program evaluation.

16 See http://coexgov.securesites.net/index.php?keyword=a432fbc34d71c7. Retrieved November 10, 2007.

17 An eminent educational psychologist and former dean of the Stanford University School of Education.

18 Schwandt (2005:286) shows that of the 29 people who constituted the original combined membership of the technical advisory panel for the WWC and the board of the Coalition for Evidence-Based Policy, over half were psychologists, economists, psychometricians, or statisticians. Another two were from applied fields that had long embraced randomized controlled trials as the methodological standard for program evaluation (medicine and criminology), and six were from private research firms and think tanks.

19 See pp. 4–5 of the call for proposals titled "Predoctoral Interdisciplinary Research Training Program in the Education Sciences" dated February 4, 2004. Available at http://www.ed.gov/programs/predoc/predoctoralrfa2004.doc. Retrieved April 28, 2008.

20 See *Resolution on the Essential Elements of Scientifically Based Research* (AERA 2003).

21 Nor did the criticism from the scientific community abate after the first few years of the Bush presidency. In February 2004, for example, a highly-publicized report issued by the Union of Concerned Scientists and signed by more than 60 of the nation's top scientists renewed earlier charges that the Bush administration routinely misrepresented scientific findings and made selections for scientific panels on the basis of prospective panelists' support for administration policies rather than scientific credentials (Brainard 2004:A18). In February 2006, Bush administration policies on scientific issues were again attacked in a highly visible manner by a number of leading scientists at a session at the annual meeting of the American Association for

the Advancement of Science (AAAS). Most notably, David Baltimore, a Nobel laureate and president-elect of the AAAS, charged that the Bush administration misuses "science policy to advance its political aims" (Byrne and Monastersky 2006:24).

22   Consider the counterfactual. In the absence of allies who could be recognized as scientists and experts who could argue the scientific merits of the new standards for education research, the lawmakers and bureaucrats' efforts to set research standards would have appeared to have been too overtly political and coercive. That is, the efforts would have revealed the power relations that in the normal course of "doing science" are concealed by the couching of debates in terms of knowledge, truth, impartiality, and objectivity (see Fuchs 1992:17). A more-or-less united front on the part of "scientists" might not have defeated the effort to establish randomized controlled trials as the gold standard for education research, but it would have cast it as an exercise of political power that (illegitimately) ran roughshod over good science.

23   The WWC guidelines did acknowledge that quasi-experiments and regression-discontinuity designs could sometimes reliably identify causal effects in education research (see Valentine and Cooper 2004), but many in the education research community still objected that the WWC's definition of legitimate "scientific" methods was overly restrictive (see Schwandt 2005; Eisenhart and Towne 2003).

24   White House press release, November 19, 2003. Available at http://www.whitehouse.gov/news/releases/2003/11/20031119-3.html. Retrieved February 9, 2008.

25   Hakuta, an educational psychologist, was not on the IES board.

26   Eric Hanushek, an economist, is the only one of the board members who is a member of the National Academy of Education, for example.

27   See www.educationaleffectiveness.org/pages/leadership/advisory.shtml. Retrieved November 8, 2007.

28   Even though the National Research Council's report *Scientific Research in Education* was contested by many within the education research community, the committee membership nonetheless drew fairly heavily on the education research community itself: fully half its 16 members had current or recent appointments in schools of education (see listing in Shavelson and Towne 2002). And, more importantly for present purposes, the volume's stance on what constitutes good research in education is far broader than the stance endorsed by the IES. Subsequent organizations that have allied closely with the IES stance include few individuals who had been on the NRC committee that produced *Scientific Research in Education*: Only two of the members of the advisory board for the Society for Research on Educational Effectiveness had been on the NRC committee, and only one member of the National Board for Education Sciences, the IES advisory board, had been on the NRC committee. Even more significantly, none of those with overlapping memberships on the NRC committee and one of these other boards were long-time members of education school faculty.

29   While the report expresses concern that the current attention devoted to randomized trials might lead to an underestimation of the value of (quantitative) analyses of large datasets for purposes of addressing questions of causality in education, many methods that in the 1990s and earlier had been widely accepted within the education research community for "causal" research were left out of consideration. The point is that while the position expressed in this report and other public statements from the leadership of the education research community expands the definition of appropriate methods for causal research beyond the randomized trial, it largely accepts the attempt by the advocates of the education sciences to limit the methods appropriate to "scientific" research or "causal" research to statistical approaches that substitute for the logic of randomized trials when they are not feasible or practical, such as fixed effects models, analyses using instrumental variables, propensity score matching, and regression-discontinuity designs.

References

American Educational Research Association. 2003. Resolution on the Essential Elements of Scientifically Based Research. Retrieved May 5, 2008 (http://www.aera.net/meeting/councilresolution03.htm).

Angrist, Joshua D. 2004. "American Education Research Changes Tack." *Oxford Review of Economic Policy* 20:198–212.

Berk, Richard A. 1981. "On the Compatibility of Applied and Basic Research: An Effort in Marriage Counseling." *American Sociologist* 4:204–211.

Berk, Richard A., Robert F. Boruch, David L. Chambers, Peter H. Rossi, and Ann D. Witte. 1985. "Social Policy Experimentation: A Position Paper." *Evaluation Research* 9:387–429.

Boruch, Robert F., Dorothy de Loya, and Brooke Snyder. 2002. "The Importance of Randomized Field Trials in Education and Related Areas." Pp. 50–79 in *Evidence Matters: Randomized Trials in*

Education Research, edited by Frederick Mosteller and Robert Boruch. Washington, DC: Brookings Institution Press.

Boruch, Robert, F.A. John McSweeney and E. Jon Soderstrom. 1978. "Randomized Field Experiments for Program Planning, Development and Evaluation: An Illustrative Bibliography." *Evaluation Review* 2:655–695.

Boruch, Robert F., David S. Cordray, Georgine M. Pion and Laura C. Leviton. 1983. "Recommendations to Congress and Their Rationale: The Holtzman Project." *Evaluation Review* 7:5–35.

Boyd-Zacharias, Jayne. 1999. "Project STAR: The Story of the Tennessee Class-Size Study." *American Educator* Summer:1–6. Retrieved November 12, 2007 (http://www.aft.org/pubs-reports/american_educator/summer99/STARSummer99.pdf).

Brainard, Jeffrey. 2004. "How Sound Is Bush's 'Sound Science'?" *Chronicle of Higher Education* 50(26):A18–A20.

Byrne, Richard and Richard Monastersky. 2006. "Nobel Laureate Assails Bush Science Policy." *Chronicle of Higher Education* 52(26):24.

Camic, Charles and Yu Xie. 1994. "The Statistical Turn in American Social Science: Columbia University, 1890 to 1915." *American Sociological Review* 59:773–805.

Campbell, Donald T. and Julian C. Stanley. 1963. *Experimental and Quasi-experimental Designs for Research*. Chicago, IL: Rand McNally.

Clifford, Geraldine Joncich and James W. Guthrie. 1988. *Ed School: A Brief for Professional Education*. Chicago, IL: University of Chicago Press.

Cole, Jonathan R. and Stephen Cole. 1973. *Social Stratification in Science*. Chicago, IL: University of Chicago Press.

Collins, Randall. 1989. "Toward a Theory of Intellectual Change: The Social Causes of Philosophies." *Science, Technology, and Human Values* 14:107–140.

Constas, Mark A. 1998. "The Changing Nature of Educational Research and a Critique of Postmodernism." *Educational Researcher* 27:26–33.

Cook, Thomas D. 1999. "Considering the Major Arguments against Random Assignment: An Analysis of the Intellectual Culture Surrounding Evaluation in American Schools of Education." Paper presented at Harvard Faculty Seminar on Experiments in Education, March, Cambridge, MA.

Cook, Thomas D. and Donald T. Campbell. 1979. *Quasi-experimentation: Design and Analysis Issues for Field Settings*. Boston, MA: Houghton Mifflin.

Cook, Thomas D. and Monique R. Payne. 2002. "Objecting to the Objections to Using Random Assignment in Educational Research." Pp. 150–178 in *Evidence Matters: Randomized Trials in Education Research*, edited by Frederick Mosteller and Robert Boruch. Washington, DC: Brookings Institution Press.

Crane, Diana. 1972. *Invisible Colleges: Diffusion of Knowledge in Scientific Communities*. Chicago, IL: University of Chicago Press.

Eisenhart, Margaret and Lisa Towne. 2003. "Contestation and Change in National Policy on 'Scientifically Based' Education Research." *Educational Researcher* 32:31–38.

Epstein, Steven. 1996. *Impure Science: AIDS, Activism, and the Politics of Knowledge*. Berkeley, CA: University of California Press.

Fiske, Edward B. 1986. "Study by U.S. Department of Education Reports on Best Ways of Teaching." *New York Times*, March 1, section 1, page 12, column 1.

Frickel, Scott and Neil Gross. 2005. "A General Theory of Scientific/Intellectual Movements." *American Sociological Review* 70:204–232.

Friedkin, Noah E. 1998. *A Structural Theory of Social Influence: Structural Analysis in the Social Sciences*. Cambridge, U.K.: Cambridge University Press.

Fuchs, Stephan. 1992. *The Professional Quest for Truth: A Social Theory of Science and Knowledge*. Albany, NY: State University of New York Press.

———. 1993. "A Sociological Theory of Scientific Change." *Social Forces* 71:933–953.

Gage, N. L. 1989. "The Paradigm Wars and Their Aftermath: A 'Historical' Sketch of Research on Teaching since 1989." *Educational Researcher* 18:4–10.

Griffith, B. C. and A. J. Miller. 1970. "Networks of Informal Communication among Scientifically Productive Scientists." Pp. 125–149 in *Communication among Scientists and Engineers*, edited by Carnot E. Nelson and Donald K. Pollack. Lexington, MA: D. C. Heath and Company.

Gueron, Judith M. 2002. "The Politics of Random Assignment: Implementing Studies and Affecting Policy." Pp. 15–49 in *Evidence Matters: Randomized Trials in Education Research*, edited by Frederick Mosteller and Robert Boruch. Washington, DC: Brookings Institution Press.

Harding, Sandra. 1991. *Whose Science? Whose Knowledge? Thinking from Women's Lives*. Ithaca, NY: Cornell University Press.

Hoffer, Thomas B., Scott Sederstrom, Lance Selfa, Vince Welch, Mary Hess, Shana Brown, Sergio Reyes, Kristy Webber, and Isabel Guzman-Barron. 2003. *Doctorate Recipients from United States Universities: Summary Report 2002.* Chicago, IL: National Opinion Research Center.
Jackson, Philip W. 1990. "The Functions of Educational Research." *Educational Researcher* 19:3–9.
Kaestle, Carl F. 1993. "The Awful Reputation of Education Research." *Educational Researcher* 22:23, 26–31.
Katz, Michael B. 1966. "From Theory to Survey in Graduate Schools of Education." *Journal of Higher Education* 37:325–334.
Kennedy, Donald. 2003. "An Epidemic of Politics." *Science* 299:625.
Labaree, David F. 2004. *The Trouble with Ed Schools.* New Haven, CT: Yale University Press.
Lagemann, Ellen Condliffe. 1997. "Contested Terrain: A History of Education Research in the United States, 1890–1990." *Educational Researcher* 26:5–17.
———. 2000. *An Elusive Science: The Troubling History of Education Research.* Chicago, IL: University of Chicago Press.
Lagemann, Ellen Condliffe and Lee S. Shulman (eds.). 1999. *Issues in Education Research: Problems and Possibilities.* San Francisco, CA: Jossey-Bass.
Lather, Patti. 2004a. "This Is Your Father's Paradigm: Government Intrusion and the Case of Qualitative Research in Education." *Qualitative Inquiry* 10:15–34.
———. 2004b. "Scientific Research in Education: A Critical Perspective." *British Educational Research Journal* 30:759–772.
Latour, Bruno. 1987. *Science in Action: How to Follow Scientists and Engineers through Society.* Cambridge, MA: Harvard University Press.
Lincoln, Yvonna S. and Gaile S. Cannella. 2004. "Qualitative Research, Power, and the Radical Right." *Qualitative Inquiry* 10:175–201.
Long, J. Scott and Robert McGinnis. 1985. "The Effects of the Mentor on the Academic Career." *Scientometrics* 7:255–280.
Michaels, David, Eula Bingham, Les Boden, Richard Clapp, Lynn R. Goldman, Polly Hoppin, Sheldon Krimsky, Celeste Monforton, David Ozonoff, and Anthony Robbins. 2002. "Advice without Dissent." *Science* 298:703.
Mitchell, Theodore R. and Analee Haro. 1999. "Poles Apart: Reconciling the Dichotomies in Education Research." Pp. 42–62 in *Issues in Education Research: Problems and Possibilities*, edited by Ellen Condliffe Lagemann and Lee S. Shulman. San Francisco, CA: Jossey-Bass.
Mooney, Chris. 2005. *The Republican War on Science.* New York: Basic Books.
Morgan, Richard. 2002. "Bill Passes to Reform Education Research." *Chronicle of Higher Education*, Nov. 8, p. 24.
National Academy of Education. 1991. *Research and the Renewal of Education: A Report from the National Academy of Education.* Stanford, CA: National Academy of Education.
National Commission on Excellence in Education. 1983. *A Nation at Risk: The Imperative for Educational Reform.* Washington, DC: The Commission.
Nature. 2001. "Problems with the President." *Nature* 410:499.
New York Times. 1985. "Education Watch: He Tests the Nation's Teachers, Schools." *New York Times*, July 21, section 4, page 9, column 1.
Olson, Lynn. 1999. "NRC Seeks New Agenda for Research." *Education Week* 18:1–2.
Rauma, David and Richard A. Berk. 1982. "Crime and Poverty in California: Some Quasi-experimental Evidence." *Social Science Research* 11:318–351.
Reuben, Julie A. 2003. "Education and the History of the Social Sciences." Pp. 622–634 in *The Cambridge History of Science*, Volume 7: *The Modern Social Sciences*, edited by Theodore M. Porter and Dorothy Ross. Cambridge, U.K.: Cambridge University Press.
Riecken, Henry W. and Robert F. Boruch. 1974. *Social Experimentation: A Method for Planning and Evaluating Social Intervention.* New York: Academic Press.
———. 1978. "Social Experiments." *Annual Review of Sociology* 4:511–532.
Robarts, James R. 1968. "The Quest for a Science of Education in the Nineteenth Century." *History of Education Quarterly* 8:431–446.
Rossi, Peter H., Richard A. Berk, and Kenneth J. Lenihan. 1980. *Money, Work, and Crime: Experimental Evidence.* New York: Academic Press.
Rossi, Peter H. and Howard E. Freeman. 1982. *Evaluation: A Systematic Approach.* 2nd ed. Thousand Oaks, CA: Sage Publications.
Rossi, Peter H. and James D. Wright. 1984. "Evaluation Research: An Assessment." *Annual Review of Sociology* 10:331–352.
Schneider, Barbara, Martin Carnoy, Jeremy Kilpatrick, William H. Schmidt, and Richard J. Shavelson.

2007. *Estimating Causal Effects: Using Experimental and Observational Designs.* Report from the Governing Board of the American Educational Research Association Grants Program. Washington, DC: American Educational Research Association.
Schwandt, Thomas A. 2005. "A Diagnostic Reading of Scientifically Based Research for Education." *Educational Theory* 55:285–305.
Scientific American. 2001. "Faith-Based Reasoning." *Scientific American* 284:8.
Shapin, Stephen. 1995. "Here and Everywhere: Sociology of Scientific Knowledge." *Annual Review of Sociology* 21:289–321.
Shavelson, Richard J. and Lisa Towne (eds.). 2002. *Scientific Research in Education.* Committee on Scientific Principles for Educational Research, National Research Council. Washington, DC: National Academy Press.
U.S. House of Representatives Committee on Government Reform—Minority Staff. 2003. *Politics and Science in the Bush Administration.* Retrieved March 19, 2008 (http://oversight.house.gov/features/politics_and_science/pdfs/pdf_politics_and_science_rep.pdf).
Valentine, Jeffrey C. and Harris Cooper. 2004. *What Works Clearinghouse Study Design and Implementation Assessment Device.* Version 1.1. Washington, DC: U.S. Department of Education.
Viadero, Debra. 1995a. "E.D. Spends Time on Task of Reshaping Research Efforts." *Education Week* 14(20):19–20.
———. 1995b. "Academy of Education Launches 3-Year Study on Improving Research." *Education Week* 14(40):6.
———. 1998. "National Academy Guides the Future of Education Research." *Education Week* 18(9):10.
———. 1999a. "Experts' Panel Seeks New Research Priorities." *Education Week* 18(29):20–21.
———. 1999b. "Panel Suggests Federal Research Priorities." *Education Week* 18(34):5.
———. 1999c. "New Priorities, Focus Sought for Research." *Education Week* 18(41):1–3.
———. 2001a. "Whitehurst Aims to Retool Education Research." *Education Week* 21(1):38–39.
———. 2001b. "Panel Defines 'Science' of Education Research." *Education Week* 21(15):12.
———. 2002a. "Bill Would Remake OERI into 'Education Sciences' Academy." *Education Week* 21(25):31.
———. 2002b. "Campbell Collaboration Seeks to Firm Up 'Soft Sciences.'" *Education Week* 21(29):8.
———. 2002c. "Ed. Dept. Picks Groups to Develop Database of Effective Practices." *Education Week* 22(1):38–39.
———. 2002d. "Ed. Dept. Quietly Funds More Experimental Studies." *Education Week* 22(15):1–2.
———. 2004. "Ed. Dept. Issues Practical Guide to Research-Based Practice." *Education Week* 23(16):12.
———. 2005. "Education Sciences Board Convenes for First Time." *Education Week* 24(23):32–33.
———. 2006a. "New Group of Researchers Focuses on Scientific Study." *Education Week* 25(21):1–2.
———. 2006b. "Breakaway Education Research Group Pulls from Diverse Disciplines." *Education Week* 26(16):11.
———. 2007. "AERA Stresses Value of Alternatives to 'Gold Standard.'" *Education Week* 26(33):12–13.
Viadero, Debra and Jessica Portner. 2000. "Research." *Education Week* 19(37):10.
Weiss, Rick. 2002. "HHS Seeks Science Advice to Match Bush Views." *Washington Post*, September 17, p. A01.
Werner, Leslie Maitland. 1986. "For a Radical Reformer, Research Is Power." *New York Times*, November 9, section 12, page 28, column 1.
Zuckerman, Harriet. 1977. *Scientific Elite: Nobel Laureates in the United States.* New York: Free Press.

CHAPTER 2

A History of Efforts to Improve the Quality of Federal Education Research: From Gardner's Task Force to the Institute of Education Sciences

MARIS A. VINOVSKIS

Educators and policymakers periodically raise concerns about the quality of federally-funded research, development, and statistics. Surprisingly little effort, however, has been made to assess the actual quality of that work by examining what has been produced. Nor do policymakers offer specific recommendations for improving federal education research agencies. During the 1990s, however, Congress became more interested in the quality and impartiality of federal education research. With the passage of the No Child Left Behind Act of 2001, the White House and the 107th Congress committed themselves to requiring the use of high-quality, scientifically-based research to improve American education.

This chapter traces some of the attempts to improve federal education research—from the recommendations of the influential 1964 Gardner Task Force on Education to the creation in 2002 of yet another federal research agency, the Institute of Education Sciences. By providing a critical narrative analysis of past federal education research initiatives, this chapter highlights the conditions that have facilitated or impeded the provision of high-quality research, development, and statistics.

Restructuring Education Research, Statistics, and Development during the Johnson Administration

Before the 1950s the federal government provided only modest assistance for education research and development (Lagemann 1997, 2000; Vinovskis 1996). Following the passage of the Cooperative Research Act of 1954, the Office of Education modestly expanded its research partnerships with colleges, universities, and state departments of education (Clark and Carriker 1961). And spurred by the Soviets' launch of the Sputnik satellite in 1957, the Eisenhower administration and the 85th Congress passed the National Defense Education Act of 1958, which provided federal education monies for science, mathematics, and foreign language instruction as well as additional education research funding (Lazarsfeld and Sieber 1964). By FY1960 the Office of Education spent more than $10 million annually for research and dissemination (Dershimer 1976).

Despite these increases in federal education research support in the 1950s, the extent and quality of education research failed to keep pace with the substantive and methodological innovations made in the other social sciences (Cronbach and Suppes 1969; Featherman and Vinovskis 2001). Indeed, Paul Lazarsfeld and Sam Sieber's survey (1964) of the quality of education research in the early 1960s was pessimistic about the quality of the next generation of researchers being trained by schools of education.

When President Lyndon B. Johnson launched the War on Poverty in 1964, education was slated to play a key role in the effort to eliminate poverty during the next decade. Yet there was considerable dissatisfaction with the leadership and research of the Office of Education in the U.S. Department of Health, Education, and Welfare. Consequently, the White House appointed John Gardner, president of the Carnegie Corporation, to chair the 1964 Task Force on Education; the panel was to assess current federal education policies and recommend ways to improve them (Dershimer 1976).

After reviewing the quality of education research and development, the Gardner Task Force complained about the scientific inadequacy and irrelevance of much of that work. The Task Force report called for the creation of at least a dozen large-scale national laboratories that would support "a massive burst of innovation" and foster a "system designed for continuous renewal, a system in which reappraisal and innovation" are an integral part of the programs (Gardner 1964:33). Rather than continuing to fund mainly "small-scale efforts operating out of a corner of a department of education," the task force advocated new institutions that would be "more closely akin to the great national laboratories of the Atomic Energy Commission and [sharing] many of their features" (Gardner 1964:34).

The recommendation of the Gardner Task Force on Education to create large-scale education laboratories was incorporated in Title IV of the Elementary and Secondary Education Act (ESEA) of 1965. Research and development funding for the Office of Education increased dramatically to $100 million in FY1967. But the decision of the Office of Education to create numerous modestly-funded laboratories, focusing more on providing regional technical assistance and local services rather than long-term research and large-scale development, undermined the original vision of the Gardner Task Force (Dershimer 1976; Vinovskis 1998a).

The 1964 Civil Rights Act called for a large-scale civil rights study, the Educational Opportunity Survey. In one of the first national education research studies of its kind, the Office of Education commissioned James Coleman to analyze 4,000 schools, a half-million students, and 60,000 teachers to determine whether schools attended by African-American students received equal resources. Surprisingly, the 1966 Coleman study found that minority schools received relatively equal funding; but the study also argued that there was little direct relationship between per pupil spending and student academic achievement once the socioeconomic background of the parents was taken into consideration. The Coleman study revolutionized social science research in education, but the report did not have much impact in the last two years of the Johnson administration. Years later, however, it was resurrected by Daniel Patrick Moynihan in the Richard M. Nixon administration and played an important role in framing its policies (Mosteller and Moynihan 1972).

The Johnson administration also devoted considerable efforts to evaluating military and social programs. Unfortunately, however, some of the assessments were hurriedly commissioned and inadequately designed, and led to considerable debates among the public and experts. The controversial Westinghouse analysis of the early childhood education Head Start program, for example, raised questions about the efficacy of that program in fostering the long-term academic achievement of disadvantaged young children (Vinovskis 2005a). And the Follow Through program, intended to help transition Head Start students move into regular classrooms, was piloted at the Office of Education in mid-1967. Follow Through was intended to be a large-scale service program; but inadequate initial funding forced Follow Through to be hastily converted to an experimental initiative (Elmore 1976; Vinovskis 1999).

There were several other major changes in education research and statistics during the Johnson administration. As part of the Office of Education's 1965 reorganization, a Bureau of Research was created to oversee education research, statistics, and development—including creation of the National Center for Education Statistics (NCES). The Bureau of Research also established the Educational Resources Information Center (ERIC), which funded a dozen clearinghouses at universities to collect and distribute education research information for classroom teachers and scholars. At the end of the decade the Exploratory Committee on Assessing the Progress of Education developed the National Assessment of Educational Progress (NAEP) to assess the academic achievement of students in the 4th, 8th, and 12th grades (Bailey and Mosher 1968; Dershimer 1976; Jones and Olkin 2004; Vinovskis 1998b).

Improving Education Research and Development in the 1970s

The incoming Nixon administration continued several of the major evaluations initiated by its predecessor (Finn 1977). The Follow Through program, for example, was revamped and expanded. The conceptual idea behind Follow

Through was planned variation—funding different types of programs to assist at-risk Head Start children move into the regular schools; and then assessing their relative effectiveness in enhancing the academic, social, and health outcomes of the participants. Many of the experimental models supported by Follow Through were not well designed or adequately implemented. Over time, most Follow Through programs simply became de facto service providers, though the rationale for the program continued to be their experimental orientation. Still, the program survived until the early 1990s. Altogether, about $1.5 billion dollars (in constant 1982–1984 = 100 dollars) was spent on Follow Through from FY1967 to FY1992—almost twice as much as was spent on the regional educational laboratories and about two and a half times what was spent on the R&D centers during those 25 years (Vinovskis 1999).

The Brookings Panel on Social Experimentation explored the ongoing Head Start and Follow Through planned variation experiments at an influential 1973 conference. At the conclusion of the conference, the organizers summarized the proceedings and called for a systematic five-stage strategy for education research and development that would require 10–12 years to complete. Their recommendations still provide one of the best frameworks for doing such work today—though they have been largely forgotten and ignored by educators and recent administrations.

> The experiment would begin as a highly controlled investigation at a single site involving random assignment to control and treatment groups and careful observations of inputs and outcomes. If the intervention appeared to have appreciable positive effects under these conditions, a couple of years would then be devoted to developing it further.... The intervention would next be tried out under natural conditions in a small number of sites.... Not until after all of this development, small-scale testing, and revision had been successfully completed would a large-scale field test be undertaken to find out how the intervention works under a variety of conditions and with a variety of populations. In the final stage, full results of the field testing and training would be disseminated to those who wanted to adopt the intervention in their own school.
>
> (Rivlin and Timpane 1975:18)

The proposal by the Brookings Panel on Social Experimentation fleshed out some of the original research and development strategy that had been proposed by the Gardner Task Force on Education a decade earlier. Unfortunately, interest in rigorous long-term development work faltered in the mid-1970s. Conservative congressional complaints about federally-funded National Science Foundation (NSF) curriculum development initiatives discouraged many R&D centers as well as regional educational laboratories from undertaking rigorous developmental work. Instead, most of the R&D centers and regional education laboratories now pursued multiple small undertakings. And the potentially promising Follow Through planned variation experiments were quietly abandoned as projects shifted their federal monies to providing technical assistance and local services rather than program assessments (Vinovskis 2001).

Despite the improvements in education research, statistics, and development in the 1960s and early 1970s, there was continued dissatisfaction with the quality and utility of the work produced through the Bureau of Research (Dershimer 1976). As a result, Moynihan, executive director of Nixon's Domestic Council, and other administration officials urged the creation of a new agency, the National Institute of Education (NIE). This idea was championed by Rep. John Brademas (D-IN), Chair of the House Select Subcommittee on Education and received bipartisan support—though most other members were either indifferent to the proposal or thought they already had enough research information to improve American schools (Sproull, Weiner, and Wolf 1978).

The National Institute of Education was established in June 1972, but never received either the funding or the political support that had been anticipated by its proponents. When the agency tried to end funding of the R&D centers and the regional laboratories because of a concern with the low quality of the research and the relatively high cost of their technical assistance, a bitter political battle ensued. The Council on Educational Development and Research (CEDaR), the lobby group for the centers and laboratories, persuaded the House and Senate appropriations committees to earmark funds for their clients—even though this meant that other NIE projects had their funding substantially reduced or eliminated (Sproull et al. 1978; Vinovskis 2001).

Whereas the initial emphasis within NIE had been on applied social science research, during the second half of the 1970s more attention was paid to basic research. At the same time, responding to practitioner and congressional criticisms, NIE also tripled its dissemination expenditures. And the National Center for Educational Statistics (NCES) expanded NAEP testing and developed the National Longitudinal Study to analyze the transition of students from high school to college or into the labor force. Even as the NCES budget grew, however, it still trailed substantially other federal statistical agencies (Jones and Olkin 2004; Vinovskis 1998a, 1998b).

Reagan Administration Attempts to Dismantle the National Institute of Education and Improve Education Statistics

Ronald Reagan's landslide presidential victory and the unexpected Republican control of the Senate emboldened Republicans to reduce the size and influence of the federal government on domestic affairs. The Reagan White House tried to abolish the recently established U.S. Department of Education; but determined Democratic congressional opposition combined with assistance from some moderate Republican lawmakers thwarted that attempt. The Reagan administration, however, reduced federal education monies in constant dollars by one-seventh from FY1980 to FY1984 (Verstegen 1990).

Conservatives also targeted NIE for elimination. They complained that the agency was staffed by liberals who slanted research for their own ideological purposes. The new NIE director, Edward Curran, refused to reappoint most of the excepted service employees (those who had been appointed for multiyear contracts) and redirected the research agenda of the agency; and Curran secretly pleaded with the White House to abolish NIE altogether. Clashes between the new NIE director and the more moderate Secretary of Education, Terrel Bell, however, resulted in the dismissal of Curran. But the internal and external political battles within NIE continued, and hampered the operation of the office (Zodhiates 1988).

Faced with the necessity to absorb major cuts in the federal budget as well as the political turmoil at NIE, the agency had its budget dramatically reduced. As NIE coped with its financial losses, the agency tried to distribute the cuts proportionately across its grantees. But CEDaR persuaded Congress to limit the R&D center and regional education laboratory losses to only 10 percent. By contrast, individual researchers, some of whom might have produced higher-quality work, did not have a comparable lobby organization to support their claims. At the same time, congressionally-mandated expenditures for programs such as ERIC and NAEP further reduced NIE's flexibility in managing the reductions. As a result, NIE funding for most other activities came to an almost complete halt (Vinovskis 1998a).

Under the leadership of Secretary Bell, the U.S. Department of Education created the National Commission on Excellence in Education. The bipartisan Commission issued its now classic 1983 report, *A Nation at Risk*, which warned that the American education system had badly deteriorated. Interestingly, the expert panel simply assumed that they already knew what had to be done and therefore additional education research and development was unnecessary (National Commission on Excellence in Education 1983:15). Thus one of the most influential panels of education experts in the early 1980s downplayed the need for any further major investments in education research and development (Vinovskis 2003).

When William Bennett replaced Bell as the Secretary of Education in 1985, he reorganized the U.S. Department of Education. The new umbrella agency for education research, statistics, and development was the Office of Educational Research and Improvement (OERI), and Chester "Checker" Finn was appointed as the new Assistant Secretary (Hertling 1985).

Concerns about the poor quality of education research and statistics continued. A National Academy of Sciences (NAS) panel that had been appointed earlier to examine NCES issued a highly critical report of that agency. Unless immediate reforms were undertaken, the NAS panel reported that "we are unanimous in our conviction that serious consideration should be given to the more drastic alternative of abolishing the [NCES] center and finding other means to obtain and disseminate education data" (Levine 1986:4). Responding to the NAS panel's criticisms, Assistant Secretary Finn and Emerson Elliott, the future first Commissioner of Education Statistics, revamped NCES into a strong statistical agency (Elliott 1989).

The Office of Educational Research and Improvement during the Bush Administration

Whereas attempts had been made in the Reagan administration to abolish NIE, during the George H. W. Bush administration the Office of Educational Research and Improvement (OERI) expanded considerably and made some improvements. His term was January 1989 to January 1993. The management of the agency was mixed—Christopher Cross and Diane Ravitch provided strong administrative and intellectual leadership; but Patricia Hines was appointed while Congress was in recess and was characterized as an unqualified conservative activist. Within that four-year period there were five changes in OERI leaders, which undermined the agency's continuity.

The OERI budget more than tripled during the Bush administration. Much of that increase, however, was not in OERI's research, statistical, or development budget, but in the transfer of other types of programs such as the Blue Ribbon Schools (which recognized schools providing high-quality education). Funding for the more traditional OERI activities such as the regional education laboratories and the R&D centers, NCES, ERIC, and field-initiated grants did grow (with most of that increase for the centers, the laboratories, and NCES). Yet the average size of the centers diminished as OERI Assistant Secretaries Finn and Cross favored funding more, but smaller, institutions (Vinovskis 1998a, 2001). The statistical work of the National Center for Education Statistics continued to improve under the guidance of NCES Commissioner Elliott. And work continued on the National Assessment on Educational Progress as interest in assessment of student achievement grew following the 1989 Charlottesville Education Summit and the announcement of the six National Education Goals (Vinovskis 1999, 2001).

Assistant Secretary Cross commissioned the NAS to assess the role of the federal government in education research and development (with particular attention to OERI). The NAS panel issued its influential 1992 report, which recommended OERI's reorganization into several R&D directorates. The report endorsed the R&D centers, but suggested they undertake additional basic research as well as "engage in more sustained efforts of applied research, development, aimed at nurturing new methods, approaches, and tools to full maturity" (Atkinson and Jackson 1992:150). At the same time, the NAS panel recommended that the "innovative methods, programs, and processes developed by the centers should be subject to a quality assurance process before wide-scale distribution" (Atkinson and Jackson 1992:150).

Whereas critics of the regional educational laboratories questioned the quality of their research and the cost-effectiveness of their technical assistance, the NAS panel recommended that the laboratories be maintained and converted to reform assistance laboratories (RALs). The NAS panel stated that "RALs would conduct a wide range of activities: applied research, development, demonstrations, evaluations, dissemination, state policy assistance, and technical assistance for the purpose of facilitating school reform" (Atkinson and Jackson 1992:152). Similar to their suggestion for the R&D centers, the panel advised that the "RALs' innovative methods, programs, and processes should be subject to a quality assurance review" (Atkinson and Jackson 1992:152).

Although OERI wanted the NAS study to assess the quality of the work produced by the centers and laboratories, the panel did not analyze in any detail the functions of these institutions or the quality of their products. This was a very unfortunate but not an unusual decision, as most earlier studies also had not analyzed systematically the quality of the center and lab work. The NAS panel acknowledged, however, that "OERI has a checkered history in respect to quality assurance" (Atkinson and Jackson 1992:126). Yet in an effort to promote long-term stability for the labs, the panel questioned the advisability of periodic competitions for these institutions (Atkinson and Jackson 1992:153).

Frustrated by the lack of information about the quality of work produced in the centers and labs, Assistant Secretary Ravitch recruited University of Michigan professor Maris Vinovskis as OERI's Research Advisor and asked him to review the research and development products produced by these institutions. Vinovskis examined the quality of work produced by five of the current 20 R&D centers (as well as two former centers); he also analyzed the research and development projects of five of the ten regional educational laboratories. Preliminary results of that investigation were shared with the interested parties in 1992, and the final report was released in mid-1993 under the Clinton administration (Vinovskis 1993).

Vinovskis praised center accomplishments, but complained that "many of the center activities are more a series of interesting and often well-done individual projects rather than part of a closely co-ordinated, ongoing research strategy" (Vinovskis 1993:86). He recommended that their budgets be directed toward a more coherent program of scientifically rigorous research and development. The overall quality of the existing work at the centers was mixed:

> On the one hand, some of the projects produced within centers have produced excellent social science research.... On the other hand, some of the research projects are so conceptually and methodologically weak that they either should never have been funded or should have been promptly improved after being funded.
> (Vinovskis 1993:88–89)

While Vinovskis also found some variation among the work of the regional education laboratories, he observed that "today, for all practical purposes, many of the labs are primarily regional institutions offering research-based technical assistance and governed mainly by their own regional boards" (Vinovskis

1993:189). The report urged OERI to explore carefully the different types of missions that the laboratories might be asked to do in the future. One possibility was "to expand the role of systematic research and development at the labs much along the lines envisioned for those institutions in the 1960s and early 1970s" (Vinovskis 1993:192). Serious questions were raised about the quality of the research and development products produced by the laboratories (with the notable exception of the Far West Laboratory). As a result, "given the unequal quality of applied and developmental research that has been encountered in this investigation, more emphasis needs to be placed on the quality of the work produced" (Vinovskis 1993:195).

After 18 months in office, Assistant Secretary Ravitch left office in January 1993 and reflected on her Washington experiences as well as the challenges facing OERI. She noted that "OERI has never had the appropriations to support a good research program." Moreover, "the agency does not have enough first-rate researchers inside the agency. There is a small cadre of able researchers in OERI, but their numbers are too few, and many are burdened with administrative duties" (Ravitch 1993:2). Unlike other major federal research entities such as NIH and NSF, OERI neither had much money to hire high-quality researchers nor was often willing to do so when staff vacancies occurred.

The "New" OERI

Congressional and White House disagreements over the powers of the proposed OERI policy oversight board initially stalled the reauthorization of the agency (Rothman 1992). The election of Bill Clinton to the White House and continued Democratic control of the House and Senate led to OERI's reauthorization on March 31, 1994 (as Title IX of the Goals 2000 Educate America Act). The new legislation called for the creation of five national research institutes (which housed the R&D centers), the Office of Reform Assistance and Dissemination (which included the regional educational laboratories), the National Center for Education Statistics, and the National Research Policy and Priorities Board (Schnaiberg 1994).

Congress made an unexpected effort to improve the scientific quality of federally-sponsored research during OERI's reauthorization. In the late 1980s and early 1990s there had been little congressional concern about the poor quality of OERI-funded education research. During the two days of OERI reauthorization hearings in March 1992 before the House Subcommittee on Select Education, however, concerns were raised about the political objectivity and quality of the work funded by the agency. Critics pointed to the absence of established scientific standards as allowing OERI to award some grants and contracts to pursue the Bush administration's partisan policies. In addition, the 1992 NAS report had called for a stronger peer review system. At the same time, the centers and laboratories, seeking to circumvent their traditional 5-year recompetitions, lobbied for renewals mainly on the basis of a successful

OERI-controlled third-year review (which certified that high-quality research had been produced) (Vinovskis 1998c).

As a result, the 1994 OERI reauthorization mandated the agency to develop and implement standards in three phases:

1. standards for the evaluation of applications for grants, contracts, and cooperative agreements;
2. standards for reviewing and designating exemplary promising programs;
3. standards for evaluating the activities and products of all recipients of OERI financial assistance.

Drafting the phase one and two standards was relatively easy because the tasks were more clearly definable and logistically manageable (especially since only applications above $100,000 required a peer review). Developing the phase three standards, however, was a more challenging task due to the large number and diversity of OERI-funded products. All grants, contracts, and cooperative agreements (not just above $100,000) were to receive both an interim and a final evaluation. Although the agency tried to deal with the mandated quality standards seriously, it failed to develop an adequate in-house evaluation system or resolve many of the problems. Yet the pioneering legislation by the 103rd Congress as well as OERI's efforts to comply acknowledged the shortcomings of federally-funded education research and reinforced the call for higher quality standards (Vinovskis 1998c).

With the 1994 reauthorization of OERI, the agency's budget increased by about 40 percent from FY1993 to FY1997—mainly due to the addition of non-research projects such as educational technology and dissemination. But while OERI funding rose during the Clinton administration's first term, its staff was reduced by one-quarter in order to provide personnel for other activities in the Department (it was the only U.S. Department of Education agency that lost such a substantial proportion of its staff). Regrettably, almost no one in the education research community publically complained at that time about this drastic staff reduction (Vinovskis 2001).

Responding to the OERI 1994 reauthorization, the agency was thoroughly reorganized; the OERI reinvention occupied much of the energy and attention of the diminished staff. Tasks such as improving the quality of the research and development as well as overseeing the larger number of the agency's grantees and contractors received less attention than was needed. The subsequent third-year reviews of the R&D centers and the regional educational laboratories, for example, did not employ the scientifically rigorous standards mandated by the 1994 OERI reauthorization (Vinovskis 2001).

Republicans unexpectedly won control of both the House and the Senate in the 1994 midterm elections and questioned the need for the U.S. Department of Education or for programs such as Goals 2000. There was also growing concern about the scientific quality of education research; some legislators remained skeptical about the quality, usefulness, and objectivity of federally-funded education research. As a result, Congress gradually paid more attention to the quality of education research as well as its incorporation into classrooms—especially in reading instruction.

Congress in 1997 asked the National Institutes of Health (NIH), in consultation with the U.S. Department of Education, to convene a national panel to assess the research basis for reading instruction in the schools, devise a strategy to disseminate information about effective reading programs, and recommend additional research for early reading development and instruction. Drawing upon the work of the National Research Council Committee on preventing reading difficulties, the 14-member National Reading Panel delivered a progress report to Congress in February 1999 (National Reading Panel 2000).

Clinton had proposed the America Reads initiative during his 1996 re-election campaign and introduced that legislation the following year. Rep. Bill Goodling (R-PA), chair of the Education and Workforce Committee, offered a GOP substitute, the Reading Excellence bill; Goodling's legislation called for training reading teachers rather than relying upon volunteer tutors as Clinton envisioned. The Goodling bill also required the use of scientifically-based reading research to guide classroom practices. Therefore, the GOP bill included a definition of scientifically-based reading research, which opponents attacked as too restrictive and inappropriately placed within the legislation. After some debate, the Clinton White House accepted the GOP's Reading Excellence bill and it passed in late 1998 (Manzo 1999).

Comprehensive school reforms also emphasized their scientific basis and focused on improving the entire school rather than just altering one or two elements. Led by Reps. David R. Obey (D-WI) and John Edward Porter (R-IL) in 1997, Congress passed the Comprehensive School Reform Demonstration program, which authorized $150 million in federal grants for low-performing schools to develop research-based school-wide reforms. The legislation emphasized the importance of using scientifically-based interventions and provided a list of 17 acceptable models—though it turned out that almost none of them had convincing scientific evidence of their ability to raise student achievement scores (Olson 1999).

As the House and Senate prepared for the 2000 OERI reauthorization, both chambers held hearings on the quality of research supported by the agency. In the House Subcommittee on Early Childhood, Youth, and Families hearings on May 4, 2000, for example, Chairman Michael Castle (R-DE) stated that "unfortunately, a significant amount of federal funding flows to programs for which there is little or no scientifically based research to demonstrate that these full-scale initiatives will increase student achievement." Castle also complained that he was "concerned with some of the findings in recent evaluations of the labs and research centers and disappointed that the Department has been less than forthcoming in providing Congress with timely information about the quality of their research and development" (U.S. House 2000:2). At a later October hearing, Castle also protested the failure of the U.S. Department of Education to provide overdue information from the Longitudinal Evaluation of School Change and Performance on the effectiveness of Title I; at that hearing he wondered whether that delay was politically motivated (Vinovskis 2002).

Several witnesses at the May 4 hearing testified to the generally low quality of education research and development sponsored by OERI, and some of them called for a more independent agency with stricter accountability for high-quality work (U.S. House 2000). As G. Reid Lyon, chief of the National Institute of Child Health and Human Development, bluntly put it, "Most education research is not well done, is not of good quality, does not inform, and should not be trusted" (Viadero 2000a:31).

Castle proposed the Scientifically-Based Education Research, Statistics, Evaluation, and Information Act of 2000 (H.R. 4875) to reauthorize OERI as an independent agency that produced quality research and development. Included in Castle's bill was a definition of high-quality scientific research. The Democrats on the Early Childhood, Youth, and Families subcommittee generally were supportive of Castle's bill, but opposed making the new agency an independent entity; a compromise was reached to have the agency remain within the U.S. Department of Education as an autonomous agency. The House subcommittee unanimously passed Castle's bill on July 26, 2000, but Senators postponed consideration until the next year (Viadero 2000b).

Responding to the congressional attempts to define more specifically scientifically-rigorous research, OERI's National Educational Research Policy and Priorities Board contracted with the National Research Council to review how scientific education research should be defined and improved. To carry out this assignment, the National Research Council created the Committee on Scientific Principles for Educational Research. The Committee decided

> not [to] attempt to evaluate the quality of bodies of existing research of existing researchers in the field, or of the existing federal research function because that would have constituted a monumental challenge and we judged it beyond the scope of our charge. Instead, we adopted a forward-looking approach that draws on lessons from history and identifies the roles of various stakeholders (e.g. researchers, policy-makers, practitioners) in fulfilling a vision for the future of education research.
>
> (Shavelson and Towne 2002:1–2)

The Committee on Scientific Principles for Educational Research explored in depth the nature of scientific work in education and related disciplines as well as briefly reviewing how other federal research agencies were organized and administered. The Committee concluded that the nature of scientific inquiry was the same in all fields—though education research was particularly challenging because the field was so broad and diverse. The Committee identified six key scientific principles that should be followed. The Committee also considered characteristics needed to design "a federal research agency to nurture a scientific culture within the agency" (Shavelson and Towne 2002:6). To achieve such an outcome,

> the agency must have an infrastructure insulated from political micromanagement, supported by sufficient and sustained resources, and led by a staff with top scientific and management credentials who have flexibility to make decisions and are accountable for them. Importantly, responsibility for the success of such an agency lies with all education stakeholders. The government cannot mandate a healthy federal role.
> (Shavelson and Towne 2002:7)

The Committee on Scientific Principles for Educational Research's report was discussed widely by both policymakers and education analysts. The Committee's analysis of scientific inquiry drew particular interest and praise, though some commentators questioned its somewhat limited definitions of scientific rigor or its lack of attention to other recent developments such as postmodernism (Berliner 2002; Pellegrino and Goldman 2002; St. Pierre 2002).

The Committee on Scientific Principles for Educational Research emphasized the responsibility of the community of education scholars for improving the quality of education research; at the same time, it opposed congressional efforts to define and mandate specific scientifically-rigorous research standards in legislation. In a summary of the report, the co-editors asked, "Why do lawmakers feel compelled to codify methods of educational research in federal statute? Perhaps it is because they do not trust the field to monitor itself" (Feuer, Towne, and Shavelson 2002:5).

Certainly there were reasons why policymakers might wonder if education investigators, as a community, were really willing or able to monitor themselves in terms of producing high-quality research. As noted earlier in this chapter, the 1992 National Academy of Sciences panel chose not to analyze the quality of OERI's work—even though the agency had initially requested it to do so; and despite the growing concerns about the quality of education research, the 2002 Committee on Scientific Principles for Educational Research also did not investigate the quality of education research or examine the OERI's operation. Similarly, the National Academy of Education's 1991 study group (the Commission on the Improvement of Education) solicited more than a dozen essays on the state of education research (Lagemann and Shulman 1999a). The essays and a related set of recommendations (Lagemann and Shulman 1999b) raised thoughtful questions about education research; but neither of the documents addressed the overall quality of federally-funded education research or what Congress and OERI specifically should do to improve that work.

Members of Congress also heard testimony from several scholars who wondered about the quality of education research, challenged the willingness of the American Educational Research Association (AERA) to develop and enforce high-quality research standards, and questioned OERI's commitment to ensuring high-quality research and development. Based upon the testimony from witnesses as well as his own observation as a former academic, Rep. Vernon J. Ehlers (R-MI) guessed that only about one-fifth of education was good. Responding to Ehlers' question of what needed to be done to improve that ratio, Maris Vinovskis asked:

> [W]ill OERI, will my colleagues in the AERA . . . tell you about which is the good 20 and which is the bad 80? We can talk all we want, but for 35 years we have had labs and centers, and who dares speak up[?] . . . What happens to those suggestions? Nothing.
> (U.S. House 2000:21)

Chairman Castle responded:

> I worry about the statement that Dr. Vinovskis made earlier, which is that nobody is willing to say that research is good or not good out there. I mean, I want to find 10 of the toughest sons-of-guns we can find out there who are willing to come in there and say this is just not working, it is not good, and this is good. And my concern is, are we just going to brush this under the rug and say, "Well, you're being resistant to change, but if you're good boys and girls, we'll give you another 5 years or 3 years," or whatever.
> (U.S. House 2000:26)

No Child Left Behind, the Institute of Education Sciences, and Education Research

George W. Bush personally was interested in helping children learn to read. Bush's mother had helped her son Neil deal with his dyslexia and promoted literacy programs when her husband was in the White House. George W. Bush's wife, Laura, also had a strong interest in reading as a teacher and librarian. When George W. Bush became Texas governor, he worked closely with NIH's Reid Lyon and other reading experts who endorsed research-based phonetics rather than a whole-language approach. As a result, Bush and his close Texas advisors, such as Alexander "Sandy" Kress and Margaret La Montagne (Spellings after her August 2001 remarriage), developed an appreciation of the importance of research in developing education reforms (Kessler 2004:56–69).

Only a few days after his inauguration, President Bush released his K–12 education blueprint, "No Child Left Behind." In that 28-page document he sketched out the main contours of his proposed legislation—including several mentions of the importance of research-based school reforms. For example, the education blueprint announced that "federal dollars will be spent on effective research based programs and practices" (Bush 2001:2). Professional development for teachers was to ensure research-based classroom practices. And early childhood reading and the Reading First initiative for children in kindergarten to the second grade called for programs utilizing "research-based pre-reading methods . . . anchored in scientific research" (Bush 2001:4).

Republicans and Democrats differed on several key aspects of the No Child Left Behind legislation, such as providing federal support for private school vouchers or appropriating even more Title I monies; but there was little disagreement on the call for using scientifically-based or research-based programs and practices—though there was not much discussion of education research by the members (U.S. House 2002a). Indeed, those terms were used more than 100 times in the final bill, and the legislation included a rather rigorous definition of scientifically-based research (the language in the section of the statute for the Reading First and Early Reading First programs was actually less demanding) (Cowan 2005).

Most commentators on the No Child Left Behind Act did not focus on the mandate for scientifically-based programs and practices. Some welcomed the greater reliance on research-based information than in the past, but wondered whether there was enough scientifically-based research available to provide adequate guidance for educators. And some education experts and organizations were concerned about the law's definition of scientifically-based research, which stressed quantitative methods and randomized field experiments at the expense of qualitative studies (Berliner 2002; Pellegrino and Goldman 2002; St. Pierre 2002). As Nel Noddings, the president of the National Academy of Education complained, "Why the emphasis on experimental and quasi-experimental research, when there's so much other good stuff out there, I don't know. I think that's a far too narrow focus" (Olson and Viadero 2002:14).

State and local administrators of No Child Left Behind were concerned about who would administer the scientifically-based research mandate and how vigorously those standards would be enforced. Unlike for some of the other No Child Left Behind provisions, the Bush administration did not pay much attention to developing and implementing the research guidelines. The U.S. Department of Education ruled that state education agencies were authorized to prevent local education agencies from using curriculum that did not meet the new standards. In December 2003 the U.S. Department of Education did issue some general guidelines to help educators select appropriate curriculum. Few states, however, implemented such curriculum requirements—in part because almost half of state and local officials felt that the U.S. Department of Education provided only poor guidance and technical assistance in this area (Center on Education Policy 2004; Cowan 2005).

The Bush administration nominated Grover J. "Russ" Whitehurst as the OERI assistant secretary on April 18, 2001. Whitehurst was an accomplished psychology professor at the State University of New York at Stony Brook and an expert in early childhood literacy. Researchers and policymakers praised the appointment of Whitehurst. Catherine Snow, past AERA president and a professor at Harvard University, said, "It's very exciting to see a serious, experienced researcher as head of OERI, and someone who understands literacy as deeply as Russ does" (Viadero 2001:26). Stanford professor and OERI's policy board director Kenji Hakuta responded, "I'm really delighted that we have a person of stellar research background to head this agency, and this is really an important time for research in education reform" (Viadero 2001:26). Whitehurst was unanimously confirmed by a voice vote of the Senate three months later (Sack 2001).

With OERI not reauthorized in 2000, the 107th Congress returned to the task the following year. Castle reintroduced his previous bill (H.R. 4875), now called the Education Sciences Reform Act of 2002 (H.R. 3801); the House Education Reform Subcommittee held hearings on the legislation on July 17, 2001 and February 28, 2002. Castle explained that he was

> seeking to insulate our Federal research, evaluation, and statistics activities from partisan or undue political influences, put the needs of our teachers and students first, insisting on the use of rigorous scientific standards to identify and disseminate effective strategies and methods, and ensure that program evaluations are impartial.
> (U.S. House 2002b:2)

The legislation called for an autonomous Academy of Sciences for education research, statistics, evaluation, and improvement within the U.S. Department of Education.

The witnesses generally supported the legislation—though there were questions about placing the NCES under the new Academy of Sciences or the need to spell out scientifically-based research in the legislation (U.S. House 2002a, 2002b). At the February hearing, Assistant Secretary Whitehurst, who had just seen the revised bill that morning, endorsed the general thrust of legislation. He stressed the need for focusing research and agreed with the National Research Council's call for establishing a "culture of science within the research agency and the Department of Education"—especially selecting good peer reviewers (U.S. House 2002b:12). Whitehurst was particularly interested in improving reading comprehension among elementary school students. Though Whitehurst was skeptical of much of the quality of education research, upon questioning he praised the contributions of some of the R&D centers (such as the work on Success for All) and acknowledged the value of the regional educational laboratories in helping implement No Child Left Behind (U.S. House 2002b:13–23).

At the hearings, there were some differences in how participants compared the quality of education research to that in other fields. As the Subcommittee was deliberating OERI reauthorization, for example, the National Research Council's panel released its report *Scientific Research in Education* (Shavelson and Towne 2002). This report was submitted by Lisa Towne to the Subcommittee members at the February hearings. The NRC panel agreed that education research was of uneven quality, but argued that this was true of most other fields. Towne and her co-editor of the report, in a subsequent publication, also acknowledged they personally shared a bias

> that the conventional wisdom about the weaknesses of scientific educational research relative to other sciences is exaggerated, and the criticisms would be equally worthy of serious investigations if leveled at other branches of the social and physical sciences or at other applied fields like medicine or agriculture.
> (Feuer et al. 2002a:5)

Some of the other witnesses at the reauthorization hearings, however, were much more critical of the overall quality of education research. Frank Newman, Professor of Public Policy and Sociology at Brown University, testified that on the basis of his three decades as a scholar and 14 years as the president of the Education Commission of the States,

> the problem with research, at least public scholarship, is not a deficiency of quantity, but of quality. The problem is that the research in this country is grossly inadequate to the task.... The problem is not whether there is anything to read, but whether there is anything worth reading.... What I learned from all of this was that too much of the research is basically opinion buttressed by anecdotes.
> (U.S. House 2002a:7)

Similarly, Jim Horne, Secretary of the Florida Board of Education, testified on behalf of the Education Leaders Council that he

> believe[d] there is a broad consensus today at the state and local levels that much of the research that has been funded and disseminated by the Federal Government has not, to date, met the same very rigorous and stringent criteria that is now defined clearly in the No Child Left Behind law.
> (U.S. House 2002b:25)

Horne went on to state that

> it is a fact that in the field, there is a sense that the credibility of this research is driven more by politics than by sound science.... I think it needs to be admitted that the canons of science haven't always

worked, even when it has been applied to education research. That is why we have so many peer reviewed reports and studies that turn out to be nothing more than ideological soap boxes.

(p. 29)

There was little disagreement among Democrats and Republicans about reauthorizing OERI, but the 107th Congress focused on passing No Child Left Behind as well as coping with the September 11 terrorist attack on the United States. Castle resubmitted his bill (H.R. 3801) on February 27, 2002 and it easily passed in the House on April 30 (Viadero 2002a). The Senate Health, Education, Labor, and Pensions Committee enacted a similar version in September, but named the new agency the Institute of Education Sciences, put greater emphasis on long-term research, and provided more autonomy for NCES (Goldstein 2002). The Senate passed the legislation in a voice vote on October 15, 2002; the following day the House accepted the Senate version (Sack 2002). On November 5, President Bush signed the Education Sciences Reform Act of 2002 and said that this "act will substantially strengthen the scientific basis" for the work of the U.S. Department of Education (Viadero 2002b:26).

Most social science researchers and policymakers were pleased overall with the Education Sciences Reform Act of 2002. James W. Kohlmoos, president of the National Education Knowledge Industry Association, which represents the regional educational laboratories, characterized the legislation as vital. Assistant Secretary Whitehurst stated that "it's a much better bill than the current statute, and provides a lot more flexibility for the department. I think it removes significant impediments to us becoming a world-class research agency, and removes any excuses for failure" (Sack 2002:22). But Checker Finn felt there were not enough major changes—such as overhauling the regional educational laboratories. As a result, Finn complained that "odds are, most money will continue to go where it's already gone. There's less here than meets the eye" (Sack 2002:22). And others worried just how independent, in practice, the Institute of Education Sciences would be from the U.S. Department of Education (Viadero 2000b).

The Bush administration waited almost two years for the creation of IES. The new IES director, Whitehurst, moved quickly to implement the major changes (some of which had been initiated even prior to the passage of the Education Sciences Reform Act of 2002). Many of the more service-oriented programs were moved from IES to other units such as the Office of Innovative Improvements (though the legislation mandated the continuation of the regional educational laboratories within IES). And Whitehurst tried to staff the new agency with more researchers.

One important step in identifying and fostering higher quality of research was the creation of the $18.5-million What Works Clearinghouse. The Clearinghouse synthesized existing research on particular topics by assessing the scientific quality and rigor of the work. Preference was given to the few education studies using randomized field trials; and rigorous experimental findings were favored over non-experimental ones. Carefully matched groups and "regression continuity designs" were also accepted; but case studies and descriptive reports did not meet the Clearinghouse standards. Results from the WWC were made available to practitioners and policymakers at a special U.S. Department of Education website (Viadero 2002c, 2004b).

Initially the Clearinghouse analyzed peer-assisted learning strategies and middle-school mathematics programs. While few studies have qualified under the stringent standards, the developers hope that the Clearinghouse will stimulate better research in the future. The Clearinghouse has been well received by researchers and policymakers. But there are complaints about the narrowness of what is defined as scientific research; and practitioners and policymakers have been disappointed by the limited number of studies deemed worthy of inclusion as well as the slow pace at which education programs and practices are assessed and the findings reported (Viadero 2004b; Viadero and Hoff 2006).

There was growing federal interest in supporting rigorous education research which employed randomized trials. Starting in the Clinton administration, several randomized experimental studies were funded to look at the 21st Century Community Learning Centers after-school program, the Even Start family literacy projects, the Upward Bound college program, the school-wide comprehensive programs, and the early childhood education studies. The Institute of Education Sciences planned in 2002 to spend $47 million over the following two years on additional randomized studies. Whitehurst denied, however, that these more rigorous analyses came at the expense of funding more traditional educational studies. "By and large, these randomized trials will be funded out of evaluation and national-activities money, and that's money that's not previously been available to the research community" (Viadero 2002d:12).

Citing the need for developing the next generation of well-trained education scholars, in February 2004 Education Secretary Paige announced a $50-million training program over the following five years. The IES-administered monies would go to doctoral programs at colleges and universities to help transform education into an evidence-based field. Ten higher education institutions would receive up to $1 million for five years to train the students (Viadero 2004a).

Another, but more controversial, IES effort to assist researchers was a three-year $760,000 grant to help start the Society for Research on Educational Effectiveness, a new organization of scholars dedicated to scientifically-oriented education research. One side effect of having such an organization is that it may generate additional support for the new IES research priorities. In an address before the Society, Assistant Secretary Whitehurst said, "I suggest as you become a little more mature as an organization that you think about adding to your mission public-policy advocacy for the type of research that you are committed to doing as individuals" (Viadero 2006e). While many individuals appreciated the need for more rigorous education research, others wondered whether the new IES-assisted society was not too narrowly focused. Harvard School of Education professor Ellen Condliffe Lagemann commented that "It's important to do very high standard work of a variety of kinds. I'm not sure creating a society around one method is sensible" (Viadero 2006a).

As IES expanded its support of rigorous research and evaluation studies as well as training researchers, the agency significantly reduced R&D center funding. Historically, the R&D centers had received a sizable share of NIE/OERI research funding; but the quality of their research products (only a few development projects were undertaken) varied considerably among the centers as well as within any particular center. Though OERI occasionally had experimented with funding small centers, the results from a rigorous research perspective were disappointing (Vinovskis 2001).

On February 4, 2004, Whitehurst announced that IES would provide up to $10 million over the following five years for four national research centers (previously the largest recipient, the Center for Research on the Education of Students Placed at Risk, had received in 1996 $27.8 million for five years). With monies for the last of the ten larger R&D centers ending in 2006, IES planned to fund another four small centers. In the past, centers had considerable autonomy in deciding which specific projects they would pursue. Now, however, Whitehurst explained that "rather than leaving it to the centers to decide on that once they're funded, we want there to be proposed specific research projects ahead of time" (Viadero 2004c:36). Moreover, the application guidelines reiterated the agency's preference for certain methodological approaches such as randomized controlled studies.

As R&D centers had provided education research funding for faculty in many colleges and universities, there was a mixed reaction to the IES's decision to fund eight small centers. On the one hand, researchers were relieved that R&D centers would continue; on the other hand, they were disappointed that the overall funding would be reduced substantially. "We've tried 'mini-centers' before and found them totally unsatisfying," commented Gerald R. Sroufe, the AERA government-relations director (Viadero 2004c: 36). Moreover, Sroufe complained that the guidelines "suggest that, instead of picking the methodology to solve the problem, you almost have to pick the problem to fit the methodology you have" (Viadero 2004c:40).

Given the cost of the R&D centers in the past and their mixed record of producing high-quality, coherent work, it is not surprising that IES sought to reduce their funding and importance. Whether the scientific quality of work produced by centers receiving only $1 or $2 million annually will be adequate remains to be seen. Moreover, the elimination of some of the traditional work of the R&D centers may leave some important gaps in the research portfolio of the agency. For example, much of the earlier influential policy analysis on systemic/standards-based reform was done by scholars such as Marshall "Mike" Smith and Jennifer O'Day through the Policy Center of the Consortium for Policy Research in Education (primary site at Rutgers University).

Will such policy analyses continue to be sponsored by IES? If not, who will provide funding for such studies? Education policy work will continue to be supported through non-profit foundations and Washington-oriented think tanks; but many of these entities have strong explicit or implicit policy preferences which may affect the proposals they fund or influence the analyses that they support. Susan H. Fuhrman, president of Teachers College, complained about the lack of IES policy-related studies. "What's happening to the big high schools left over when small high schools are taken out? Now that's a big policy question, and it's hard to think of where in IES you could propose this" (Viadero 2006d).

Doing rigorous scientific education studies by themselves is not enough to improve American education. We must systematically develop, implement, and test rigorously those research findings in different settings so that teachers and administrators have a better idea of the likely impacts of various programs and practices on children's academic achievement. As was discussed earlier, the 1970s Brooking Panel on Social Experimentation laid out a thoughtful and practical five-stage model of systematic program development that might require 10–12 years to complete (depending in part on how much high-quality work had already been done on the proposed intervention).

While there were some earlier efforts at long-term systematic development, there has been very little work along these lines in OERI for the past two decades. One notable exception has been the development of Success for All through the Center for Research on Effective Schooling for Disadvantaged Students (primary site at Johns Hopkins University)—though a more rigorous evaluation design from the very beginning would have been helpful. When Whitehurst testified before the House Subcommittee on Education Reform, he pointed to Success for All as a good example of OERI research being translated into practice (U.S. House 2002b:16). Will programs such as Success for All be developed by the IES's new centers? If not, should IES provide monies for long-term development elsewhere rather than mainly funding more short-term scientifically-based experiments and evaluations?

The decision to reduce spending on R&D centers is not necessarily bad, but care should be taken that the quality of research produced by these new centers really will be scientifically sound and useful. At the same time, IES may need to reconsider its overall portfolio of research, development, evaluations, and statistics to ensure it has an adequate balance of initiatives to enhance student learning. With the demise of the larger R&D centers, should IES need to provide alternative programs to fund projects such as policy studies? What about more qualitative education studies from humanities and the social sciences—is there a place for them any more in IES? And who will design and fund large-scale long-term development programs? Does IES have any plans for designing and implementing ambitious projects such as NIH's multimillion dollar, 30-year research project on reading, which has played such a key role in the Bush administration? Or is such work better left to other federal agencies such as the

National Institute of Child Health and Human Development or the National Science Foundation—especially since IES funding is limited and the overall quality of the agency's research staff still needs improvement?

When Congress created IES as an autonomous unit within the U.S. Department of Education, it mandated that the IES director, with independent advice from the Education Sciences Board, set the direction and priorities of the new agency. The Board would approve the director's research priorities as well as assess the work of IES. Unfortunately, it took Congress three years to reauthorize OERI; President Bush signed the Education Reform Act into law on November 5, 2002 (Viadero 2002b). Yet the White House did not nominate members for the Education Sciences Board until December 2003 (Robelen 2003). And nearly another year passed before the Senate approved the nominees (Viadero 2004d). As a result, the 15-member Education Sciences Board only met for the first time on February 8, 2005—well after many of the important decisions about the agency's operation and direction had already been made. As C. Kent McGuire, the OERI assistant secretary under President Clinton, put it, "There's no getting around the fact that some bets have already been placed" (Viadero 2005a:34).

In addition, as IES was being organized it still lacked some key administrators. For example, since 1999 the National Center for Education Statistics had lacked a permanent commissioner. Mark S. Schneider, the well-respected former chair of the political science department at the State University of New York at Stony Brook, was not confirmed as the permanent NCES commissioner until October 2005 (Viadero 2005b). Under such circumstances, will the agency be as independent and influential as it was under Emerson Elliott, the first NCES commissioner? Frederick M. Hess, director of policy studies at the American Enterprise Institute, observed, "One of the problems . . . has been that, without a strong leader, it's easy for an agency with more conventional, statistics-gathering responsibilities to get overlooked or marginalized" (Samuels and Viadero 2005:34).

The Institute of Education Science has made considerable improvements and progress in fostering more rigorous, scientifically-based research through many of its new grants and contracts. The pace of those improvements, however, has sometimes been slow. Inspired by the standing review committees of the NIH and the National Science Agency, for example, IES has been developing plans to assemble outside panels of experts to help assess research applications as well as review selected reports published under the name of the U.S. Department of Education. In January 2006 the Education Sciences Board formally approved the process for helping evaluate new proposals as well as signing off federally-funded education reports (Viadero 2006b).

At the same time, however, IES has made much less progress in assessing the quality of much of the work produced by grantees or contractors (such as the R&D centers and the regional educational laboratories it inherited). Under the 1994 OERI reauthorization, the agency was mandated to create and implement phase three standards for assessing all of the work sponsored by OERI. Since IES was not created until November 2002, in the first two years of the Bush administration the agency was still operating under the previous authorization and therefore had to comply with the phase three standards as well (though not everyone at the time was aware of that obligation). Moreover, under the 1994 OERI reauthorization, the agency was expected routinely to conduct a third-year review of the R&D centers and the regional educational laboratories (as well as monitor the work of those entities on an ongoing basis). Indeed, members of Congress such as Rep. Castle had criticized OERI during the Clinton administration for failing to carry out such reviews carefully and objectively.

As the Bush administration proposed to eliminate the regional educational laboratories, it would have been useful to members of Congress to have an objective analysis of the scientific quality of lab products and recommended practices—either through a thorough third-year review or rigorous ongoing monitoring of their work. Absent that information, several Democratic and GOP members of Congress as well as some of the invited witnesses emphasized the value of regional educational laboratories for schools in their congressional districts (U.S. House 2002a, 2002b). Without any recent systematic evidence contrary to that testimony, Whitehurst and other administration witnesses repeatedly failed to persuade Congress to stop supporting the regional educational laboratories, reduce their overall funding, or to transfer them out of IES. Indeed, the continued lack of a rigorous evaluation of the regional educational laboratories contributed to the Bush administration being forced to hold another system-wide lab competition and awarding more than $326 million to ten regional educational laboratories for the next five years—monies that might have been better spent on other IES priorities (Viadero 2006c).

Many of OERI's programs were transferred to other agencies such as the Office of Innovative Improvements. Are the research and evaluation projects there being rigorously developed, implemented, and evaluated using scientifically-based methods? Whereas IES is trying to fund only the most rigorous, scientifically-valid studies, the Office of Innovative Improvements supports a wide variety of projects, such as the Teaching of American History program and the provision of school choice programs. Yet almost none of these projects, such as the $120 million spent annually to improve the teaching of American history, have employed randomized field studies or controlled experiments. As a result, despite repeated congressional calls for high-quality research-based products and practices under No Child Left Behind, the U.S. Department of Education in practice applies different quality standards for assessing reading research than for evaluating American history instruction (Vinovskis 2005b, forthcoming).

Most observers praise IES for improving the rigor of education research, though some question the agency's more narrow methodological focus as well as its choice of issues to investigate (Viadero 2006d). At the same time, critics accuse the Bush administration of generally misusing research to pursue its partisan policies. Especially on science-related issues such as the environment and global warming, some scholars have charged the administration with suppressing and distorting research (Shulman 2006).

The federal government's use of education research, however, generally has not received the same level of scrutiny and criticism. But serious questions are now being raised about the Reading First programs funded under No Child Left Behind. Critics charge that the U.S. Department of Education "stacked" the panels for evaluating the annual billion-dollar Reading First applications as well as improperly influencing local schools' and districts' reading curricula and assessments (Manzo 2006). The matter is now being investigated by the U.S. Department of Education's Inspector General as well as the GAO. Rep. George Miller (D-CA) charged that "this was a concerted effort to corrupt the process on behalf of partisan supporters, and taxpayers and school children are the ones who got harmed by it" (Manzo 2006:24). This widely-discussed and well-publicized event reminds us of the periodic charges of possible biases in the uses of education research by earlier administrations as well; it also raises questions about the proper roles and involvement of IES and the education research community in dealing with such controversies.

Concluding Observations

Education research has not been a high priority for most of the public and policymakers. Everyone has been to school and many of us have had our children attend as well. As a result, many individuals already consider themselves knowledgeable about schools and how to improve them. In addition, many educators and policymakers believe we already possess enough research to improve schools; the problem they see is the need to disseminate those findings and implement them.

At the same time, others regard existing education research as neither reliable nor useful. They point to the poor quality of the research—often citing the lack of scientific rigor of those studies. Some believe that decisionmakers and analysts slant research findings to fit their ideological or policy predispositions. And there are complaints that much of the research funded is not designed to provide principals or teachers with useful school or classroom information.

The quantity and quality of education research has been limited by the inadequate funding. In the first half of the twentieth century, much of education research was funded by non-profit foundations and local colleges and universities. Since the 1950s and 1960s, however, the federal government has played a much larger role in funding education research, statistics, and development. Yet when the Reagan White House and Congress reduced federal education spending, research funding was particularly drastically cut.

In the last 40 years, periodic efforts have been made to improve or reorganize federal education research agencies and strategies: developing R&D centers and regional educational laboratories; creating the National Institute of Education; founding the Office of Educational Research and Improvement; reorganizing OERI in 1994; and establishing the Institute of Education Sciences in 2002. These changes indicate continued interest in federal education research as well as frequent disappointment with earlier reforms. Moreover, the numerous reorganizations have been time-consuming and hindered efforts for long-term planning and program development.

Throughout the past four decades the federal education research agencies generally have not adequately ensured high-quality, scientifically-rigorous work. In the past, close monitoring of the quality of the products from research grants and contracts has not been a major focus in Washington; moreover, many of the agency staff have lacked the training and professional experience necessary for assessing research quality. And agency directors and staff sometimes have felt politically constrained from enforcing rigorous quality standards for some of the grantees and contractors.

Overseeing the quality of the work produced is made more difficult by the lack of agreement on what tasks federal research agencies should undertake or even what constitutes research. Much of the responsibility of NIE, OERI, and even IES today has been not only to direct and assess different types of research, but to offer related services such as disseminating information and providing technical assistance to K-12 teachers in the field. Indeed, actual research usually has been only a small part of the overall portfolio of an agency's activities. At the same time, there are considerable differences of opinion among educators, policymakers, and researchers on what constitutes legitimate research and how it should be pursued methodologically. And there is no consensus on whether that research should be solicited from individual researchers or organizations such as the R&D centers or the regional educational laboratories.

Reacting against the recent congressional efforts to become more involved in specifying and implementing quality standards for research, the Committee on Scientific Principles for Educational Research has recommended that the task be left to the education research community. Certainly it would be better if the field of education studies would take more responsibility for research quality; but unfortunately their involvement to date has not been sufficient to ensure high-quality work. The American Educational Research Association, for example, has a diverse membership in terms of interests and research skills; and AERA has not been in the forefront of setting or assessing rigorous, high quality standards for qualitative and quantitative work.

The National Academy of Education as well as National Academy of Sciences panels on education research have made valuable contributions to the analysis of the nature of education research; but they have tended to stay away from actually examining and commenting on the quality of federally-funded education research. Perhaps their recent explorations of scientifically-based education research will encourage them also to assess the actual quality of federally-funded research, development, and statistics produced by IES and other agencies such as the Office of Innovative Improvements or the National Science Foundation.

Throughout the debates on the nature and reliability of federal education research, some Democratic and Republican policymakers have worried periodically about the role of politics in setting federal research agendas, evaluating education programs, and producing research as objectively as possible. Concerns about the possible political one-sidedness of most educational researchers have also been raised as potentially affecting how studies are conducted and interpreted.

On the other hand, researchers have challenged the long-standing congressional interference with the operation of federal education agencies by mandating that R&D centers as well as the regional educational laboratories have to be funded—even though there have been frequent questions about the overall quality of their work. At the same time, the recent interest in improving the quality and use of federally-funded education research in No Child Left Behind and the creation of the Institute of Education Sciences has come from the bipartisan leadership of the 107th Congress.

Although one might question some of the mandates about scientifically-based education research or how these standards are being applied in practice by IES or the Office of Innovative Improvements, we should welcome the recent attention by policymakers to the importance of research, development, and statistics in improving American education. Particularly encouraging is the growing awareness of the need to support and produce high-quality work as well as to develop appropriate mechanisms to assess it more critically than we have in the past.

References

Atkinson, Richard C. and Gregg B. Jackson (eds.). 1992. *Research and Education Reform: Roles for the Office of Educational Research and Improvement.* Washington, DC: National Academy Press.

Bailey, Stephen K. and Edith K. Mosher. 1968. *ESEA: The Office of Education Administers a Law.* Syracuse, NY: Syracuse University Press.

Berliner, David C. 2002. "Educational Research: The Hardest Science of All." *Educational Researcher* 31(8):21–24.

Bush, George W. 2001. "No Child Left Behind." Washington, DC: The White House.

Center on Education Policy. 2004. *From the Capital to the Classroom: Year 2 of the No Child Left Behind Act.* Washington, DC: Center on Education Policy.

Clark, David L. and William R. Carriker. 1961. "Educational Research and the Cooperative Research Program." *Phi Delta Kappan* 42:226–230.

Cowan, Kristen Tosh. 2005. *The New Title I: The Changing Landscape of Accountability.* Washington, DC: Thompson Publishing Group.

Cronbach, Lee J. and Patrick Suppes (eds.). 1969. *Research for Tomorrow's Schools: Disciplined Inquiry for Education.* New York: Macmillan.

Dershimer, Richard A. 1976. *The Federal Government and Education R&D.* Lexington, MA: Lexington Books.

Elliott, Emerson J. 1989. "New Directions and Initiatives at NCES: Implications for Educational Research, Policy, and Practice." *Educational Researcher* 18(3):11–16.

Elmore, Richard F. 1976. "Project Follow Through: Decision-Making in a Large-Scale Social Experiment." Ph.D. dissertation, Graduate School of Education, Harvard University, Cambridge, MA.

Featherman, David L. and Maris A. Vinovskis. 2001. "Growth and Use of Social and Behavioral Science in the Federal Government since World War II." Pp. 40–48 in *Social Science and Policy Making: A Search for Relevance in the Twentieth Century*, edited by David L. Featherman and Maris A. Vinovskis. Ann Arbor, MI: University of Michigan Press.

Feuer, Michael, J., Lisa Towne, and Richard J. Shavelson. 2002. "Scientific Culture and Educational Research." *Educational Researcher* 31(8):4–14.

Finn, Chester E., Jr. 1977. *Education and the Presidency*. Lexington, MA: Lexington Books.

Gardner, John. 1964. "Report of the President's Task Force on Education." Austin, TX: LBJ Presidential Library.

Goldstein, Lisa Fine. 2002. "Senate Panel Passes Federal Research Bill." *Education Week* 22(5):24, 27.

Hertling, James. 1985. "Finn to Head Reorganized Research Unit." *Education Week* 4(40):14–15.

Jones, Lyle V. and Ingram Olkin (eds.). 2004. *The Nation's Report Card: Evolution and Perspectives*. Bloomington, IN: Phi Delta Kappa Educational Foundation.

Kessler, Ronald. 2004. *A Matter of Character: Inside the White House of George W. Bush*. New York: Sentinel HC.

Lagemann, Ellen Condliffe. 1997. "Contested Terrain: A History of Education Research in the United States, 1890–1990." *Educational Researcher* 26(9):5–17.

———. 2000. *An Elusive Science: The Troubling History of Education Research*. Chicago, IL: University of Chicago Press.

Lagemann, Ellen Condliffe and Lee S. Shulman (eds.). 1999a. *Issues in Education Research: Problems and Possibilities*. San Francisco, CA: Jossey-Bass.

———. 1999b. "Next Steps: Reflections on Education Research and Ways the National Academy of Education Might Help to Further Strengthen It." Unpublished manuscript, National Academy of Education, Washington, DC.

Lazarsfeld, Paul F. and Sam D. Sieber. 1964. *Organizing Educational Research*. Englewood Cliffs, NJ: Prentice-Hall.

Levine, Daniel B. (ed.). 1986. *Creating a Center for Education Statistics: A Time for Action*. Panel to Evaluate the National Center for Education Statistics, Committee on National Statistics, National Research Council. Washington, DC: National Academy Press.

Manzo, Kathleen Kennedy. 1999. "Reading-Achievement Program Is Off to a Quiet Start." *Education Week* 18(18):21, 25.

———. 2006. "Scathing Report Casts Cloud over 'Reading First'." *Education Week* 26(6):1, 24–25.

Mosteller, Frederick and Daniel P. Moynihan (eds.). 1972. *On Equality of Educational Opportunity*. New York: Vintage Books.

National Commission on Excellence in Education. 1983. *A Nation at Risk: The Imperative for Educational Reform*. Washington, DC: U.S. Government Printing Office.

National Reading Panel. 2000. *Report of the National Reading Panel: Teaching Children to Read: An Evidence-Based Assessment of the Scientific Research Literature on Reading and Its Implications for Reading Instruction: Reports of the Subgroups*. Washington, DC: National Institute for Literacy.

Olson, Lynn. 1999. "Researchers Rate Whole-School Reform Models." *Education Week* 18(31):1, 14–15.

Olson, Lynn and Debra Viadero. 2002. "Law Mandates Scientific Base for Research." *Education Week* 21(20):1, 14–15.

Pellegrino, James W. and Susan R. Goldman. 2002. "Be Careful What You Wish For—You May Get It: Educational Research in the Spotlight." *Educational Researcher* 31(8):18–20.

Ravitch, Diane. 1993. "The State of the Agency." *OERI Bulletin* 1:2.

Rivlin, Alice M. and P. Michael Timpane. 1975. "Planned Variation in Education: An Assessment." Pp. 1–21 in *Planned Variation in Education: Should We Give Up or Try Harder?*, edited by Alice M. Rivlin and P. Michael Timpane. Washington, DC: Brookings Institution Press.

Robelen, Erik W. 2003. "13 Nominated to New Panel Overseeing Federal Education Research." *Education Week* 23(15):23.

Rothman, Robert. 1992. "With Death of O.E.R.I. Bill, Reorganization Put Off." *Education Week* 12(6):22.

Sack, Joetta L. 2001. "Rush of Confirmations Populates Paige's Executive Suite." *Education Week* 20(43):36, 41.

———. 2002. "Research Bill, after Stall, Sails to Passage." *Education Week* 22(8):18, 22.

Samuels, Christina A. and Debra Viadero. 2005. "Bush Nominates Commissioner for Statistics Agency." *Education Week* 24(44):28, 34.

Schnaiberg, Lynn. 1994. "O.E.R.I. Compromise Strikes Balance on Who Will Control Research Agenda." *Education Week* 13(26):17.

Shavelson, Richard J. and Lisa Towne (eds.). 2002. *Scientific Research in Education*. Committee on Scientific Principles for Educational Research, National Research Council. Washington, DC: National Academies Press.

Shulman, Seth. 2006. *Undermining Science: Suppression and Distortion in the Bush Administration.* Berkeley, CA: University of California Press.
Sproull, Lee, Stephen Weiner, and David Wolf. 1978. *Organizing an Anarchy: Belief, Bureaucracy, and Politics in the National Institute of Education.* Chicago, IL: University of Chicago Press.
St. Pierre, Elizabeth Adams. 2002. "'Science' Rejects Postmodernism." *Educational Researcher* 31(8):25–27.
U.S. House. 2000. Subcommittee on Early Childhood, Youth and Families. *Hearings on Options for the Future of the Office of Educational Research and Improvement.* 106th Cong., 2nd sess. Washington, DC: U.S. Government Printing Office.
———. 2002a. Subcommittee on Education Reform. *Hearings on From Research to Practice: Improving America's Schools in the 21st Century.* 107th Cong., 1st sess. Washington, DC: U.S. Government Printing Office.
———. 2002b. Subcommittee on Education Reform. *Hearings on the Reauthorization of the Office of Educational Research and Improvement.* 107th Cong., 2nd sess. Washington, DC: U.S. Government Printing Office.
Verstegen, Deborah A. 1990. "Educational Fiscal Policy in the Reagan Administration." *Educational Evaluation and Policy Analysis* 12:355–373.
Viadero, Debra. 2000a. "Competing Plans Offered to Shield Research from Political Influences." *Education Week* 19(35):31.
———. 2000b. "House Plan Would Create Research 'Academy'." *Education Week* 19(43):30.
———. 2001. "Bush Chooses Childhood-Literacy Expert to Head OERI." *Education Week* 20(32): 26.
———. 2002a. "Research Bill Clears House without Fuss. *Education Week* 21(34):1, 21.
———. 2002b. "New Research Agency's Independence in Question." *Education Week* 22(11):26, 29.
———. 2002c. "Draft Standards for 'What Works' Released." *Education Week* 22(13):10.
———. 2002d. "Ed. Dept. Quietly Funds More Experimental Studies." *Education Week* 22(15):1, 12.
———. 2004a. "Grant Program Unveiled for Researcher Training." *Education Week* 23(22):21.
———. 2004b. "'What Works' Research Site Unveiled." *Education Week* 23(42):1, 33.
———. 2004c. "Next-Generation Research Centers Unveiled." *Education Week* 23(23):36, 40.
———. 2004d. "Senate Panel Approves Research Board Members." *Education Week* 24(5):23.
———. 2005a. "Education Sciences Board Convenes for First Time." *Education Week* 24(23):32, 34.
———. 2005b. "Senate Confirms Head of NCES." *Education Week* 25(10):25.
———. 2006a. "New Group of Researchers Focuses on Scientific Study." *Education Week* 25(21):1, 16.
———. 2006b. "Review Process for U.S. Education Research Approved." *Education Week* 25(21):24.
———. 2006c. "Control of Regional Education Labs Shifting." *Education Week* 25(29):32, 34.
———. 2006d. "IES Gets Mixed Grades as it Comes of Age." *Education Week* 26(5):1, 8–9.
———. 2006e. "Breakaway Education Research Group Pulls from Diverse Disciplines. *Education Week* 26(16):11.
Viadero, Debra and David J. Hoff. 2006. "'One Stop' Research Shop Seen as Slow to Yield Views that Educators Can Use." *Education Week* 26(5): 8–9.
Vinovskis, Maris A. 1993. *Analysis of the Quality of Research and Development at the OERI Research and Development Centers and at the OERI Regional Educational Laboratories.* Washington, DC: OERI, U.S. Department of Education.
———. 1996. "The Changing Role of the Federal Government in Educational Research and Statistics." *History of Education Quarterly* 36:111–128.
———. 1998a. "Changing Federal Strategies for Supporting Educational Research, Development, and Statistics." Background paper for the National Educational Research Policy and Priorities Board U.S. Department of Education, Washington, DC.
———. 1998b. *Overseeing the Nation's Report Card: The Creation and Evolution of the National Assessment Governing Board* (NAGB). Washington, DC: National Assessment Governing Board, U.S. Department of Education.
———. 1998c. An Analysis of the Proposed Phase Three Standards for the Conduct and Evaluation of OERI Activities." Unpublished background paper prepared for the Office of Educational Research and Improvement (March 26). OERI, U.S. Department of Education, Washington, DC.
———. 1999. *History and Educational Policymaking.* New Haven, CT: Yale University Press.
———. 2001. *Revitalizing Federal Education Research and Development: Improving the R&D Centers, Regional Educational Laboratories, and the "New" OERI.* Ann Arbor: University of Michigan Press.
———. 2002. "Missing in Practice? Development and Evaluation at the U.S. Department of Education." Pp. 120–149 in *Evidence Matters: Randomized Trials in Education Research*, edited by Frederick Mosteller and Robert Boruch. Washington, DC: Brookings Institution Press.

——. 2003. "Missed Opportunities: Why the Federal Response to *A Nation at Risk* Was Inadequate." Pp. 115–130 in *A Nation Reformed? American Education 20 Years after* A Nation at Risk, edited by David T. Gordon. Cambridge, MA: Harvard Educational Publishing Group.

——. 2005a. *The Birth of Head Start: Preschool Education Policies in the Kennedy and Johnson Administrations*. Chicago, IL: University of Chicago Press.

——. 2005b. "Comment by Maris A. Vinovskis." Pp. 74–80 in *Brookings Papers on Education Policy: 2005,* edited by Diane Ravitch. Washington, DC: Brookings Institution Press.

——. Forthcoming. "History Assessments and Elementary and Secondary Education." In *History Education Policy*, edited by Robert Bain and Robert Orrill.

Zodhiates, Philip. 1988. "Bureaucrats and Politicians: The National Institute of Education and Educational Research under Reagan." Ed.D. dissertation, Graduate School of Education, Harvard University, Cambridge, MA.

PART **II**
Seeking Rigor; Finding Rigor

CHAPTER 3

Assessing Quality in Educational Journals

BARBARA SCHNEIDER*

Over 50 years ago, Robert Merton (1968), a major figure in sociology credited with advancing the concept of sociology of science, systematically described how important publication in top-tier journals was to an academic's career. Publication in top-tier journals continues to be an academic's currency; the more one publishes in high-quality journals, the more an individual acquires prestige, recognition, and access to research funding opportunities (Diamond 1986).[1] It is not just publication that has value; an academic's promotion and influence within the academy are also enhanced by the number of times he or she is *cited* in top journals. Moreover, journal publication and citation serve as markers of organizational status and prestige as well as the standing of individuals within the academy: Rankings of universities and the departments within them are also partially determined by the number of articles in particular journals that are published by faculty members. In short, publication and citation in top-tier journals matter for scientific recognition and standing; and they matter in education much as they do in the natural and social sciences.

Although the value of publication is widely regarded as important in education, strong criticisms have been raised concerning the quality of research and the articles based on these studies that appear in educational journals (Shavelson and Towne 2002; Towne, Wise, and Winters 2004). Education is not the only field that has been the recipient of public criticism; it has, however, been the target of more recent attention and rebuke. Many of these criticisms suggest that the studies reported in education journals are not scientifically rigorous; that findings, especially those using specific methodologies, cannot be replicated; and that even the replicable results are often not relevant or useful to professional educators or policymakers (Lagemann 1996, 2000). If the quality of research being conducted in education were of lesser quality than that in other fields of inquiry, one might expect that the journals would be of lower quality and that the editorial and peer review processes would be much less stringent, resulting in a higher proportion of manuscript acceptances. Are scientific educational journals weaker in quality than other social science journals? This question cannot be answered without first exploring some of the widespread concerns about most journals, before determining whether education is an anomaly. Who and what gets published in journals, whether the process is fair, reliable, and valid, and if journals are actually fulfilling their perceived function as receptors and depositories of knowledge accumulation have been seriously questioned by scientists across diverse disciplines including, but not limited to, economics, medicine, psychology, and sociology (Blank 1991; Chubin and Hackett 1990; Fletcher and Fletcher 1997; Lamont and Mallard 2005). This chapter reviews some of the critiques of journals as a source of knowledge accumulation and examines whether there is something uniquely different about the education journal publication process and the quality of the journals that publish work in this field.

Ranking Scientific Journals

Most scientific journals are accessible through printed pages, online in protected websites, or in strictly electronic form. Within disciplines there is a hierarchical structure whereby some journals are rated within their respective fields as being of higher quality than others. Quality is certainly relative. What, then, can be relied upon to rank and distinguish journals, particularly in the social sciences? Presently there are no standards that distinguish quality among the journals. In the absence of defined criteria, academics, college administrators, and funding agencies generally turn to information provided by the Institute for Scientific Information (ISI Web of Science), an electronic global database that contains lists of peer-reviewed journals, to determine which journals and authors are having the most influence in and out of their respective fields. ISI is something of a monopoly, as only a limited number of other databases can compete with the depth and range of its holdings and search capacities. ISI claims to provide a comprehensive database of the world's most important and influential research (Testa 2004). It is important to underscore that comprehensive does not necessarily mean inclusive, as ISI does not purport to include all journals—only ones that meet its inclusion criteria.

A system of ranking suggests that one journal is better than another by a defined set of criteria. Although the criteria for ranking journals are often subject to dispute, one standard often used by the academy is citation count—that is, the number of times certain work is cited in published material in specific or related fields. The underlying assumption being made is that articles more frequently cited are making greater contributions to the field than those less cited. Critics of citation analysis maintain that what gets published in the journals is biased by self-citation, size and specialization of the field, type of research conducted, and the peer review process itself (see Campanario [1998a] and Armstrong [1997] for reviews of fairness, reliability, and empirical studies of peer-reviewed journals). Not all references to reported findings are positive, and some manuscripts cite other authors as exemplars of flawed research, oftentimes as justification for their own design and analysis. Some articles have high citation counts because they are seen as integral to a discipline's canon, and the positive or negative qualities associated with the concepts, results, and/or conclusions function as part of the historical narrative. Despite these criticisms, citation count continues to be one of the principal measures for rating journal quality.

Indexing Journals for Quality

Viewed historically, the ranking of scientific journals by citation count is a fairly recent development, as the ability to distinguish quality among the journals requires some type of indexing system. Electronic citation indexing became a viable option for the scientific community in the 1950s, when the federal government allocated considerable resources to the technological development of such a system. As scientific information burgeoned across disciplinary fields, there was a pressing need for a method of indexing and retrieval that was broader in scope and more technologically efficient than subject-specific indexes that were currently in place.

At the time, Eugene Garfield, a Ph.D. in structural linguistics, quickly recognized the value computers could have in capturing information, synthesizing it, and reconfiguring it in unique ways whereby researchers could, by searching a database, obtain information produced by other scientists that described both their methodology and their results. He and his associates embarked on a series of studies that showed how electronic citation indexing allowed for the retrieval of information that subject-specific indexing could not. Working first in the sciences, Garfield developed a national citation database that subsequently led to the first edition of the *Science Citation Index®* (SCI®), a multidisciplinary citation index launched in 1963. (See Thomson Scientific [2005a] and Cawkell and Garfield [2001] for a more complete history of citation indexing.) SCI soon evolved into a greater entity encompassing a wider range of disciplines; in 1972 it was joined by the Social Sciences Citation Index® and in 1978 by the Arts & Humanities Citation Index®. This database was soon modified for online hosts and CD-ROM format (Szigeti 2001).

As the technology advanced, within a relatively short period of time SCI was transformed into the Institute for Scientific Information (ISI). This entity underwent another transformation in 1997 when the ISI Web of Knowledge (a fully integrated research system within a Web-based environment) was launched (see Szigeti 2001).

Once the ISI citation database files were made available via a Web-based interface, bibliographic retrieval was substantially improved by the ability to capture both points in time and multidisciplinary work. Researchers are now able to trace what research influenced an author's work (the "Cited References" hyperlink), and through a new component that keeps track of papers presented at meetings (Related Records®) learn how academic research is having an impact on the scholarly research community across disciplines in seemingly unrelated fields.

The evolution of ISI within a 40-year period symbolizes more than a technological advance for compiling and cross-listing information, as the computer search capacities allow for tracking information not only on journals, but also on conceptual areas and individuals. The transparency of knowledge production by journal type, author affiliations, and progression of ideas and the speed by which these topics can be amassed is transforming many aspects of the research process and the potential to uncover bias and particularistic criteria in the publication of certain articles. With the ISI database one can investigate which journals are more likely to publish innovative work, more open to different methods, and less discriminatory with respect to characteristics of the authors, including gender and institutional affiliation.[2]

Indeed, the complexity and richness of the ISI database appears to be outpacing the capacity of researchers who are interested in tracing how knowledge is developing and which fields and methods are having the most influence on scientific discovery and policy. Accessing multidisciplinary content sources across the globe has become critical, especially for researchers working on an original discovery or synthesizing information. With worldwide information merely a tap and click away, the need to discriminate between solid research and studies plagued by error and fraud has elevated the value and necessity of monitoring the quality of what is published in traditional and electronic media.

Distinguishing Quality among the Journals

In our increasingly accessible, expanding information environment it would seem that it is critically important to distinguish quality from quantity. This, however, does not seem to be the case as analyses by researchers at ISI have shown that a relatively small number of journals publish the majority of significant scientific results (Testa 2004). Although approximately 2,000 journals now account for about 85% of published articles and 95% of cited articles, recent analyses show that a core of only 150 journals account for half of what is cited and one-quarter of what is published. However, this core is not static; its basic composition changes over time (see Testa 2004). This concentration of citations within a few journals suggests an inherent selectivity system operating among the journals, with the most critical and path-breaking results being published in journals that have more status among the relevant readership than others.

Even though only a relatively small number of journals are frequently cited, all journals entered into the ISI system have undergone an evaluation for inclusion in its database. According to ISI reports, nearly 2,000 new journal titles are reviewed by the staff annually, but only 10–12% of the journals are selected into the databases (Testa 2004). Electronic journals, irrespective of field, undergo the same selection process as journals in print media. Journals currently in the database are continuously reviewed to ensure that they continue to maintain the standards and relevance to ISI products.

Several factors are taken into account when evaluating whether a journal will be incorporated in the database, including (1) publishing standards, (2) expert review, and (3) citation analysis. Basic publishing standards include timeliness of publication, peer review procedures, and whether the journal adheres to common international editorial conventions. With respect to timeliness, a journal must be published according to its stated frequency to be considered for initial inclusion. The ability to publish on time implies a healthy backlog of manuscripts, and a journal's viability is considered to be waning when it appears chronically late (e.g., weeks or months after its cover date). Determinations with respect to timeliness are usually made on the basis of reviewing at least three issues. International editorial conventions require that articles must provide retrievable sources, full bibliographic information, address information for authors, and informative titles for both journals and articles. Application of the peer review process is another indicator of the journal's publishing standard, suggestive of both the overall quality of the research presented and the comprehensiveness of the references cited (Testa 2004).

In addition to these publishing standards, ISI employs a group of editorial experts to review the content of journals being considered for inclusion. For a new journal to be included the editors must decide that its content would enrich the existing database (i.e., that the topic is not already adequately covered by other, currently indexed journals). This evaluation component of the ISI database is least specified and it is unclear if other content considerations are taken account, who the experts are, or how much weight their decisions have in determining whether a journal is added to the database.

The final criterion, citation count, is the most comprehensive and quantitative aspect of the journal evaluation process. For newer journals the editors examine the publishing record of the journal's authors and editorial board members, noting where their articles have been published and if their work has been cited. Because the number of journals varies greatly among disciplines, discipline-specific citation rates also differ. Smaller specialty fields do not generate as many articles or citations as larger fields, particularly in some of the sciences. In some fields, such as the arts and humanities, it may take a relatively long time for an article to attract a number of citations; however, in other areas, such as the natural sciences, it is not unusual for citation numbers to peak after only a few years. Citations in social science journals tend to follow the same pattern found in the natural sciences—a linear rise, peak, and decline.

Education scholarship, perhaps even more so than other disciplines in the social sciences, is primarily based on pressing contemporary problems and their solutions. This emphasis on solving real-life problems is reinforced by federal and not-for-profit research support directed at designing and implementing organizational reforms, pedagogical and curricular innovations, and the privileging of certain methodological approaches. While this type of work legitimizes education as a field of study, it also affects the types of scholarly work that is produced. Given its focus on applied problems, it is not surprising that educational scholarship tends to yield citation counts with immediate high spikes and subsequent lower plateaus. This phenomenon tends to support the impression that education research is based on popularized notions rather than on sustained scientific research and evidence, even though its citation patterns mirror those found in the social and natural sciences.

Several types of citation data are used to determine journal quality, including overall citation rate, impact factor, and an immediacy index. Briefly, the overall citation rate is the number of times a journal has been cited. The impact factor is the number of times a journal has been cited in the past year divided by the number of articles published by the journal in the past two years. The immediacy index is the average number of times in its yearly publication cycle an article is cited.

One issue with using overall citation rates as an indicator of quality is self-citation. Self-citation refers to the number of times a journal is cited in articles it publishes. Testa (2004) provides an example of a hypothetical journal cited 15,000 times including 2,000 times the journal cites itself. The self-cited rate is 2/15, or 13.3%. A journal's self-citation rate may indicate something about the field it represents; a high self-citation rate may mean that the field is small or isolated. Multidisciplinary journals tend to have lower self-citation rates. Approximately 80% of the journals among ISI have a self-citation rate of less than 20% (see McVeigh 2002).

The impact factor and the immediacy index are often used by administrators in evaluating grant applications and by faculty in making promotion and tenure decisions. The impact factor has been regarded as a surrogate for expected performance. Recently published papers which receive high numbers of citations, especially among more junior scholars, are often seen as indicators of promising academic success. This reliance on impact factors has continued and there is evidence it is expanding, despite the fact that considerable controversy surrounds its application. Research has shown that a few years of article citation data are not necessarily predictive of sustaining contributions or career accomplishments (Pudovkin and Garfield 2002; Seglen 1997).

Journal impact factors are influenced not only by subject field and author characteristics but also by the nature of the work itself. Review articles are generally cited more frequently than typical research articles, as they serve as a guide to prior literature, especially in journals that limit references. Similarly, methodological articles tend to have higher impact scores, although journals devoted to methods tend not to have unusually high impact scores (Garfield 1994).

Education Journals within the ISI Database

Within the massive ISI database, there are approximately 150 journals classified as education journals. These journals are divided into three categories, including education and education research, educational psychology, and special education. Owens and Schneider examined the ISI holdings and contrasted them with those included in the Educational Resources Information Center (ERIC), a database of educational journals, reports, and conference papers.[3] In 2002 the ERIC database included 1,016 education journals. Although the ERIC list was considerably larger, there were several journals listed in ISI that were not listed in ERIC. The education journals in ISI not listed by ERIC tended to be international journals and journals in the fields of psychology and development. ERIC also listed a number of journals that appeared in the ISI holdings but were not considered "education journals." These journals were for the most part disciplinary based, such as the *American Historical Review*, the *American Sociological Review*, and *Cognitive Psychology*.

From these rather crude comparisons, it is clear that there are a number of education journals not included in the ISI database, and that is indeed disconcerting. The proliferation of journals in education that seemingly do not measure up to the standards set by traditional science and social science citation indexes suggests that perhaps too much information of dubious quality is saturating the field of education. It is important to underscore that education is not the only field where journal proliferation is increasingly a problem. As reported by Lawrence Altman and William J. Broad (2005) in the *New York Times*, the number of international scientific journals has risen dramatically, nearly doubling in 15 years (15,300 in 1980 to 29,098 in 2005).

The educational journals published by the U.S. professional education scientific research association, the American Educational Research Association (AERA), listed in ISI include the *American Educational Research Journal*, *Educational Evaluation and Policy Analysis*, *Journal of Educational and Behavioral Statistics*, *Review of Educational Research*, and *Review of Research in Education*. The average citation count for these journals is higher than the average citation count for all of the 153 education journals listed in ISI. The impact factor of AERA journals is also higher than the average education journals in the ISI database. The average immediacy index for the AERA journals is only slightly below that of the average ISI education journals but considerably lower than for journals published by the American Psychological Association (APA), such as the *Counseling Psychologist*, *Educational Psychologist*, and *School Psychology Review*.

One of the education-related journals in the ISI database with the highest citation count is *Child Development*; within a year, it is cited nearly 12 times more often than journals published by AERA. *Child Development* is a multidisciplinary journal and in it one finds articles by educational researchers, educational psychologists, sociologists, and those who work in human development. This is one instance where multidisciplinary affiliations tend to strengthen the prestige of the journal, perhaps because the journal also publishes authors who work in high-status fields such as cognitive science and health and medical specializations. Additionally, *Child Development* is published more often than AERA journals and has a higher page count. These facts are important to note as journals that publish more often and contain more articles have a better chance of being cited. *Child Development* has four times the number of pages, taking into account word count per page, than, for example, *Educational Evaluation and Policy Analysis*.

Journal citation represents only one indicator of journal selectivity; another measure of selectivity is made on the basis of manuscript acceptance and rejection rates. Acceptance and rejection rates are not part of the ISI database but are commonly available through professional association websites or publications. For the year 2002 the average acceptance rates for the AERA journals were *American Educational Research Journal* approximately 10%; *Educational Evaluation and Policy Analysis*, 16.5%; *Journal of Educational and Behavioral Statistics*, 27%; and the *Review of Educational Research*, 13%. In this same time period, the acceptance rate for the *American Sociological Review*, regarded as the flagship journal of the American Sociological Association (ASA), was 16.1% (these percentages have been considerably lower in recent years). The acceptance rate for *Child Development* was 8%. It is interesting that *Child Development*, with the highest citation rate, has more pages, but also receives one and a half times as many manuscripts and has a lower acceptance rate than any one of the AERA journals—suggesting that page count alone is not a robust indicator of quality.

The rejection rates of AERA journals seem to be within the range of the more prestigious journals in psychology and sociology. The most selective journals have rejection rates of 70% and these rejection rates tend to be quite similar from one year to the next (Cicchetti 1997). Rejection rates tend to remain consistent even when there are fluctuations in manuscript submissions or journals are given page limitations (Cicchetti 1997). This pattern of rejection and acceptance rates is similar to that resulting from the review of grant proposals and fellowship applications (Lamont and Mallard 2005).

Acceptance and rejection rates are fundamentally the consequence of the peer review process, a process that appears to function fairly similarly across journals. Journal peer review is commonly perceived as the mechanism for ensuring that the articles published are of high quality. Researchers who study publication practices and peer review in medicine and the behavioral sciences find generally that there is more agreement on rejection than on article acceptance (Armstrong 1997; Bakanic, McPhail, and Simon 1987; Cicchetti 1997). As shown above, the education journals, specifically those published by

AERA listed in ISI, have rejection and acceptance rates similar to those in other social science fields.

The peer review process has been challenged as being conservatively biased, publishing material that tends to sacrifice scientific innovation for improved consensus among independent sets of reviewers (Campanario 1998a; Hackett and Chubin 2003). Empirical studies show that accepted articles tend to privilege quantitative methodologies and authors in more prestigious institutions (Bakanic et al. 1987; Campanario 1998b; Lamont and Mallard 2005). Recognizing criticisms and concerns about the peer review process throughout the sciences and social sciences, the question remains—is there something unique to the peer review process that allows for the publication of manuscripts in education journals that are of lesser quality and relevance to the field than those found in other journals?

Peer Review and Its Application to Education

The purpose of peer review is to assist editors in selecting the best articles for publication and to improve the quality of submitted work. Common practice in journals is that an editor will identify two or three external reviewers who are experts in some aspect of a submitted manuscript (content and/or methodology), external to the journal staff, and free from financial or other conflicts of interest regarding the content of the manuscript or relationship with the author. Manuscripts are sent to reviewers who are asked to judge the quality of the paper based on a set of guidelines developed by the editor and editorial board, including criteria such as the completeness of information, clarity, balance in presenting results, and contribution to the field. It is the last criterion, contribution to the field (which tends to imply originality), that has proved to be the most elusive and created considerable controversy among those interested in judging the quality of peer review.

In many professional associations (including AERA, APA, and ASA), the procedure for selecting editors of the association's journals begins with a request for nominations from a search committee (often a subcommittee of a publications board). Letters are sent out to individuals inviting them to apply for the position. According to Campanario (1998b), it is not unusual for 50–80% of invited nominees to decline to apply, primarily because of the heavy burden of work associated with editorial positions. Reviewing résumés, publication records, and letters of application, the committee rank-orders the candidates. The publication committee then (usually in executive session) reviews the recommendations and invites the highest-ranked candidate to accept the position.

Individual editors are responsible for selecting their own editorial boards, and the criteria they use for identifying suitable candidates are unclear. Research on the selection and qualifications of editorial boards is dated and inconsistent, suggesting that arguments that editors and editorial board members of education journals are less qualified and capable than editors and editorial members of journals in other fields are spurious and based on mere speculation. What does appear to be the case (based on research conducted in the 1980s and 1990s) is that in both the sciences and the social sciences most editorial board members have published in their fields, although not necessarily in the journal on whose board they were invited to serve (Campanario 1998a).

Editorial board members serve as reviewers for the manuscripts; however, the bulk of reviewing is done by outside peer reviewers. Peer review is a voluntary task, sometimes undertaken to learn about recent advances in the discipline (Yankauer 1990), gain recognition from the field (Yankauer 1990), and provide service to the field. Peer review is also a time-consuming process. It has been estimated that an average reviewer spends from two to six hours reviewing a manuscript, with younger, less experienced reviewers tending to give longer, more comprehensive reviews than those more senior in the field (Evans et al. 1993; Lock and Smith 1990; Yankauer 1990). Referees often evaluate several manuscripts from different journals at a time (Garfunkel et al. 1990), as good reviewers are more likely to attract more invitations to review (LaFollette 1992).

Reviewer recommendations differ from one another and, as Cicchetti (1991) has shown, there are low levels of reliability between the recommendations of journal referees, regardless of whether the reviewers are assessing manuscripts in medical, physical, or social sciences. Average reliabilities among reviewers for most journals, regardless of field, rarely rise above 0.40, which is relatively low, and in many instances the coefficient is close to 0.01. It is not unusual for an author to receive comments from one reviewer who finds the work meritorious of publication, while a second reviewer may judge the paper to be unworthy of publication. Reliabilities among reviewers and between reviewers and editors can be improved by increasing the number of reviewers. However, as Cicchetti (1991) points out, adding reviewers leads to higher rejection rates, as the more reviewers, the more likely one is to detect a fatal flaw in the work.

Not unexpectedly, most authors are critical of the reviews they receive (Armstrong 1997). Decisions on publication are made by the editor, who takes advice from the external reviewers and sometimes from local editorial staff. Few manuscripts are accepted outright, and most authors are invited to revise their manuscripts and resubmit them. The revision process is generally perceived as a way to further strengthen the quality of the manuscript, although in most journals revisions do not ensure publication. Goodman and colleagues (1994) conducted a study to determine if the peer review process increased the quality of the manuscripts. Using manuscripts submitted to the *Annals of Internal Medicine*, they divided manuscripts into two groups, one that was originally submitted and another that had been revised based on peer review. The manuscripts were then given to a group of experts who judged the quality of the manuscripts. Based on empirical ratings, the manuscripts significantly improved. This is only one study, yet it would seem that by having experts in the field review the work and provide constructive feedback, the quality would improve and the probability of overstating its contribution to knowledge would be tempered.

The majority of top-tier refereed journals require referees to review manuscripts that have been blinded—that is, any author-identifying information has been removed from the manuscript. It is often argued that the blinding process removes bias and with it the potential for reviewers to give friends or rivals different treatment in the review process. In the *Journal of General Internal Medicine* a random study took over 100 manuscripts and gave them to two groups: one received manuscripts including authors' names, the other received manuscripts where this information had been blinded. Editors then judged the quality of the reviews in the two groups. The blinded reviews were judged higher in overall quality, and the reviewers of these manuscripts were rated as having done a better job at judging the importance of the research question, targeting key issues, and critiquing methods. Blinded reviews were not, however, more thorough, constructive, fair, or courteous (McNutt et al. 1990). In another study, Blank (1991) allocated 1,498 manuscripts submitted to the *American Economic Review* to two groups, one with the authors' identities and affiliations removed from the cover and first page (referred to as double-blinded), the other with identifying information retained in the manuscript sent to reviewers (who remained anonymous to authors, thus referred to as "single-blinded"). Only 53% of reviewers in the double-blind group failed to guess the author; this group Blank refers to as "truly blinded." Acceptance rates were lower, and reviewers were more critical when the reviewer was unaware of the author's identity and affiliation.

With respect to general guidelines for journal peer review, such as the selection of editors, editorial boards, and reviewers, the blinding of manuscripts, and criteria for publication, the AERA education journals are similar to those in the sciences and social sciences. They have similar rejection and acceptance rates, and it would seem they are not more or less likely than other journals to achieve high consensus on whether a manuscript should be published. These education journals are not outliers with respect to the common procedures followed by most peer-reviewed journals. *For those education journals not included in the ISI, the process for peer review is less clear, as there are no delineated standards regarding the publication process.*[4]

What Gets Published?

With the increasing emphasis on publication within the academy and especially publication in top-ranked journals, it is not surprising that the information base for peer review and editorial decisions has grown and among researchers a relatively new specialization termed "journalology" is gaining recognition (Fletcher and Fletcher 1997). Essentially, there appear to be two distinctive types of journal research. The first, as discussed earlier, focuses on empirical studies that examine the number and kinds of reviewers, whether they agree, prevalence of statistical errors in publishing, and how often articles are cited and by whom. The second are in the more subjective realm and address how journal editing should be done to ensure fairness and honesty as well as the confidentiality and the anonymity of research participants (Stamp 1997). Other pressing concerns relate to reviewer favoritism, self-interest, and negligence, including the inability to detect problems such as plagiarism or fraud (Campanario 1998b). In both instances, scholars contend that some sort of bias enters into the review process, resulting in evaluation errors that lead to the publication of manuscripts of low quality or the reification of existing theories or empirical findings.

These concerns result in two types of errors: a Type I error occurs when the journal publishes papers of low quality; a Type II error occurs when the journal fails to publish quality papers that should have been published. Criticisms of education articles tend to focus on Type I error, arguing that too many of the articles being published are of low quality, which may be directly related to the extensive outlet of journals for education manuscripts. Campanario (1998b) suggests that publication of low-quality articles is likely to be the consequence of reviewer negligence and favoritism. These concerns commonly levied against education are also found throughout the natural and social sciences. Charges of papers with fabricated data are not unknown in the sciences, as evidenced by the recent controversy regarding the results of a cloning experiment reported in *Science* (Kennedy 2006). Scandals involving plagiarized papers are found across the disciplines, most recently in the field of history (see Crader 2002; History News Network 2005; *USA Today* 2002). Results of experiments are also subject to classic mistakes, including one controversial economics study that contained a programming error that led to results that were the opposite of those originally published (Pressman 1994).

Reviewers' favoritism is evident, as it has been shown that reviewers are more likely to accept and review favorably those papers that employ similar theoretical paradigms and research methodologies to their own (Guetzkow, Lamont, and Mallard 2004). Referees are also more likely to favorably review manuscripts where the suspected authors are connected to the reviewer in some way, such as having been a mentor at the institution in which the reviewer was trained. Another argument concerning bias in the evaluation of manuscripts targets the discrimination reviewers sometimes display toward certain categories of people, favoring particular epistemological approaches and other cognitive categories that serve as proxies for other characteristics such as gender, race, or institutional affiliation (Clemens et al. 1995; Lamont and Mallard 2005).

In education, the likelihood of reviewer favoritism may be exacerbated by the large number of Ph.D. researchers trained in prestigious research universities. Studies show that reviewers tend to be employed in more prestigious universities and in the fields with which the author is affiliated. The number of Ph.D.s in education is higher than in many other fields, even among those seeking research careers (see Groen and Rizzo 2004; Hoffer et al. 2005). The pressure on these individuals to publish is similar to that in the other social sciences. Second, the insularity of educational training within colleges and schools of education may also contribute to reviewer favoritism. Even though education tends to be multidisciplinary in its content, it is difficult to recruit referees outside the field, who already are likely to be overburdened with reviewer commitments in their own discipline.

Whither Education in the Hierarchy of Science?
Education articles rarely tend to be cited in other social science journals; part of the explanation for this may be traced to the types of work published in education journals. The most serious problem education faces is its position in the hierarchy of science, that is, having an identifiable epistemological style that characterizes the research and scholarship of the work published within it.[5] Lamont and Mallard (2005) have developed a conceptual frame for describing what they term the social styles of research, which consist of four distinctive epistemological styles: constructivist, comprehensive, positivist, and utilitarian. The constructivist style is used by scholars who seek to give voice to minorities or to embrace their indigenous concepts. The comprehensive style is used by scholars who adopt an interpretative or theoretical approach to understand social phenomena, whereas the positivist style is used by those who adopt a hypothesis and quantitative approach to solving an empirical puzzle. Finally, those with a utilitarian style adopt hypotheses and employ deductive and quantitative approaches to analyze social problems and generate policy-oriented knowledge. Fields such as history and humanities could be characterized as primarily comprehensive and constructivist, whereas comprehensive and positivist styles dominate the social sciences (sociology and political science), with the exception of economics, which tends to adopt a positivist and utilitarian approach. The physical and natural sciences would also fall within this category. This typology is particularly helpful for understanding what type of work is privileged within certain fields and why education may be perceived as something of an outlier, as it tends to encompass all four styles. The recent movement within education as evidenced in the No Child Left Behind legislation, which mandates the funding of more research in the experimental tradition that relies on randomized control trials, has placed the work of some education scholars closer to that of economists and the physical and natural sciences. Nevertheless, education studies overall seem to be a hodgepodge of all four styles, with fewer studies in the positivist and utilitarian domains.

It has been argued that different fields would be better served by adjusting the review process criteria toward sensitivity or selectivity. Sensitivity refers to selecting manuscripts that rate high on originality, whereas selective criteria would filter out studies of dubious quality or significance. Within a field, certain problems or objectives may be better served by a review system adjusted toward sensitivity or selectivity. Selectivity might work best on problems situated within well-developed theoretical frameworks with clearly established methods, whereas sensitivity may be preferred when the problem or object is ill-defined or when there is little agreement about the most promising approach (Hackett and Chubin 2003). It could be argued that education research fits more closely the sensitivity model than the selective one.

The problem with the sensitivity model is that, because the field of education is so large and diverse, it is difficult to reach a shared consensus on the most valid theoretical models and methodological approaches. Kuhn (1970) argued that the sciences are organized so that those fields without a high level of consensus on the theory and approach rest at the bottom of the hierarchy and are viewed in the pre-paradigmatic state. But in the instance of education, some work, especially in early literacy, is highly developed (see Snow, Burns, and Griffin 1998), whereas in teacher preparation and professional development the research is less cohesive (Darling-Hammond, Berry, and Thoreson 2001; Goldhaber and Brewer 2000; Ingersoll 2001). One could argue that in other fields there are similar problems, with certain specializations sharing a particular theory and methodology that is not necessarily consistent with other general trends in the discipline. However, as Lamont and Mallard (2005) have shown, there is an epistemological style that binds them. This is less the case in education, as recently evidenced by the criticisms of the NRC report *Scientific Research in Education* (see, e.g., *Qualitative Inquiry*, volume 10, number 1, 2004; *Teachers College Record*, volume 107, number 1, 2005).

Why Journal Quality Is Important

Within most science and social science fields, scholars tend to rely on the number of publications appearing in commonly recognized top-tier refereed journals as one key marker of a field's research quality and influence (Campanario 1998a). Looking at the ISI numbers with respect to citation counts and acceptance and rejection rates, the educational journals in ISI measure up to those in other social science fields, and this includes those published by AERA. And the peer review process, at least as described in publication manuals, follows accepted procedures. What, then, appears to be contributing to this perception of poor quality?

The first problem is that one rarely hears of high-quality work not having a home in the educational journals, suggesting that the authors of such manuscripts may be turning to journals in the social sciences for publication where more prestige is likely to accrue to the individual. Some scholars may turn to their disciplinary homes for more theoretical work where they are more likely to achieve legitimacy in their home discipline and leave the applied work for education research journals. If the best work is migrating outward, this reduces the quality of what gets published.

For example, some major issues in education such as the negative effects of curricular differentiations on learning, especially for poor and minority students, and the inequitable distribution of social and material resources for instruction, including the basis on which teachers organize classes for instruction, appeared first in sociology journals (see Dreeben 1994; Schneider 2003). Even the concept opportunity to learn, a key educational idea, first appeared in a sociology journal (Sorenson and Hallinan 1977). A similar argument can be made for psychology, where educational psychologists are more likely to place their more conceptual work in psychology journals. Based on citation analyses, it would appear that researchers tend to seek recognition in journals in their own fields rather than ones such as education that are multidisciplinary and viewed as practical rather than theoretical and rigorous.

Second, in the social science journals, education articles tend not to be cited. The lack of education research citations in the more disciplinary-oriented journals contributes to the insularity of education and, given its size, contributes to the impression of low-quality work being published. In some sense this second point is tied to the first; scholars trained in a discipline look to their field first for publication and then cite the work in that discipline. Authors realize citing the work of others in one's field is critical in terms both of reviewers likely to review the manuscript and of evidence of the author's knowledge of seminal work in a particular field. There is little to be gained in the review process by citing work in education when writing for economics, psychology, or sociology journals. This problem is further compounded in the educational journals, where citing work in the disciplines other than education enhances the perceived value of the scholarly work. The fewer the educational citations, the more likely it is that the work, whether theoretical or empirical, will be seen as representing highly valued disciplinary scholarship, especially in relation to education which cannot claim a disciplinary home.

A third and perhaps more compelling reason may be that the nature of the work in education is so eclectic in style that it is viewed as having an ambiguous scientific approach. If an anthropologist chooses to conduct work on an indigenous culture, the academy tends to perceive this work as authentically representing the discipline. What are the intellectual boundaries of education that are considered as authentic in the field? This question is far more difficult to answer, yet without a bounded scientific content and approach it seems that education is unlikely to change its position in the hierarchy of science. Right or wrong, one's position in the hierarchy of science bestows certain prestige and legitimacy even in the face of fraud or plagiarism, which is unfortunately becoming increasingly publicized in the health and medical sciences.

One way to build consensus is to begin to share some commonly held standards, and these would apply to journal quality. While scientists agree strongly that the contribution an article makes to a given area of inquiry and the quality of the research design are the most critical criteria for judging the merit of proposed or published research, they have not been able to agree on what these concepts entail. There are different understandings of what constitutes scientific inquiry, evidence, and interpretations. Frickel and Gross (2005) argue that intellectual self-concepts framed around micro-level processes can spur larger social change. Thinking about this with reference to education, there are several ways in which these micro-level processes can help to build consensus that may lead to more normative ideas of scientific inquiry. The first would be to develop a coherent knowledge base in education, which could be partially accomplished by conducting systematic reviews of high-quality research. The Campbell Collaboration in the science, health, and policy fields, and the What Works Clearinghouse in education, are designed to synthesize existing work on a particular topic and are moving toward this aim.

The ability to conduct such reviews depends quite strongly on the quality of the evidence that is available in the field and how it is described in both form and content. Several initiatives seem directly relevant to this objective. The first is to have educational journals require structured abstracts.[6] Abstracts are brief summaries of articles that typically include the research question, mode of inquiry and, if empirical, information on the population, measures, and analytic approach, findings, and conclusions. Abstracts facilitate the process of conducting systematic reviews, enhancing the likelihood that relevant work can be identified, and findings and conclusions reviewed in relationship to other work in a specific field. The requirement for abstracts is complementary with another mechanism for achieving consensus on quality of evidence—the institution of journal reporting standards. Most professional fields have explicit guidelines for preparing manuscripts for publication. AERA (2006) has taken a major step in this direction and has developed reporting standards for empirical research published in its journals and has recently turned to standards for scholarship in fields such as educational history.[7]

Data sharing and encouraging the conduct of studies that replicate findings is another way to enhance consensus in a field. Sharing data among researchers working on similar problems can promote knowledge development. By reanalyzing data and/or integrating it with new information, researchers can verify or challenge existing assumptions (see Schneider 2003). The value of data sharing is growing in importance among all the sciences, and most of the professional and scientific associations have ethics codes that require investigators to share data once results are published.[8] Data sharing also encourages replication. Certainly, through replication it is possible to test theories, achieve greater generalizability of results, and chart new areas for study. Replication of studies in education is not a common phenomenon; however, when it occurs it can be a powerful tool for reexamining results and policy directions.[9] For example, Ehrenberg, Goldhaber, and Brewer (1995) were able to show through reanalyses of two national datasets, the Equal Opportunity Survey and the National Education Longitudinal Study of 1988, the importance of teacher subjective evaluations and how they influence students' aspirations and academic course taking.

Finally, there is a need to improve the peer review process. The need for information is placing traditional peer review processes under considerable threat. School personnel, parents, and policymakers want to know what works today, what will change practice. Authors are responding to these pressures (and sometimes personal recognition) by bypassing journals and announcing their findings directly to the press. Traditional peer review does not fit well in our impatient and information-hungry society. The growth of electronic publishing, the rising costs of paper publication, and delays in the flow of information, some have argued, may make peer review obsolete (Fletcher and Fletcher 1997). Others, however, maintain that conventional paper publication in leading journals will continue to be the preferred method of scientific exchange, the primary indicator of quality for rankings of faculty and institutions, and the key safeguard against author misconduct (Cicchetti 1993). While seen as partially flawed, peer review is generally perceived as better than having no external system of quality control.

All journals appear to be plagued with the same problems. There is a clear bias toward rejection, certain methods, and characteristics of the author, including their institutional affiliation. Research literature suggests that peer review of manuscripts suffers from both low reliability and questionable validity. Yet it has been argued that scholars can be trained to be better reviewers, and the expectation is that with such training they will act as better safeguards against publishing work that is of low quality or rejecting work of high quality (see Cicchetti 1991 on this point). One suggestion is that editors select reviewers on the basis of the manuscript's scientific content, rather than selecting reviewers randomly or on the basis of their similar specializations. Cicchetti (1991) argues that by selecting reviewers for their complementarity rather than similar backgrounds, the reliability and validity of peer review should increase.

Even in the absence of clear criteria for identifying high-quality manuscripts, peer reviewers can become more skilled at identifying inappropriate methods, measures, and results, more sensitized to issues of fairness, and more open to originality. The call for more training is a message being sent by those working in education and in other fields, including medicine and the social science disciplines. This idea is widely supported, and a recent NRC report, *Advancing Scientific Research in Education* (Towne, Wise, and Winters 2004), recommended that more systematic efforts be undertaken for the professional development and training of peer reviewers.

Regardless of perceptions, there does not seem to be a crisis with respect to educational journals in the ISI database. Those educational journals included in ISI databases resemble other natural and social sciences and their problems are much the same as those of journals in other fields. However, in the field more generally there is a numbers problem, in that there are many more educational researchers than researchers in other fields, as well as many more journals. The sheer number of people in the education research enterprise raises questions about its quality—how can so many people all be engaged in high-quality work? Moreover, among this large number there are researchers who self-publish and publish in venues that do not have the same scholarly standards and criteria that characterize journals in the ISI database. This also contributes to the perceived quality problem, although, as shown in this chapter, journal proliferation outside of the ISI realm is not unique to education.

What does seem unique to education is its eclectic epistemological style, and this may be contributing to the notion of a rudderless field where anything goes as research. The prevailing view is that education research is flawed in some fundamental way, and there have been a number of efforts including federal legislative mandates, national panels, and funds for research that privilege some methodological paradigms such as random controlled trials (RCTs) to make education research more scientifically rigorous (Schneider et al. 2007). Presently, there are few publication outlets for this work, although the new *Journal of Research on Educational Effectiveness* has been created to apply "principles of scientific inquiry to the study of educational problems."[10]

One of the challenges for RCTs, because of their design, is the focus of the work and the complex infrastructure needed to undertake them. However, increasingly, researchers expert in this methodology have been advocating larger, more complex designs that specify the necessary components in the infrastructure to carry out the rigor of implementation required in RCTs.[11] The tension lies in that although this type of work has high value for scientific research in education, there are few publication outlets for it in education journals and only a limited number of researchers trained to evaluate the contribution and quality of such designs. Nonetheless, for those who advocate and support these research paradigms that focus on cause-and-effect relationships for improving education and bringing promising interventions to scale, this scientific intellectual movement represents a major shift in the conduct of education research and ultimately the type and quality of subsequent scholarly publications (Schneider and McDonald 2007).

As with most shifts in intellectual focus, there is likely to be dissent and resistance. Some scholars have argued quite vehemently that the current emphasis on scientific principles in education research is constraining originality and eliminating certain paradigms as being valuable for understanding problems in education (Bloch 2004; Popkewitz 2004). Given the contentiousness within the field, beginning at the micro level seems a more reasonable direction, which may lead to a more unified understanding of what is high-quality research in education. These micro efforts are evident in AERA's initiative to establish standards for publication in its journals, the movement toward structured abstracts, and the efforts on the part of professional associations to take on a more directive role in the training of editors and peer reviewers—all of which help to create a consensus for what constitutes high-quality research and scholarship.

These micro efforts toward building a consensus on high-quality research and scholarship are one way in which the field of education can enhance the field's research quality and its influence in the scientific literature and its value to educational enterprise more generally. Will these micro initiatives dramatically change impressions of the quality of educational journals and the work on which it is based? Probably not in the short term, but if such initiatives continue, and the field itself continues to take on the role of monitoring and providing incentives to those who work and publish in education, the future may be more promising than some have envisioned. If education research is to be viewed as more scientifically rigorous as a field, it is imperative that the quality of its journals is enhanced and the processes by which journal quality is achieved are thoughtfully and carefully undertaken. For the quality of research in a field's scientific journals is the marker of the standing and vitality of the field. A critique of the work in a field's top journals is a critique of the field as a whole.

Notes

* This material is based upon work supported by the National Science Foundation under Grant No. 0129365. Any opinions, findings, and conclusions or recommendations expressed in this material are those of the author(s) and do not necessarily reflect the views of the National Science Foundation.

1. The importance of publication in top-tier journals is not strictly a U.S. phenomenon. In the United Kingdom, public universities receive funding in part based on the results of a national Research Assessment Exercise (RAE). The significance of high-quality research output as evidenced by publication in top-tier journals makes publication records important factors in recruiting, particularly near the end of individual RAE cycles. Guidelines for assessing the quality of research and the distribution of funds can be found at http://www.rae.ac.uk/.

2. A number of researchers have criticized citation counts as problematic but with the ISI database it should be possible to test some of these criticisms with sophisticated analytic methods. Empirical work on journal citation has been minimal whereas the research on access to the journals that is the process of peer review is more extensive (see Campanario 1998a, 1998b). It should be possible to use citation count as an outcome measure to test some of the allegations especially with respect to journal conservatism and bias.

3. These calculations were made for a presentation at the Committee on Research on Education at the Center for Education at the National Academies, November 2003 by Ann Owens and Barbara Schneider. Documentation for them was presented at the workshop, and reference to these documents can be found in the National Research Council report 2005. All of the journal titles for these examples can be found on the Data Research and Development Center website (http://drdc.uchicago.edu/). ERIC is currently being reorganized and it may be that in the future these two lists will not be as discrepant.

4. I was unable to find recent published material that described standards for accepting or rejecting manuscripts in other databases that contain education journals not listed in ISI.

5. Cole (1983), using the propositions defined by Comte, which posit that sciences progress through ordained stages of development and at different rates, shows that science knowledge, especially new discoveries, occurs in multiple disciplines, and there is considerable disagreement concerning which discoveries will be significant. Hierarchy of science refers to the ranking of paradigm development (theory and methodology) among the disciplines, with physics at the top, followed by chemistry, biology, economics, psychology, political science, and sociology. For knowledge to accumulate in any discipline, Cole finds that there has to be some minimal level of paradigmatic consensus. Cole's perspective on the hierarchy of science has been revisited by Lamont and Mallard (2005), who have developed an epistemological typology that they map onto various disciplines. Instead of adopting a development model of cognitive consensus, they have identified different epistemological perspectives as a way of distinguishing the work that generally characterizes particular disciplines.

6. This recommendation was made in the NRC report *Advancing Scientific Research in Education* (Towne, Wise, and Winters 2004).

7. AERA recently appointed a committee of scholars representing different epistemological styles to work on a set of guidelines for journal reporting in its publications. Such efforts can foster a shared discourse and perhaps lead to some common understandings on what constitutes scientific research in education.

8   Data sharing was another recommendation of the NRC report *Advancing Scientific Research in Education*.
9   The lack of replication in educational studies is not only a U.S. problem. Tooley (2001), in a study of 264 articles in the top three British education journals in ISI from 1994 to 1996, found that there were no replications of earlier research.
10 See http://www.educationaleffectiveness.org/pages/publications/journals.html. Retrieved October 12, 2007.
11 Infrastructure here includes the steps regarding safeguards for ensuring randomization, fidelity of implementation, and limiting attrition.

References

Altman, Lawrence K. and William J. Broad. 2005. "Global Trend: More Science, More Fraud." *New York Times*, December 20, page F1 (http://www.nytimes.com/2005/12/20/science/20rese.html?_r=1&scp=1&sq=global+trend%3A+more+science+more+fraud&st=nyt&oref=slogin).
American Educational Research Association. 2006. "Standards for Reporting on Empirical Social Science Research in AERA Publications." *Educational Researcher* 35(6):33–40.
Armstrong, J. Scott. 1997. "Peer Review for Journals: Evidence on Quality Control, Fairness, and Innovation." *Science and Engineering Ethics* 3:63–84.
Bakanic, Von, Clark McPhail, and Rita J. Simon. 1987. "The Manuscript Review and Decision-Making Process." *American Sociological Review* 52:631–642.
Blank, Rebecca M. 1991. "The Effects of Double-Blind Review versus Single-Blind Reviewing: Experimental Evidence from the *American Economic Review*." *American Economic Review* 81:1041–1067.
Bloch, Marianne. 2004. "A Discourse that Disciplines, Governs, and Regulates: The National Research Council's Report on Scientific Research in Education." *Qualitative Inquiry* 10:96–110.
Campanario, Juan Miguel. 1998a. "Peer Review for Journals as It Stands Today, Part 1." *Science Communication* 19(3):181–211.
——— 1998b. "Peer Review for Journals as It Stands Today, Part 2." *Science Communication* 19(4):277–306.
Cawkell, Tony and Eugene Garfield. 2001. "Institute for Scientific Information." Pp. 149–160 in *A Century of Science Publishing: A Collection of Essays*, edited by Einar H. Fredriksson. Amsterdam, NL: IOS Press.
Chubin, Daryl E. and Edward J. Hackett. 1990. *Peerless Science: Peer Review and U.S. Science Policy*. Albany, NY: State University of New York Press.
Cicchetti, Domenic. 1991. "The Reliability of Peer Review for Manuscript and Grant Submissions: A Cross-disciplinary Investigation." *Behavioral and Brain Sciences* 14:119–186.
———. 1993. "The Reliability of Peer Review for Manuscript and Grant Submissions—It's Like Déjà-Vu All Over Again." *Behavioral and Brain Sciences* 16:401–403.
———. 1997. "Referees, Editors, and Publication Practices: Improving the Reliability and Usefulness of the Peer Review System." *Science and Engineering Ethics* 3:51–62.
Clemens, Elisabeth, Walter W. Powell, Kris McIlwaine, and Diana Okamoto. 1995. "Career in Print: Books, Journals and Scholarly Reputations." *American Journal of Sociology* 101:433–494.
Cole, Stephen. 1983. "The Hierarchy of Sciences." *American Journal of Sociology* 89:111–139.
Crader, Bo. 2002. "A Historian and Her Sources." *The Daily Standard*. Retrieved December 28, 2005 (http://www.weeklystandard.com/Content/Public/Articles/000/000/000/793ihurw.asp).
Darling-Hammond, Linda, Barnett Berry, and Amy Thoreson. 2001. "Does Teacher Certification Matter? Evaluating the Evidence." *Educational Evaluation and Policy Analysis* 23:57–77.
Diamond, Arthur M., Jr. 1986. "What Is a Citation Worth?" *Journal of Human Resources* 21:200–215.
Dreeben, Robert. 1994. "The Sociology of Education: Its Development in the United States." Pp. 7–52 in *Research in Sociology of Education and Socialization*, vol. 10, edited by Aaron M. Pallas. Greenwich, CT: JAI Press.
Ehrenberg, Ronald G., Dan D. Goldhaber, and Dominic J. Brewer. 1995. "Do Teachers' Race, Gender, and Ethnicity Matter? Evidence from National Educational Longitudinal Study of 1988." *Industrial and Labor Relations Review* 48:547–561.
Evans, Arthur T., Robert A. McNutt, Suzanne W. Fletcher, and Robert H. Fletcher. 1993. "The Characteristics of Peer Reviewers Who Produce Good Quality Reviews." *Journal of General Internal Medicine* 8:422–448.
Fletcher, Robert H. and Suzanne W. Fletcher. 1997. "Evidence for the Effectiveness of Peer Review." *Science and Engineering Ethics* 3:35–50.

Frickel, Scott and Neil Gross. 2005. "A General Theory of Scientific/Intellectual Movements." *American Sociological Review* 70:204–232.
Garfield, Eugene. 1994. "The Impact Factor: ISI." The Institute for Scientific Information (now Thomson Scientific). Retrieved December 27, 2005 (http://scientific.thomson.com/free/essays/journalcitationreports/impactfactor/).
Garfunkel, Joseph M., Martin H. Ulshen, Harvey J. Hamrick, and Edward E. Lawson. 1990. "Problems Identified by Secondary Review of Accepted Manuscripts." *Journal of the American Medical Association* 263:1369–1371.
Goldhaber, Dan D. and Dominic J. Brewer. 2000. "Does Teacher Certification Matter? High School Teacher Certification Status and Student Achievement." *Educational Evaluation and Policy Analysis* 22:129–145.
Goodman, Steven, Jesse Berlin, Suzanne W. Fletcher, and Robert H. Fletcher. 1994. "Manuscript Quality before and after Peer Review and Editing at *Annals of Internal Medicine*." *Annals of Internal Medicine* 121:11–21.
Groen, Jeffrey A. and Michael J. Rizzo. 2004. "The Changing Composition of American-Citizen PhDs." Cornell Higher Education Research Institute Working paper #48). Retrieved December 29, 2005 (http://www.ilr.cornell.edu/cheri/wp/cheri_wp48.pdf).
Guetzkow, Joshua, Michele Lamont, and Gregoire Mallard. 2004. "What Is Originality in the Humanities and Social Sciences?" *American Sociological Review* 69:190–212.
Hackett, Edward J. and Daryl E. Chubin. 2003. "Peer Review for the 21st century: Applications to Education Research." Paper presented at the Workshop on Peer Review of Education Research Grant Application, National Research Council Workshop, December 25, Washington DC.
History News Network. 2005. "How the Goodwin Story Developed." Retrieved December 28, 2005 (http://hnn.us/articles/590.html#beam10-6-05).
Hoffer, Thomas B., Vincent Welch, Jr., Kimberly Williams, Mary Hess, Kristy Webber, Brian Lisek, Daniel Loew, and Isabel Guzman-Barron. 2005. *Doctorate Recipients from United States Universities: Summary Report 2004*. Chicago: National Opinion Research Center. Retrieved December 29, 2005 (http://www.norc.uchicago.edu/issues/sed-2004.pdf).
Ingersoll, Richard M. 2001. "Rejoinder: Misunderstanding the Problem of Out-of-Field Teaching." *Educational Researcher* 30:21–22.
Kennedy, Donald. 2006. "Responding to Fraud." *Science* 314:1353.
Kuhn, Thomas S. 1970. *The Structure of Scientific Revolutions*. 2nd ed. Chicago, IL: University of Chicago Press.
LaFollette, Marcy C. 1992. *Stealing into Print: Fraud, Plagiarism, and Misconduct in Scientific Publishing*. Berkeley, CA: University of California Press.
Lagemann, Ellen Condliffe. 1996. "Contest Terrain: A History of Education Research in the United States, 1890–1990." *Educational Researcher* 26(9):5–17.
———. 2000. *An Elusive Science: The Troubling History of Education Research*. Chicago, IL: University of Chicago Press.
Lamont, Michele and Gregoire Mallard. 2005. "Peer Evaluation in the Social Sciences and the Humanities Compared: The United States, the United Kingdom, and France." Report prepared for the Social Science and Humanities Research Council of Canada.
Lock, Stephen and J. Smith. 1990. "What Do Peer Reviewers Do?" *Journal of the American Medical Association* 263:1341–1343.
McNutt, Robert A., Arthur T. Evans, Robert H. Fletcher, and Suzanne W. Fletcher. 1990. "The Effects of Blinding on the Quality of Peer Review." *Journal of the American Medical Association* 263:1371–1376.
McVeigh, Marie E. 2002. "Journal Self-Citation in the Journal Citation Reports—Science Edition: A Citation Study from the Thomson Corporation." Retrieved December 27, 2005 (http://scientific.thomson.com/free/essays/journalcitationreports/selfcitation2002/).
Merton, Robert K. 1968. *Social Theory and Social Structure*. New York: Free Press.
Popkewitz, Thomas S. 2004. "Is the National Research Council Committee's Report on Scientific Research in Education Scientific? On Trusting the Manifesto." *Qualitative Inquiry* 10:62–78.
Pressman, Steven. 1994. "Simultaneous Multiple Journal Submissions: The Case Against." *American Journal of Economics and Sociology* 53:316–333.
Pudovkin, Alexander I. and Eugene Garfield. 2002. "Algorithmic Procedure for Finding Semantically Related Journals." *Journal of the American Society for Information Science and Technology* 53:1113–1119.
Qualitative Inquiry. 2004. Symposium on Scientific Education Research. 10:5–129.
Research Assessment Exercise 2008. Retrieved December 29, 2005 (http://www.rae.ac.uk/).
Schneider, Barbara. 2003. "Sociology of Education: An Overview of the Field at the Turn of the Twenty-First Century." Pp. 193–226 in *Stability and Change in American Education: Structure, Process,*

and Outcomes, edited by Maureen T. Hallinan, Adam Gamoran, Warren Kubitschek, and Tom Loveless. Clinton Corners, NY: Eliot Werner Publications.

Schneider, Barbara and Sarah-Kathryn Mcdonald (eds.). 2007. *Scale-Up in Education:* Volume II: *Issues in Practice*. Lanham, MD: Rowman and Littlefield.

Schneider, Barbara, Martin Carnoy, Jeremy Kilpatrick, William Schmidt, and Richard J. Shavelson. 2007. *Estimating Causal Effects Using Experimental and Observation Designs: A Think Tank White Paper*. Washington, DC: American Educational Research Association.

Seglen, Per O. 1997. "Why the Impact Factor of Journals Should Not Be Used for Evaluating Research." *British Medical Journal* 314:498–502.

Shavelson, Richard J. and Lisa Towne. 2002. *Scientific Research in Education*. Committee on Scientific Principles for Educational Research, National Research Council. Washington, DC: National Academies Press.

Snow, Catherine E., M. Susan Burns, and Peg Griffin (eds.). 1998. *Preventing Reading Difficulties in Young Children*. Washington, DC: National Academies Press.

Sorenson, Aage B. and Maureen T. Hallinan. 1977. "A Reconceptualization of School Effects." *Sociology of Education* 50:273–289.

Stamp, Arthur. 1997. "Using a Dialectical Scientific Brief in Peer Review." *Science and Engineering Ethics* 3:85–98.

Szigeti, Helen. 2001. "The ISI Web of Knowledge Platform: Current and Future Directions." Retrieved December 27, 2005 (http://scientific.thomson.com/free/essays/isiplatform/wokplatform/).

Teachers College Record. 2005. "A Symposium on the Implications of the Scientific Research in Education Report for Qualitative Inquiry." 107:1–58.

Testa, James. 2004. "The ISI Database: The Journal Selection Process." Retrieved December 27, 2005 (http://scientific.thomson.com/free/essays/selectionofmaterial/journalselection/).

Thomson Scientific. 2005a. "History of Citation Indexing." Retrieved December 27, 2005 (http://scientific.thomson.com/knowtrend/essays/citationindexing/history/).

——. 2005b. "Social Sciences Citation Index®." Retrieved December 27, 2005 (http://scientific.thomson.com/products/ssci/).

Tooley, James. 2001. "The Quality of Educational Research: A Perspective from Great Britain." *Peabody Journal of Education* 76:122–140.

Towne, Lisa, Lauress L. Wise, and Tina M. Winters (eds.). 2004. *Advancing Scientific Research in Education*. Committee on Research in Education, National Research Council. Washington, DC: National Academies Press.

USA Today. 2002. Purloined letters. *USA Today*. Retrieved December 28, 2005 (http://www.usatoday.com/news/opinion/2002/02/27/edtwof2.htm).

Yankauer, Alfred. 1990. "Who Are the Peer Reviewers and How Much Do They Review?" *Journal of the American Medical Association* 263:1338–1340.

CHAPTER 4

Can Non-randomized Studies Provide Evidence of Causal Effects? A Case Study Using the Regression Discontinuity Design

LARRY V. HEDGES
JENNIFER HANIS-MARTIN

It is difficult to evaluate arguments about the quality of education research as a whole because the field of education research is such a large and diverse enterprise. Little effort has yet been devoted to understanding the field itself. There is no consensus on how to define an educational researcher; little good information about the number of educational researchers (by any sensible definition); and little information on the resources devoted to education research, the productivity of educational researchers, or the productivity of the field as a whole. Empirical evidence about the field would certainly inform analysis of education research and its successes or failures. In the absence of good empirical evidence, we are led to argument by exemplars (in the best case, existence proofs), anecdotes, and logical reasoning informed by meager empirical evidence.

In this spirit, it seems clear that some parts of education research can sit comfortably within related disciplines such as economics, psychology, or sociology. Few would argue that education research which appears in the top economics journals such as *Journal of Political Economy*, the *Quarterly Journal of Economics*, or the *American Economic Review* is of inferior quality. Similarly, few would argue that education research that appears in top psychology journals such as *Psychological Review*, *Developmental Psychology*, or *Cognitive Psychology* is in some way "poor quality" because it focuses on educational issues. These journals are so selective that anything selected for publication there is virtually guaranteed to be of the same quality as the best work in the discipline. One could make the same argument about education research that appears in prestigious journals in other disciplines as well. Thus because education research does appear in these outlets (as well as even more prestigious ones such as *Science*), there are existence proofs that suggest that at least certain types of education research *can* be of high quality.

The problem with this approach to evaluating education research as a whole is that most of it (as well as most research in the relevant disciplines themselves) does not appear in the handful of top disciplinary journals. A great deal of education research appears in the much larger number of disciplinary outlets of lesser quality and in outlets that specialize in education itself. Moreover, much education research (but it is unclear just how much) relates not to theoretical concerns that drive much (but not all) disciplinary research, but to practical concerns of evaluating the consequences of educational policies, practices, or services or to the improvement of education practice. For example, the U.S. regional educational laboratories embody precisely this applied mission (see Chapter 2). We might call this kind of research *applied research* to emphasize that the origins of the research problems lie in practice, not theory, per se.

Applied research need not be of poor quality. Much of the research in the health sciences (medicine, public health, prevention sciences) is applied research because it is driven by practical aims of improving health or health care. Fields such as statistics, engineering, and computer science also have very substantial applied research components. Agriculture is a particularly interesting case of an applied research field, and one to which we will return later. None of these fields in general seems to suffer from claims that the research is of particularly low quality or is subject to attendant cries for reform. Applied research does, however, face difficulties that are not faced by purely disciplinary research.

Applied researchers, including those interested in educational policy, often face the dilemma of how to obtain evidence that can inform policy decisions within a time frame to be useful and at a cost that is acceptable. In some cases, policy decisions are recurring or they can be anticipated enough in advance to obtain resources for and organize programs of research that are dedicated to providing research input to policy decisions in a timely manner. Unfortunately, this situation seems rarer than situations in which the need for evidence emerges before a well-articulated research program has been put in place, let alone reaches fruition. One hope for applied social research articulated by Donald Campbell (1969) as his hope for an "experimenting society" was that it would be possible to improve our social knowledge (including knowledge about education) from the use of data collected in connection with natural variation in policy regimes. His use of the term "experiment" was not restricted to designed experiments with random assignment, but the more general idea of planned variation in policies. In other words, as we made the wisest decisions possible about social policy (including education), he hoped we could improve our practical understanding in order to make wiser decisions in the future.

This has proven more difficult than Campbell envisioned. Arguably the most notable product of this effort has been the development of a large literature on the difficulty of the problem and possible, although not always satisfactory, solutions. Much of the research literature on evaluation research in the last 40 years has addressed these problems (see, e.g., Shadish, Cook, and Campbell 2002). A parallel literature in econometrics (see, e.g., Heckman 1979; Manski 1995) and statistics (see Rosenbaum 1995; Rubin 2006) addresses many of the same questions, with a particular focus on the difficulty of making inferences about cause from naturally occurring data (that is, in the absence of random assignment).

The difficulty of the problem of making causal inferences in the absence of randomized experiments has led most statisticians and some social and educational researchers to question its feasibility and to call for the use of randomized experiments whenever possible. The US Institute of Education Sciences (IES) was created to improve the quality of research evidence in education. From its inception, IES was motivated by the belief that randomized experiments should be used whenever possible to evaluate causal effects of education interventions, products, and services. Advocates of randomized experiments point to the difficulties identified by evaluation researchers, econometricians, and statisticians, and also to the positive experience of other applied fields that eventually adopted randomized experiments as the gold standard for causal inference.

Agriculture is an instructive example. Ronald A. Fisher, who later became famous for developing modern experimental design and for his contributions to statistics and genetics, was hired in 1920 at Rothamsted agricultural station to carry out decidedly non-experimental analyses of the extensive records of crop yield data that had been collected there over 100 years of research. They hoped that he could use statistical methods to sort out the various confounding factors of rainfall, temperature, soil fertility, differences in drainage, etc. that bedeviled their agricultural data. Indeed, Fisher's first paper at Rothamsted (Fisher 1921) was an attempt to do just that. In it he applied the methods of statistical control (the same methods widely used in quantitative education research today) to try to understand the myriad of confounding factors that had affected Rothamsted agricultural data. He even carried out qualitative work to sort out anomalies due to factors that included social interventions (e.g., the introduction of compulsory schooling laws and later legislation to enforce them, and thus the availability of cheap labor in the form of school-age boys to weed fields). Fisher (1921) concluded that the magnitude of the confounding effects was often so much larger than the systematic effects of interest that better methods were needed. The better methods he invented included the randomized experiment and much of classical experimental design.

Those who advocate experimentation as a solution to the low quality of education research might point to the history of agricultural research. Before the invention and rapid adoption of the randomized experiment, it is difficult to identify rapid progress in agricultural research. There were technological innovations (the steel plow, the reaper, mechanical tractors) that permitted cultivation of lands not easily cultivated before and more efficient cultivation or harvesting of crops, but these were not based on fundamental knowledge about how crops grow, how farms should be organized, or what interventions would be most efficacious. In the first two decades after randomized experiments were introduced into agriculture, there was rapid progress, producing knowledge that not only changed practice in agriculture but is credited with a major role in helping avoid severe food shortages in Britain during World War II, when it was much more difficult to import food (see Healy 1995).

Advocates of experiments might also point to the experience of medicine, which adopted randomized trials as the gold standard for assessing causal effects more recently than agriculture. Throughout the 1930s, studies were conducted that increasingly approximated randomized experiments, usually using some form of alternating assignment rather than randomization (see Matthews 1995). The first modern randomized trial was conducted in 1946 (Medical Research Council 1948). Since that time, medicine has embraced the use of randomized experiments just as strongly as agriculture (Matthews 1995).

As a professional statistician and professor of statistics, the first author agrees with the position that randomized experiments are the strongest available method for assessing causal effects of interventions, products, and services. Even when there are alternatives that also provide unbiased estimates of causal effects, properly designed randomized experiments provide the most efficient estimates of causal effects (that is, they provide estimates with the smallest uncertainty among all methods using the same sample size). Randomized experiments are also usually easier to organize than alternative methods that in some cases can also provide unbiased estimates of causal effects. Finally, the logic of randomized experiments is easier to explain to users of the information they generate and thus they are more transparent.

However, it is important to recognize that assessment of causal effects of interventions, products, and services that are already developed is only a small part of education research (even of its most applied incarnations). Experiments are not well suited to what is arguably the largest portion of the education research enterprise. For example, experiments have little role in the assessment of the status of education (such as the survey and census work carried out by the National Center for Education Statistics, the International Association for the Evaluation of Academic Achievement, and the Organisation for Economic Co-operation and Development's (OECD) Programme on International Student Assessment[1]). Large-scale experiments have little role in the *development* (as opposed to evaluation) of new products, interventions, and services (including curriculum and instructional methods). Experiments likewise have little role in the discovery of basic process in reading, mathematics, and science learning.

Even for the evaluation of causal effects, where randomized experiments have the profound advantages described above, experiments are not always feasible. Sometimes they are not feasible because of political or organizational considerations. Other times, they are not feasible because they will take too long to carry out. In other cases, they are judged to be too expensive. Even the

Institute for Education Sciences, a major advocate of experiments, has found that it cannot carry out all of its evaluations using randomized experiments (major examples are its evaluation of the Reading First Program and its evaluation of the Math Science Partnership Program).

How Can Valid Causal Inferences Be Achieved in the Absence of Randomization?

The problem of making valid causal inferences in the absence of randomization has been a topic of intensive research in evaluation, economics, and statistics during the last 50 years. Most of this work focuses on the specific problem of estimating the causal effect of a treatment on an outcome. We want to estimate the causal effect of the treatment by comparing the mean outcome in a group of individuals who received the treatment with that of a group who did not receive the treatment. If individuals are assigned to these groups randomly (and there are no other disturbing influences), then the mean difference is an estimate of the causal effect of the treatment (relative to the control condition) (see Rubin 2006). If individuals are not randomly assigned to the groups, then the mean difference is generally not an estimate of the causal effect of the treatment.

If the mechanism by which each individual is selected into one group or another is known in detail, then estimation of causal effects *may* be possible in the absence of randomization. (In fact, the reason that causal effects can be estimated under conditions of random assignment is that the selection mechanism *is* known precisely: every individual has a 50% chance of being selected into the treatment group.) Most approaches to causal inference in non-experimental studies are attempts to find at least an approximation to the selection mechanism. Some approaches do this explicitly by estimating a selection model as a function of explicit covariates (see, e.g., Heckman 1979). Other approaches do so by explicit matching on individual variables or composites such as propensity scores (see Rosenbaum 1995; or more generally Rubin 2006). Still other approaches (e.g., instrumental variables methods) do so indirectly by trying to find exogenous variables that are associated with selection (see, e.g., Angrist, Imbens, and Rubin 1996). Of course, the validity of all of these methods involves assumptions which are as necessary to the validity of the causal inference as randomization is in experiments, but, unlike the randomization in experiments, they are not under the direct control of the researcher.

Sometimes the selection function is not random, but *can* be easily understood. When assignment to treatments (that is, selection) is made explicitly on the basis of an observed covariate, it is possible to obtain unbiased estimates of causal effects of the treatment (see Rubin 1977). Such situations arise when "treatments" are assigned to the most needy (e.g., compensatory education) or the most meritorious (e.g., fellowships or prizes).

The remainder of this chapter focuses on the problem of evaluation of a program in which random assignment was not feasible: A postdoctoral fellowship program providing a very expensive "treatment" (one year's salary). However, even if resources had not been a consideration, random assignment would have been antithetical to the explicit purpose of the program: improving the quality of education research by advancing the careers of the most promising young educational researchers. The approach used to evaluate this program illustrates one promising strategy for conducting non-experimental evaluations that can provide a strong basis for causal inference.

The Problem: Evaluating Postdoctoral Fellowship Programs

Many institutions (including the National Institutes of Health, the National Science Foundation, the Mellon Foundation, the Robert Wood Johnson Foundation, the Spencer Foundation, and the WT Grant Foundation) fund postdoctoral fellowship programs or early career fellowships for young faculty to enhance the research careers of the recipients. It is difficult to evaluate such programs because recipients of fellowships typically *do* have more successful academic careers than non-recipients. However, this need not be a causal effect of the program because the individuals who are selected to receive fellowships are more promising than those not selected. This is of course a classic example of the selection problem described, for example, by Shadish et al. (2002).

One such postdoctoral fellowship program has been run by the National Academy of Education (NAE) since 1986 with funding from the Spencer Foundation. The program has the goal of enhancing the quality of education research by improving the human infrastructure for education research. To accomplish this goal, each year the fellowship program provides postdoctoral fellowships to 25–30 young scholars who are within five years of receiving their doctorates in various fields. The fellowships provide one year's salary to give an opportunity for scholars already involved in education research to carry out substantial projects absent the typical obligations of faculty members. This helps fellows advance their research agenda and their careers.

The principal problem in evaluating the impact of a fellowship program on scholars' careers is that in any comparison of those awarded fellowships (the treated group) with those who applied but were not awarded fellowships (the control group), we would *expect* the treated group to have outcomes superior to the control group. After all, the treated groups were judged to be *better* by the fellowship committee before treatment. Even if the treatment makes no difference, they should still be somewhat better than the control group at the time that the outcomes are measured.

First we must evaluate how much better we should expect the treatment group to be if there were no treatment effects, and then determine whether the treatment group is better than would be expected on this basis. The difference between how much better we would expect the treatment group to be (if there were no treatment effect) and how much better it actually *is* will be the treatment effect. Thus it is essential to determine the nature of the selection process that yields the treated and untreated groups, and the degree to which the information used for selection can also predict outcomes.

The NAE/Spencer postdoctoral fellows are chosen by selection committees that use a variety of information to make their selections. These selections are made in two stages. In each year there are typically about 180 applicants for fellowships. About 60 of these 180 are typically selected as semifinalists and subjected to further evaluation, and about 25 to 30 fellows are eventually selected from among the semifinalists. One important source of information is a set of ratings of both the candidate and the proposed fellowship project by four members of the National Academy of Education. Each of these ratings is made on a five-point numerical scale, and both the individual scores and the total score across raters are available to the committee in its deliberations. Fellows are not selected using these ratings alone—each case is discussed at length and a decision is made by the committee as a whole. However, committee members have often remarked that their decisions are remarkably close to the decisions they would have made if they had relied solely on the numerical ratings. That is, the selection committee largely acts *as if* it made fellowship selections by ranking candidates according to their average numerical scores and selecting those with the highest scores as the fellows. Consequently, it seems reasonable to evaluate the effects of the fellowship program as if selections were made according to the numerical rankings. That is, the average of the numerical scores becomes the covariate used for assignment to treatment.

A research design in which assignment is made according to a covariate in this way has been called the regression discontinuity design. It was originally described by Thistlethwaite and Campbell (1960) (and later elaborated in Campbell and Stanley 1963) as a design particularly suitable for evaluating the effects of fellowships or prizes, but has been used in a variety of applications in program evaluation and economics since that time (see Trochim 1984). In this design the assignment of subjects to the treatment group depends on their score on a covariate. Subjects are assigned to the treatment group if their scores on the covariate exceed a specific threshold (e.g., all those with ratings greater than 25 receive a fellowship and those with ratings of 25 or below do not receive a fellowship). The covariate is correlated with the outcome variable, and this correlation is exploited to obtain an estimate of the treatment effect.

If the covariate X is correlated with the outcome Y, then there is some regression function $f(X)$ that is the value of the outcome expected for subjects who have covariate value X. If we have data on X and Y values for subjects in the treatment and control groups, we can estimate the regression function from the data. The regression function can be estimated separately for subjects in the treatment and control groups. Call the regression function estimated from the control group $f_C(X)$ and call the regression function estimated from the treatment group $f_T(X)$. Let t be the value of the covariate that is the threshold between receiving the treatment (or not).

We evaluate the treatment effect by examining the predictions of the two regression functions at t. If there is no treatment effect, then the two regression functions come together at t. That is, $f_C(t) = f_T(t)$. Suppose, however, that the treatment has the effect of increasing the outcome score of everyone who receives it by a certain amount (say five points on the outcome scale). Then $f_T(t) = f_C(t) + 5$, so the two regression functions will not come together. The regression function for the treatment group will be five points higher than that for the control group at t. That is, the regressions will be *discontinuous* at t (hence the name of the design).

Figure 4.1 shows the situation when the regression functions are linear. The first panel (Figure 4.1a) illustrates the case of no treatment effect, where the regression lines come together at $t = 25$. The second panel (Figure 4.1b) illustrates the case of a five-point treatment effect, where there is a gap or discontinuity of five points at $t = 25$ indicating the treatment effect.

Implementation Issues

The description of the regression discontinuity design above posits that individuals receive the treatment if and only if their covariate scores are larger than the cutoff. Rubin (1977) showed that when assignment is strictly according to covariate scores, the regression discontinuity design yields exactly unbiased estimates of treatment effects. The regression discontinuity design is often implemented imperfectly, with assignment according to covariate scores imperfectly implemented. When assignment is not *strictly* according to covariate scores, estimates of treatment effects are not necessarily unbiased (Trochim 1984).

Imperfect implementation is also a common feature of social experiments with many designs, including those with random assignment, where there are often cases of individuals switching between the treatment to which they were assigned and other treatments. Just as imperfect implementation in randomized experiments introduces the potential for bias in estimation of treatment effects, imperfect implementation of the regression discontinuity design introduces potential for bias in estimates of treatment effects.

In the case of this fellowship program, the decision to award fellowships to applicants is based on a lengthy discussion of the details of each case, including, but not limited to, the numerical evaluation scores from the four readers of the application. Because the assignment of applicants to fellowships was not *intended* to be based strictly on the covariate (the average of NAE evaluation scores from four readers of the application), it is not surprising that assignment did not perfectly correspond to covariate scores (that is, assignment was not a perfect implementation of the regression discontinuity design). However, the assignment realized comes rather close to assignment based on the covariate. If we simulate the behavior of the selection process by assignment via selection using a cutoff score (using a slightly different cutoff each year), 84% (380 of 455) of the assignment decisions would be made correctly. That includes 85%

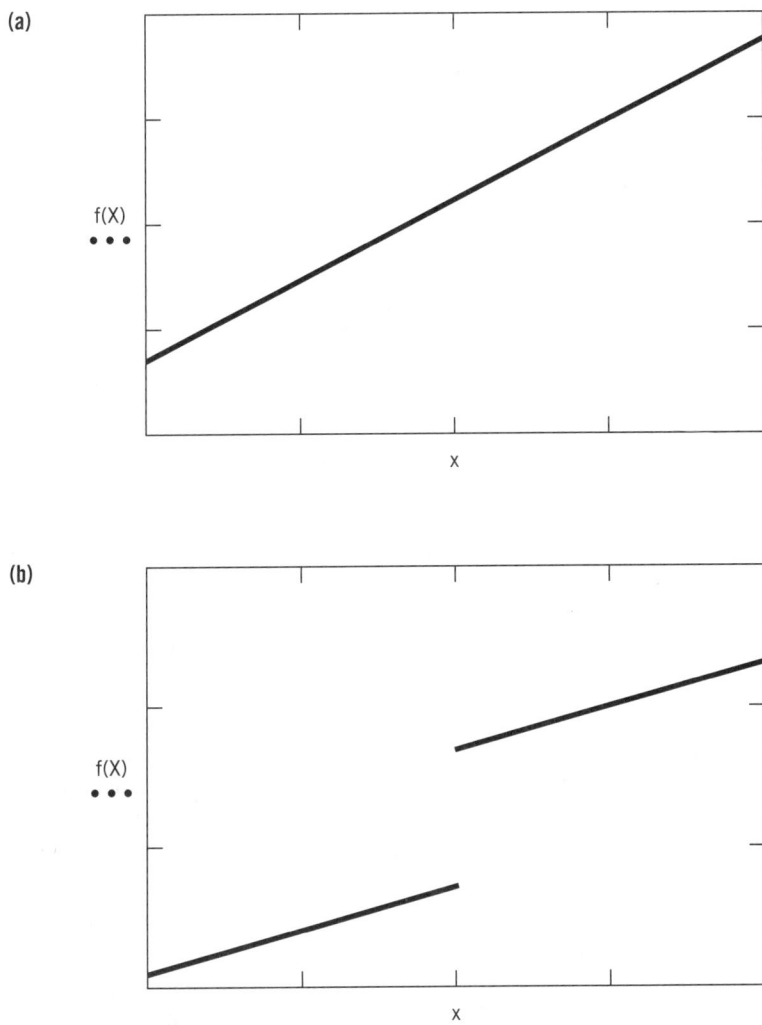

Figure 4.1 Linear regression of outcome on covariate with (a) no treatment effect and (b) five-point treatment effect

(250 of 294) of the fellows would have been correctly classified and 81% (130 of 161) semi-finalists would have been classified correctly. The fact that 16% of the assignment decisions were not made strictly in accordance with the covariate raises the possibility that bias could be introduced into estimates of the treatment effect.

It is difficult to assess how large these biases might be. However, it may be useful to compare the magnitude of the imperfect implementation in this study to that of other highly regarded, but imperfectly implemented, evaluation studies. One comparison is the Tennessee class-size experiment, which has been called "one of the great experiments in education in U.S. history" (Mosteller, Light, and Sachs 1996:814). Implementation of this experiment was also imperfect. For example, switching from assigned class sizes to the other class size (principally from regular-sized to small classes) would compromise the validity of that experiment in a manner analogous to assignment that was not according to the covariate in this study. Approximately 8–9% of students assigned to regular-sized classes switched to small classes each year during the four years of the Tennessee class-size experiment (see Nye, Hedges, and Konstantopoulos 2000). The magnitude of the imperfections of implementation in this study therefore appears to be similar to that in the Tennessee class-size experiment—an experiment widely held up as an exemplar of the "gold standard."

It may also be worth noting that the amount of missing data (which could also compromise the validity of inferences) is also considerably less in this study than in the Tennessee class-size experiment, where attrition was of the order of 20% per year (Nye et al. 2000). Therefore, while this study is clearly an imperfect implementation of a regression discontinuity design, it does not appear to be *more* imperfect than other studies that are regarded as providing conclusive social evidence.

Efficiency Considerations

While the regression discontinuity design is capable of providing unbiased estimates of treatment effects without randomization, the design has one important limitation compared to randomized experiments. It is not as efficient. That is, the statistical power of the test it provides for treatment effects is typically lower than the power of the test in the corresponding randomized experiment. The reason this is true becomes clear when one compares the analysis used in the regression discontinuity design with that used in the corresponding randomized experiment. The test for treatment effects in the randomized experiment might be derived by regressing the outcome variable on a dummy variable for treatment assignment. The test for treatment effects in the regression discontinuity design must include both a dummy variable for treatment and the covariate used for assignment, but these two predictors are necessarily correlated with one another. This correlation introduces colinearity that increases the standard error of the estimate of treatment effect in the regression discontinuity design compared to that in the randomized experiment. For example, in this study the correlation was $r = 0.61$. The effect of this correlation is to increase the standard error of the estimate of the treatment effect by a factor of $1.60 = 1/\sqrt{(1 - 0.61^2)}$ compared to a randomized experiment with the same sample size (see, e.g., Cook and Weisberg 1999:234). Another way of thinking of this is to say that a regression discontinuity study with sample size N has the same power as a randomized experiment with a sample size $N' = 0.37N$.

The study reported in this chapter has a total sample size of $N = 455$, which may sound rather large, but because of the inherent power limitations of the regression discontinuity design, it has roughly the same power as the corresponding randomized experiment with total sample size $N = 291$. Moreover, this study does not have equal numbers of individuals in the treatment and control groups (this is called an unbalanced design in the experimental design literature). This further reduces the power compared to the ideal (balanced) experiment. Taking the effects of imbalance into account, the present study has about the same power as a balanced randomized experiment with a total sample size of $N'' = 267$.

Efficiency is of interest because it determines statistical power. Cohen (1977) suggested a now widely used convention that a treatment effect of $\delta = 0.20$ (in standard deviation units) is "small" and a treatment effect of $\delta = 0.50$ is "medium." This study would have only a 23% chance of detecting a "small" effect and a power to detect a "medium" effect of 86%. Consequently, the findings of this study should be interpreted in light of what is certainly modest power to detect small effects, but somewhat higher power to detect larger effects.

Outcomes

It is not obvious that academic career success can be described by any single measure. Indeed, career success would seem to have several dimensions, and any or all of these might be considered as outcomes for this evaluation. Perhaps the most obvious dimension of success for a scholar is research productivity measured by publications or presentations at professional meetings. A second dimension is one of influence on the research of others measured by citations, prizes, fellowships, editorships, invited lectureships, etc. A third dimension of success of a scholar is the ability to garner resources to support research efforts, as measured by success in obtaining research grants. A fourth dimension of success might be the rank or prestige of the academic position occupied by an individual. We discuss measures of each of these dimensions below.

RESEARCH PRODUCTIVITY

Faculty performance has traditionally been assessed by "straight counts" (Lindsey 1980) of publications such as articles in peer-refereed journals, books, monographs, edited volumes, book chapters, and presentations at professional meetings (Braskamp and Ory 1994; Braxton and Bayer 1986; Miller 1972, 1987; Seldin 1984). This approach is appealing in part because measurement is straightforward, and the information is usually readily available, and verifiable. However, straight counts alone may be insufficient to judge a scholar's productivity.

Several different weighting schemes for forming composite from measures of different kinds of publications have been suggested in the literature (Braxton and Bayer 1986; Braxton and Toombs 1982; Cartter 1966; Crane 1965; Glenn and Villemez 1970; Knudsen and Vaughn 1969; Lightfield 1971; Manis 1951; Wilson 1964). There have been different suggestions about how to deal with multiple authorship on publications. For example, there is concern that publications having two or more authors should be considered differently than those with just one author, and that first authors should be weighted differently than co-authors (Lindsey 1980). After carrying out sensitivity analyses addressing these issues, we were somewhat surprised to find that the results did not vary greatly with different weighting schemes. Consequently, we report here the simplest approach, one that reports different kinds of publications individually as well as together, distinguishing between books, edited volumes, book chapters, book reviews, and peer-reviewed articles.

Scholarly Influence

Another important element of a scholar's career success is the influence his/her work has on the rest of the scholarly community. One way of measuring an individual's influence is to examine citation of that scholar's work (Centra 1993). Since citation counts can be viewed as an indirect method of ascertaining peer judgments, Gordon (1982) considers citation counts to be one of the better indicators of visibility and value of research. Using the *Social Science Citation Index* (SSCI) in conjunction with participants' vitae, we were able to count citations of the scholars' publications from years four, five, and six following their fellowship, or fellowship applications (in the cases of semifinalists). We identified these years as relatively high-publication years by looking at publication rates of a random sample of fellows and semifinalists from each of the cohorts over the course of their careers so far.

Another way that scholars influence the work of others is through their participation in the peer review process. Perhaps the most influential individuals in this process are the editors, associate editors, and editorial board members who select peer reviewers and make decisions about publication of others' manuscripts in light of input from peer reviewers. We coded whether individuals had been appointed to editorships, associate editorships, and membership on editorial boards of academic journals.

Garnering Research Support

Another dimension of a scholar's success is their ability to garner the financial support necessary to carry out their research program. This support is more tangibly provided through an individual's receipt of research grants. There is evidence that research grants have recently become more important in evaluating scholars' research performance than they have been historically (Centra 1993). And as with publications, not all grants are equal or should be treated equally. Grants also carry with them varying levels of prestige, with a grant from the National Science Foundation being perceived as more prestigious than one received from an institutional research fund (Braxton and Bayer 1986). In an effort to capture differences in prestige, in addition to looking at a straight count of all grants, we also separate grants into two categories, distinguishing federal grants from all other grants.

ACADEMIC RANK

The final dimension of career success we consider is the scholars' success in climbing the academic career ladder. Few of the scholars in the study were assistant professors in 2003, at the time of data collection. Thus we used a simple dichotomous variable to measure academic rank: full professor and other.

The need to consider not one but a number of diverse outcomes is not unique to this program. We believe that an important feature of many educational programs is that their goals are not restricted to a single easily measured outcome, as is often the case in medicine or agriculture. Instead they are better captured by several outcomes, which are often weakly correlated. Thus a key difficulty in carrying out meaningful evaluations of educational programs is devising measures of distinct outcomes, evaluating the impact of the program on each, and integrating those impacts into a single interpretation.

Results

Overall Sample

We began with a universe of 369 individuals who were selected as fellows and 249 individuals who were semifinalists (but not selected as fellows) during the years 1986 to 1999. We have secured contact information for 402 of the fellows (96% of the population of fellows) and 327 semifinalists who did not later become fellows (83% of the population of semifinalists). After multiple follow-ups of non-respondents (including telephone calls), we have obtained an overall response rate of 81% (82% from fellows and 78% from semifinalists) of those whom we contacted. Each respondent provided us with a current curriculum vitae that included information about employment history, publications, presentations, honors, grants received, and courses taught.

We developed a form for coding information from vitae to provide the dependent variables and classification information for our analyses. The data and results are for 13 cohorts of fellows and semifinalists.

POTENTIAL BIASES IN THE SAMPLE

Regression discontinuity analyses control for selection biases if there is no attrition, but differential attrition can introduce biases (just as it can in experiments). Thus, to assure the validity of the conclusions drawn, it is important to determine whether there is substantial differential attrition. The response rate of individuals who could be located was high in both groups (semifinalists and fellows), 78% and 82% respectively, for an overall response rate of 81%. Thus we believe that there is no substantial potential for bias due to differences in response patterns of the individuals we were able to locate.

However, the differential between groups in the proportion of individuals that could be located is somewhat higher (96% for fellows versus 83% for semifinalists). The methods we used relied on Internet searches, letters to previous addresses, and telephone calls to previous employing institutions and educational institutions. It seems likely that individuals we were *unable* to locate were substantially less professionally active and less connected to professional networks than were the individuals we *were* able to locate. If this is the case, we would expect that the individuals we were unable to locate would exhibit less career success (on the measures used in this study) than the individuals we were able to locate. Because the proportion of semifinalists we were unable to locate is considerably larger than the corresponding proportion of fellows, the individuals we were unable to locate should introduce a negative bias into the estimate of the effect of the fellowship. That is, the potential bias would make the fellowship look *less* effective than it was, so the study should yield a conservative estimate of the treatment effect.

Analytic Model

Although we have illustrated the logic of the regression discontinuity design above with only a single predictor variable, in most cases somewhat more complex analyses are dictated by the details of the study context. This was true in our study as well and we used a slightly more complex model specification in our analyses.

The sample included individuals who were fellows and semifinalists over a 13-year period (1986–1998). Because we measured career outcomes for the period after the fellowship decision, some individuals accrued outcomes over a longer time period than others (as much as a decade longer). Presumably a longer time period should lead to greater absolute accomplishment. That is, length of time period is confounded with measures of accomplishment. While this should not bias estimates of treatment effects, it should add noise to the evaluation of treatment effects. To control for length of time after the fellowship decision, we included a covariate that was the log of the number of years from the fellowship decision to the time of data collection in 2003. We carried out sensitivity analyses using several similar measures such as (unlogged) number of years since the fellowship decision, the use of the square root, and the use of a linear term plus the log term. There were no qualitative differences in results as a consequence of the particular functional form of this variable. Again, this illustrates the greater attention that must be paid to understanding and specifying the potential causal mechanisms when research is based on quasi-experimental rather than experimental methods.

We anticipated that some semifinalists would obtain other fellowships that would provide benefits similar to those of the NAE/Spencer fellowship. We discovered that 80 of the semifinalists obtained some other fellowship (Mellon fellowship, NSF Young Investigator Award, NIH Early Career Award, W. T. Grant fellowship, etc.) or a research grant of sufficient size to permit substantial release from teaching duties. Because the purpose of this evaluation was to determine the effects of the NAE/Spencer Postdoctoral Fellowship Program, and not whether it was more effective than other alternative fellowship programs, we included an indicator of whether semifinalists had received another fellowship that provided release time.

Therefore the final analytic model included four independent variables: an indicator for receiving an NAE/Spencer fellowship, the average NAE evaluation score, the log of the number of years since the fellowship decision, and an indicator for receiving another fellowship. The quantitative dependent variables used in this study all had skewed distributions, with most individuals having rather small values and a few individuals having much larger values. Consequently, we log-transformed these variables before using them as dependent variables in the regression analyses. One of the dependent variables we used, faculty rank, was recoded into a dichotomous variable with one value corresponding to the rank of full professor, the other corresponding to all other ranks or positions. Our analyses of the effect of the fellowship on faculty rank used this dichotomous outcome in a multiple logistic regression with the same four independent variables as the other regressions.

Analytic Results

In this study, as in most evaluations of educational programs, we examined several dimensions of outcome (in this case career success), and within each dimension we often had more than one particular outcome measure. The dimensions of career success included research productivity, influence on the work of others, the ability to obtain support for research, and academic rank. Each of these outcome measures is analyzed separately, and in each case we try to judge whether the size of the effect obtained is likely to be of practical importance. Finally, the separate analytic results must be integrated in some way to reach overall conclusions about program effects.

Table 4.1 gives the means and standard deviations of the measures of numbers of publications for each group (in both the original and the log-transformed metric) for fellows and semifinalists separately. The table shows that, as expected, the mean for fellows is higher than that for semifinalists on each of these measures except number of books. Table 4.2 gives the means and standard deviations of number of editorial positions for each group, the number of citations, numbers of grants received, and academic rank (in both raw and log-transformed metric) for fellows and semifinalists separately. The table shows that, as expected, the mean for fellows is higher than that for semifinalists on each of these measures. We briefly summarize the results of each of the regression analyses below, including an indication of the size of the estimated fellowship effect in each case.

RESEARCH PRODUCTIVITY

The fellowship had a significant positive effect on the unweighted (log) total number of publications (including book reviews) ($p < 0.05$). The estimated effect of the fellowship (regression coefficient for the fellowship dummy variable) implies that an individual who is a fellow will have about 30% more

TABLE 4.1 Measures of productivity: mean numbers for fellows and semifinalists

	Semi-finalists		Fellows	
	Mean	(SD)	Mean	(SD)
Articles	11.91	10.97	12.46	12.18
Books	1.01	1.86	0.93	1.29
Edited volumes	0.76	2.05	0.92	1.71
Book chapters	6.22	6.60	7.12	7.11
Book reviews	1.86	3.81	2.60	4.36
Total publications[a]	19.90	16.67	21.42	18.25
Total publications[b]	21.76	17.76	24.02	19.66
Log(Articles)	2.09	1.04	2.17	0.99
Log(Books)	−0.02	0.85	0.05	0.76
Log(Edited volumes)	−0.25	0.81	−0.05	0.82
Log(Book chapters)	1.36	1.17	1.58	1.06
Log(Book reviews)	0.14	1.09	0.38	1.18
Log(Total publications)[a]	2.65	0.95	2.78	0.87
Log(Total publications)[b]	2.74	0.95	2.90	0.83

a. Excludes book reviews
b. Includes book reviews

total publications than they would if they were only a semifinalist. Looking at the effects of the fellowship on each of the components of this total yields a similar pattern, but not always statistical significance.

The fellowship had a significant positive effect on the (log) number of book chapters published ($p < 0.05$), and positive but insignificant effects on the (log) number of refereed journal articles published ($p = 0.27$), the (log) number of books published ($p = 0.15$), and the (log) number of edited volumes published ($p = 0.27$). However, the size of these estimated effects was not negligible. They suggest that an individual who is a fellow will have about 43% more book chapters, 19% more articles, 21% more books, and 27% more edited volumes than they would if they were only a semifinalist. We judge these effects to be large enough to be important, and they are qualitatively consistent.

SCHOLARLY INFLUENCE

The fellowship had a significant effect on the (log) number of appointments as journal editors, associate editors, or members of editorial boards ($p < 0.05$) and an insignificant effect on the (log) number of citations to the individual's work ($p = 0.06$). The estimated effect of the fellowship implies that an individual who is a fellow will have about 40% more editorial appointments and 49% more citations than they would if they were only a semifinalist. Once again, these effects appear to be qualitatively consistent.

TABLE 4.2 Measures of influence, resources, and prestige: mean numbers of editorial positions, citations, and grants received

	Semi-finalists		Fellows	
	Mean	(SD)	Mean	(SD)
Measures of influence				
Editorial positions	1.53	2.13	2.29	2.72
Citations	40.66	112.24	48.66	116.56
Log(Editorial positions)	0.21	0.99	0.54	1.02
Log(Citations)	1.28	1.97	2.09	1.94
Measures of resources				
Grants received	5.96	5.86	6.84	5.92
Federal grants received	0.99	1.69	1.25	1.92
Other grants received	4.98	5.54	5.59	5.39
Log(Grants received)	1.34	1.19	1.57	1.08
Log(Federal grants received)	−0.06	0.88	0.10	0.91
Log(Other grants received)	1.15	1.16	1.34	1.10
Measure of prestige				
Rank	0.32	0.47	0.40	0.49

GARNERING RESEARCH SUPPORT

The fellowship had a significant positive effect on the (log) total number of research grants received and also on the number of federal and non-federal grants when these were disaggregated (all $p < 0.001$). The estimated effect of the fellowship implies that an individual who is a fellow will have about 129% more non-federal grants than they would if they were only a semifinalist. The estimated effect of the fellowship for the number of federal research grants implies that an individual who is a fellow will have about 80% more federal grants than they would if they were only a semifinalist. The estimated effect of the fellowship for the total number of research grants implies that an individual who is a fellow will have about 90% more grants than they would if they were only a semifinalist.

ACADEMIC RANK

The fellowship had a positive effect on the likelihood of attaining the rank of professor, but this effect was not statistically significant ($p = 0.34$). The estimated effect of the fellowship (the regression coefficient for the fellowship dummy variable) can be expressed as an odds ratio of 1.45, meaning that the odds of an individual attaining the rank of professor are 1.45 times as large if they are a fellow as they would have been if they were only a semifinalist.

Discussion

The design and analytic strategy used to estimate these effects was not a randomized experiment. A randomized experiment would not have been feasible for two reasons. First, the evaluation was only considered necessary when, after almost 20 years of support, the foundation providing the funding indicated an interest in learning about evidence that the program was having the desired effects. It would have taken another 10 to 15 years to accumulate enough experimental data for an evaluation (at the same rate of funding). Second, it is unlikely that either the National Academy of Education or the Spencer Foundation would have agreed to random assignment of expensive fellowships to possibly undeserving individuals. Such a design would likely have been deemed just too costly to obtain the information desired from the evaluation, and even if cost were no object, random assignment might have been ruled out as inconsistent with the meritocratic goals of the program.

The design chosen was well suited to the purpose. Even though the study was imperfectly implemented as an example of its type (regression discontinuity studies), we do not believe that the imperfections in implementation are profound enough to overturn the findings of this study. This study is about as well implemented as other studies that are considered not only trustworthy but exemplary, such as the Tennessee class-size experiment (Nye et al. 2000). The study reported here illustrates how reliable causal inferences can be obtained from studies that are not randomized experiments. It provides evidence that the postdoctoral fellowship program studied here had positive effects on four dimensions of academic career success, although the evidence is stronger in some areas than others. There is evidence that the program causes consistent, positive, and (sometimes) statistically significant effects on research productivity, as measured by total publications, books, edited volumes, book chapters, and journal articles. There is also evidence that the program causes positive and statistically significant effects on the influence of individuals on the work of others, as measured indirectly by appointments to editorial positions and directly by citation counts. There is evidence that the program causes positive and statistically significant effects on individuals' ability to garner resources to support their research as measured by number of research grants obtained. Finally, the evidence is weaker that the program causes more rapid promotion to the rank of professor—while effects are positive, they are far from statistically significant.

Perhaps as important as the existence of positive program effects is the fact that they are large enough to be of policy importance. The estimated effects on research productivity were of the order of 20% to 40%. This is a very substantial increase in research productivity. The effects on influence were even larger: 40% more editorial positions and 49% more citations. The effects on research funding were larger still, with the fellowship leading to 80% more federal grants and 90% more non-federal grants. The effect on attaining the rank of professor was positive, but far from statistically significant, making the findings on this dimension the weakest.

This case study also illustrates a weakness of alternatives to randomized experiments: they are not as efficient, leading to statistical tests that are not as powerful as an experiment with the same total sample size might have been. Many of the findings in this study are almost, but not quite, statistically significant. Although this is the largest evaluation study it was possible to carry out (we included essentially all of NAE/Spencer postdoctoral fellows whose fellowship was awarded long enough ago for effects to have plausibly been realized), it was not large enough to provide powerful statistical tests of effects that might be anticipated.

Randomized experiments have substantial advantages for evaluating causal effects of interventions when they are feasible, and they are probably feasible in more settings than their detractors would claim. Yet they are not feasible in all settings, or with all kinds of interventions. Randomization is much less feasible when the intervention is a complex multistage intervention taking place over the course of time. For example, instructional interventions taking place over several years are very difficult to investigate using random assignment alone (Cohen, Raudenbush, and Ball 2003). Similarly, situations where individuals may be assigned to receive treatments, but the individuals decide whether to use the treatments, introduce complexities that experiments are not suited to answer. In such situations, experiments can provide estimates of the causal effect of the *assignment* to treatment, but cannot provide estimates of the causal effect of the *use* of treatments. A classic example is the case of voucher programs. Experiments can provide estimates of the causal effect of being assigned to receive vouchers, but not of the causal effects of actually *using* those vouchers.

Note
1   See www.pisa.oecd.org.

References
Angrist, Joshua D., Guido W. Imbens, and Donald T. Rubin. 1996. "Identification of Causal Effects Using Instrumental Variables." *Journal of the American Statistical Association* 90: 431–442.
Braskamp, Larry A. and John C. Ory. 1994. *Assessing Faculty Work: Enhancing Individual and Institutional Performance*. San Francisco, CA: Jossey-Bass.
Braxton, John M. and Alan E. Bayer. 1986. "Assessing Faculty Scholarly Performance." *New Directions for Institutional Research*, No. 50 13(2):25–42.
Braxton, John M. and William Toombs. 1982. "Faculty Uses of Doctoral Training: Consideration of a Technique for the Differentiation of Scholarly Effort from Research Activity." *Research in Higher Education* 16:265–286.
Campbell, Donald T. 1969. "Reforms as Experiments." *American Psychologist* 24:409–429.
Campbell, Donald T. and Julian Stanley. 1963. *Experimental and Quasi-experimental Designs for Research*. Chicago, IL: Rand McNally.
Cartter, Allan. M. 1966. *An Assessment of Quality in Graduate Education*. Washington, DC: American Council on Education.

Centra, John A. 1993. *Reflective Faculty Evaluation: Enhancing Teaching and Determining Faculty Effectiveness.* San Francisco, CA: Jossey-Bass.
Cohen, David K., Stephen W. Raudenbush, and Deborah Loewenberg Ball. 2003. "Resources, Instruction, and Research." *Educational Evaluation and Policy Analysis* 25:119–142.
Cohen, Jacob. 1977. *Statistical Power Analysis for the Behavioral Sciences.* Revised ed. New York: Academic Press.
Cook, R. Dennis and Sanford Weisberg. 1999. *Applied Regression Including Computing and Graphics.* New York: Wiley-Interscience.
Crane, Diana. 1965. "Scientists at Major and Minor Universities: A Study of Productivity and Recognition." *American Sociological Review* 30:699–714.
Fisher, Ronald A. 1921. "Studies in Crop Variation. I. An Examination of the Yield of Dressed Grain from Broadbalk." *Journal of Agricultural Science* 11:107–135.
Glenn, Norval D. and Wayne Villemez. 1970. "The Productivity of Sociologists at 45 American Universities." *American Sociologist* 5:244–251.
Gordon, Michael D. 1982. "Citation Ranking versus Subjective Evaluation in the Determination of Journal Hierarchies in the Social Sciences." *Journal of the American Society for Information Science* 33:55–57.
Healy, M. J. R. 1995. "Frank Yates, 1902–1994: The Work of a Statistician." *International Statistical Review* 63:271–288.
Heckman, James J. 1979. "Sample Selection Bias as a Specification Error." *Econometrica* 47:153–161.
Knudsen, Dean D. and Ted R. Vaughn. 1969. "Quality in Graduate Education: A Re-evaluation of the Rankings of Sociology Departments in the Cartter Report." *American Sociologist* 4:1, 12–19.
Lightfield, E. Timothy. 1971. "Output and Recognition of Sociologists." *American Sociologist* 6:128–133.
Lindsey, Duncan. 1980. "Production and Citation Measures in the Sociology of Science: The Problem of Multiple Authorship." *Social Studies of Science* 10:145–162.
Manis, Jerome G. 1951. "Some Academic Influences upon Publication Productivity." *Social Forces* 29:267–272.
Manski, Charles F. 1995. *Identification Problems in the Social Sciences.* Cambridge, MA: Harvard University Press.
Matthews, J. Rosser. 1995. *Quantification and the Quest for Medical Certainty.* Princeton, NJ: Princeton University Press.
Medical Research Council. 1948. "Streptomycin Treatment of Pulmonary Tuberculosis." *British Medical Journal* 2:769–782.
Miller, Richard I. 1972. *Evaluating Faculty Performance.* San Francisco, CA: Jossey-Bass.
———. 1987. *Evaluating Faculty for Promotion and Tenure.* San Francisco, CA: Jossey-Bass.
Mosteller, Frederick, Richard J. Light, and Jason A. Sachs. 1996. "Sustained Inquiry in Education: Lessons Learned from Skill Grouping and Class Size." *Harvard Educational Review* 66:797–842.
Nye, Barbara, Larry V. Hedges, and Spyros Konstantopoulos. 2000. "The Effects of Small Classes on Achievement: The Results of the Tennessee Class Size Experiment." *American Educational Research Journal* 37:123–151.
Rosenbaum, Paul R. 1995. *Observational Studies.* New York: Springer-Verlag.
Rubin, Donald B. 1977. "Assignment to Treatment Group on the Basis of a Covariate." *Journal of Educational Statistics* 2:1–26.
———. 2006. *Matched Sampling for Causal Effects.* New York: Cambridge University Press.
Seldin, Peter. 1984. *Changing Practices in Faculty Evaluation.* San Francisco, CA: Jossey-Bass.
Shadish, William R., Thomas D. Cook, and Donald T. Campbell. 2002. *Experimental and Quasi-experimental Designs for Generalized Causal Inference.* Boston, MA: Houghton Mifflin.
Thistlethwaite, Donald L. and Donald T. Campbell. 1960. "Regression-Discontinuity Analysis: An Alternative to the Ex Post Facto Experiment." *Journal of Educational Psychology* 51:309–317.
Trochim, William M. K. 1984. *Research Design for Program Evaluation: The Regression-Discontinuity Approach.* Thousand Oaks, CA: Sage Publications.
Wilson, Logan. 1964. *The Academic Man: A Study in the Sociology of a Profession.* New York: Octagon Books.

CHAPTER 5

Blending Quality and Utility: Lessons Learned from the Education Research Debates

SHERI H. RANIS[*]

The heated exchanges between those who accept and reject the proposition that randomized controlled trials are the "gold standard" for scientific research in education have turned primarily on methodological virtues. The push to establish randomized controlled trials as the method of choice for education research, however, has also been animated and driven by the position that "good" research—inquiry and/or findings—informs, influences, or directly guides educational policy and practice. This preoccupation with the *utility* of education research has not been thoughtfully examined by most of those engaged in the current methodological debates: claims about rigor and quality are conflated with issues of research use in ways largely unacknowledged.

In this chapter I show that the utility of education research became a "resonant problematic": a core rationale behind the education sciences movement. A resonant problematic is a required underlying support for the kind of social and political movement that Walters has described in Chapter 1. It is a diagnosis of the problem that requires solving, packaged together with a series of assertions about remedies to solve that problem. In essence, the resonant problematic is a conceptual plank upon which a movement and its discourse can be built.

Research utility surfaced as a resonant problematic when a set of policy influentials persistently criticized education research for its lack of connection to solutions for education policy and practice. *Both* science *and* utility were raised as rationale for a new hierarchy of research methods, and frequently these two features were closely intertwined in the discourse. A corollary to this point of view was the assertion that educational policymakers and practitioners are the primary audiences for and consumers of education research and that positioning education research in service to that constituency was of the highest priority. During the period of time we are examining, this escalated rhetoric around utility was coupled with a series of dramatic institution-building efforts: the redirection of federal research grant dollars and construction of a new research infrastructure such as the establishment of new quality vetting mechanisms like the What Works Clearinghouse, doctoral and postdoctoral training programs, and the creation of a new academic association and journal to institutionalize the education sciences.

To more fully understand what has animated the controversy over upgrading the quality of education research, then, we must more closely examine how the theme of research utility was articulated and embedded in the education research quality debates. The call to make education research more useful is part of a larger intellectual context, and thus I begin with a discussion of persistent calls for a linking of quality and utility across much of the social sciences. I then turn to the attempt to rapidly put into place structures to make education research more useful to policymakers and practitioners through research infrastructure building, and close this chapter with thoughts about whether or not the resonant problematic of research utility has outlived the movement that brought it so much attention.

The Resonant Problematic: Education Research's Utility as a Proxy for Quality

Preoccupations about the utility of education research have shaped the current debates about quality and rigor of the field. These debates are neither new nor unique to education research.[1] What has been novel about the education conversation is the proposition that research quality can be *judged* by research utility: that utility is a key *measure* of quality. This is a largely new and vehemently articulated standard—one that has been broadcast in a manner with which the scholarship community in education has had difficulty coping. Let us briefly delve more deeply into broader arguments around research utility from the academy's perspective, and consider where in that complex topography the enterprise of education research can be found.

The view that education research must serve to inform education policy and practice hearkens back at least to the work of John Dewey ([1916] 1976; [1927] 1988). Without question, calls for research to more strongly "influence" policy and practice have also been persistent during more current public discussions (Hess 2008). Research's role in education policy and practice is variously described as weakly wrought influence, low in relevance, of limited usefulness, low-impact, or ineffective. These terms are used interchangeably in most recent discussions, blended with complaints about the field's lack of rigor and overall poor quality.

Conflating quality with utility implicitly reifies a certain kind of inquiry: It compels and places greater value on questions concerning impact and effect of actions and events, thus elevating a particular form of causal research method and a particular line of research, namely the assessment of the efficacy of educational treatments or interventions. In the logic of this conception, abstract and historical work, the messy up-front conceptualizations and context setting, questions about the causal effects of naturally-occurring phenomena or processes that cannot be experimentally manipulated, and the synthesis of existing knowledge or reexamination of assumptions are not highly valued pursuits. The fundamental rationale underlying scholarship is also up for questioning: Research for research's sake, as well as the iterative production of new knowledge, cannot be considered as worthy of investment of time, effort, and resources as determinations of causality in intervention or treatment efficacy settings.

In essence, if research that proves effect is the most important and meaningful intellectual path, then researchers are compelled to focus on proposing and testing solutions rather than specifying the complexity of the problem being addressed. In opposition to more diffuse and diverse notions of how education research can be conducted, what questions should be asked and what its outcomes should be, solution finding and new knowledge that is at least applied and at best operationally oriented become the top priority when utility is the primary yardstick for judging the quality of research. As noted by the National Research Council's 2002 report *Scientific Research in Education*:

> [M]ore than ever before citizens, business leaders, politicians and educators want credible information on which to evaluate and guide today's reform and tomorrow's education for all students. Driven by the performance goals inherent in standards-based reforms, they seek a working consensus on the challenges confronting education, on what works in what contexts and what doesn't, and on why what works does work. Simply put, they seek trustworthy, scientific evidence on which to base decisions about education
>
> (Shavelson and Towne 2002:22)

With the intertwining of utility with the notion of experimental methods as the premium methodological choice, educational researchers faced a challenging, tight argument for the realignment and restructuring of the education research enterprise. However, educational researchers are only the latest group of social scientists to be confronted with this kind of challenge—which we should acknowledge is driven both by outside forces and by the social sciences themselves. Consider the social science enterprise as a whole. It is an ironic and obvious fact that given the premise that all social research is concerned with understanding the complexity inherent in human phenomena, social problem-solving has been a goal of scholarship at least as long as philosophies of science have been debated (for a recent round of debate see Steinmetz 2005) as well as the preoccupation of various kinds of non-academic-sourced research by academically trained researchers that have developed over the past decades (Hess 2008; Price 2005). Not surprisingly, then, questions of the relationship between research quality and utility have been raised in recent years in many social science fields. An example of the persistent nature of this preoccupation is the establishment in 2007 of a new National Research Council committee charged with examining the "quality and utility of social science research."[2]

Nowhere is the impulse to judge the quality of research by its utility as strong, however, as in applied social fields. In the United States, reaction to persistently egregious and confounding social inequities like poverty and racism spurred the creation of whole fields of ostensibly applied inquiry such as public health, urban studies, policy studies, social work and criminology, among others. Bringing intellectual firepower to bear to illuminate beliefs, practices, institutions, and systems that perpetuate inequity and injustice is an impulse shared by most of those who pursue applied social research, including education research.

In this sense, utility is indisputably a powerful idea. But its articulation and disposition in scholarship continue to be hotly disputed throughout the social sciences as well as in applied social fields, often argued in close association with questions around the academy's proximity and independence from the rest of society. These persistent tensions about interacting with the public sphere, much less focusing on finding solutions for social ills, are constantly being sorted out in American social research, even to the extent of fighting over the proper terms of art for use in the debate.[3]

What constitutes "necessary knowledge" (to use Ellen Lagemann's term) and how it is produced includes a wide spectrum of views. At one end is socially relevant social science, which incorporates theoretical, historical, and non-constructivist approaches to understanding but hooks the question being answered to what our social world needs to know. Socially-relevant social science is currently translating into notions of socially-engaged disciplinary study such as public sociology (see Calhoun 2005). A compelling and similar conceptualization of the dynamics of approach and connections between research and use is Donald Stokes' notion of "Pasteur's Quadrant," which allows that work directed at pressing and practical problems can be pursued by both theoretical/abstract and problem-centered strategies. Stokes termed the latter "use-inspired research" (Stokes 1997).

At the other end of the spectrum, moving well beyond the notion of research being loosely coupled to utility, sits instrumentally-constructed social research strictly aligned with finding solutions. In this conception, quality certainly means utility, with the quickest road to answers through the exploration of causality as practiced by positivist scientific inquiry. Stokes termed this line of inquiry "Edison's Quadrant." Scholarship steps through posing problems or puzzles inspired by or from real-world situations, expressing a hypothesis about causality, which in turn produces warrants for those hypotheses, setting up a test and ultimately demonstrating evidence (or lack or evidence) of effect, begetting a concrete finding. To close the utilitarian loop, the finding provides an answer to all or part of the posed problem or puzzle. This approach deflects questions and findings away from elements of education or any complex social phenomena that do not seem to be addressable through interventions and treatments. This kind of instrumentalism, as Walters observes in Chapter 1, has galvanized the growth of evaluation analysis in many social policy domains.

The location of the education debate in this social science-wide maelstrom is complex. As already noted, education research is a field that inherently honors research for the social good, which is a tacit acknowledgment of the importance of research's utility, as opposed to research for research's sake. For this reason, the present education research community's chafing about the conflation of quality and utility takes some unpacking. The conflict seems to arise from three subthemes: the perceived limitation around definitions of what deep understanding entails, the focus on the promotion of a limited spectrum of methods that are supposedly fit for testing remedies, and the consequently limited range of questions to which researchers are directed to pay attention.

This is a community that honors usefulness but is not prepared to think that research should only be engaged in pursuit of seeking solutions. A glance at the presentations of any annual meeting of the American Educational Research Association (AERA) underscores that educational researchers are anything but complacent: education reform is the overwhelming preoccupation of the majority—as a subject of study and/or a personal mission. Nevertheless, as Schneider points out in Chapter 3, reviewing education research journals, the preponderance of education scholarship is anything but utilitarian in its approach. Also, as Phillips illustrates in Chapter 7, educational researchers find it difficult to be streamed or compelled to honor a single goal for intellectual pursuit—a function of the fact that education research has always made a place for multidisciplinary approaches to the study of education systems, teachers, students, and school practices, pulling generously on philosophical, historical, sociological, and anthropological frames.

By its very porous and diffuse construction as a field of inquiry, deeper understanding of the complex issues, problem specification, data gathering, and analysis stem from multiple and often competing bodies of knowledge in education research. Even when buffeted by epistemological fads and fancies, these angles provide breadth and depth to the knowledge base: this multiplicity of approaches has led to a layered and complex understanding of education as a phenomenon, as acknowledged by those who have attempted to define the field and consider future directions for it (Louie 2007; Ranis and Walters 2004; Shavelson and Towne 2002).[4]

These multiple points of attack and frameworks undoubtedly enrich us. But when utility is raised as the crucial filter through which value is assigned to research, questions of theory, history, context, as well as cultural and political screens diminish greatly in importance. Research that illuminates complexity but does not necessarily involve solution seeking is seen as less valuable. A hierarchy of what constitutes "necessary knowledge" is thus forged, as is the closely linked reification of purported superior methods.

Mobilizing for Utility

The genesis of the low utility charge and the rise of education science occurred in a near-perfect storm of developments, some of the most prominent of which included a series of reports sponsored by the National Academy of Education (NAE) on education research quality, the creation of a working group of experts at the National Research Council (NRC) determined to reenvision the production of education research through an entity called the Strategic Education Research Partnership (SERP), the work of the National Academy of Education–Social Science Research Council (NAE-SSRC) Joint Committee on Education Research, which began to examine how best to study the quality and health of the education research enterprise, and the deliberations of a congressionally-mandated oversight group in advance of the reauthorization of the U.S. Department of Education's Office of Educational Research and Improvement (OERI). The culmination of this series of events was the creation of the new Institute of Education Sciences (IES) in the U.S. Department of Education in 2002 along with the passage of the No Child Left Behind Act, both of which are described in some detail in Chapters 1 and 2. The creation of the IES signaled a fundamental change in federal policy: Henceforth, federal investment in education research was to respond to questions of concern from policymakers and practitioners as a matter of highest priority.

However, asserting utility as a resonant problematic required not just a statement of the lack of utility present in education research, but remedies to connect up research with policy and practice. Whether considered a kind of "parallel play" between the two domains that mirror each other but have little contact (Cohen and Barnes 1999) or a "dysfunctional market place" where perverse incentives steer researchers away from core questions of practice and practitioners opportunistically and selectively can pluck answers from research (Goldhaber and Brewer 2008), operationalizing that connection required some creative and rapid engineering on the part of federal authorities.[5]

The U.S. Department of Education took a number of significant steps to help policymakers and practitioners identify the research findings they could trust as guidelines for policy and practice. In essence, they constructed a knowledge-sorting infrastructure to bridge and enhance information flow between education research producers and consumers. The advocates of education research reform within the U.S. Department of Education started by financing two national efforts to spur evidence-based research to identify effective education interventions: the What Works Clearinghouse (WWC) and the Best Evidence Encyclopedia (BEE). Also during this period, elements of the social research community banded together to collate and analyze evidence of effective social policies, including education, through the creation of the Campbell Collaboration. The creation of these vetting structures personifies the resonant problematic of education research's utility and its conflation with issues of research quality. These developments also raise important questions about where authority rests to make determinations of quality and utility as well as about what process should be used to make those determinations.

Just prior to the reorganization of OERI into the Institute for Education Sciences (IES) in 2002, U.S. Department of Education leadership launched the WWC with the mission of providing systematic analysis of the scientific evidence of what works in education by establishing standards for the review and synthesis of existing research. The creation of the WWC not only buttressed the new orientation of IES toward methodological rigor; ostensibly it was formed to support the requirement that school systems select programs of curriculum, instruction, and assessment using scientifically-based evidence, as required by the No Child Left Behind Act.

The WWC focused singularly on the efficacy of education interventions and treatments, with a topical agenda determined by a mixture of expert and public nominations. Reviews were executed on individual studies, clusters of studies about particular interventions, and by clusters of studies dealing with interventions aimed at particular topic areas.

Controversy and anger from the field grew from the start over the methods used by the WWC to determine standards of evidence because the filter for inclusion in these reviews was, unabashedly, the gold standard of randomized controlled trials (RCTs). The methodology used to rate interventions was formal meta-analysis, which as applied by the WWC holds that causality—the finding that a program or an intervention has an effect on the people that are exposed to it—can only be made when fully randomized controlled trials are testing those interventions. Topical studies were judged on their suitability for inclusion in WWC reviews based on how well their research designs met the RCT standard.

The criteria for inclusion in WWC's reviews meant that most existing education studies were labeled "did not meet standard" and could not be incorporated into those meta-analytic exercises. For example, only four studies out of the 158 considered met standard for a 2006 WWC meta-analysis of middle-school math programs, with another 17 included with evidentiary reservations. Assignment of that status to specific studies was made public on the WWC website and caused a ruckus when the first WWC analyses began to roll out in 2004. To researchers named as having "not met standard" the Department of Education seemed to be vilifying the quality of their research (Viadero 2004).

Over time the WWC made some changes. It reconsidered the issue of rigorous research designs that were not strict RCTs, allowing that regression discontinuity analysis could also be considered rigorous enough to make limited causal inferences and that some additional quasi-experimental designs might also lead to some limited degree of certainty about causal claims.

However, even as the door to acceptable evidentiary standards opened a bit wider, researchers continued to chafe. Critics noted that even the small stream of studies that met WWC standard were not always suitable to be formally compared.[6]

Added to this, the review of particular curriculum and instruction interventions, often owned by publishing houses, was limited to effectiveness studies in the public domain or those voluntarily submitted by the commercial sector. Publishing houses did not rush to comply with the WWC mandate. It is unclear, however, whether this was attributable to the time and cost of pursuing RCT, discomfort with the appropriateness of that approach, or some other reason. The necessity of addressing the education materials providers' disinclination toward transparency apparently did not gain traction with federal sponsors. As noted by a former key education figure in the Bush administration, Reid Lyon:

> What I continue to argue to the consternation of commercial basal program publishers and private vendors is that at some point, education must become more serious about holding commercial publishers of educational materials accountable for the effectiveness of their programs. Establishing effectiveness and defining explicitly the conditions under which programs, approaches, and strategies are effective takes the basic effectiveness variable off the table. A focus can then be placed on determining why programs are effective in one context and not in others. This moves the analysis to issues related to teacher familiarity with, and competence in providing the program, and the essential implementation factors that can make or break a program's effectiveness—proven or not.
>
> (Shaughnessy 2008)

Intentionally or not, WWC review was a degree of scrutiny that curriculum and instruction originators/owners could all too easily ignore and federal authorities did not step up and engineer either incentives or requirements for compliance. The stumbling block here was not the utility question per se, as it was with many in the education research community. Rather, it was about resisting the call to rigorously demonstrate product effectiveness in a manner similar to the way that drug companies are required to demonstrate the effectiveness of new drugs before they can be brought to market.

As bad publicity mounted and the rollout of new reviews proceeded slowly (only two WWC topical reviews were produced from 2002 to 2006, along with fewer than two dozen reports on specific interventions), the IES financed a new research center in 2004 led by Robert Slavin at Johns Hopkins University. The Best Evidence Encyclopedia was an additional platform for figuring out effective education interventions and practices.[7] As suggested by its name, the BEE honored the hierarchy of methods used by WWC but used somewhat looser criteria for inclusion in reviews concerning research design, including duration of trials, sample size, and peer review, among other attributes.[8] The BEE was conceived as a more user-friendly tool for school-practitioner audiences shopping for evidence-based best practices under pressure from No Child Left Behind.

Interestingly, despite their having similar goals and the same funding source, Slavin joined the chorus of those critical of the WWC and calling for its reorganization and institution of more broadly conceived screens for rigor around research design (Slavin 2007). However, the BEE suffers from the same low flow of analyses that hinders the WWC: a relatively small amount of intervention and program studies that meet its standards can be reviewed. For example, an examination of effective middle- and high-school math curricula found only 13 out of 81 programs suitable for review while a similar review of reading programs for grades 6–12 found that only 10 studies out of 61 could be considered by the BEE process.

Contrast the WWC and the BEE with an organization originating from the research community itself that predated the creation of the IES: the Campbell Collaboration. This organization was created in 1999 by a group of primarily university-based researchers with a goal of bringing to social research the robustness and rigor provided by systematic reviews in health and medical research. The Campbell Collaboration focused on creating registries covering three social research domains: crime and justice, education, and social welfare. The Campbell Collaboration functioned quietly without much recognition from the broader education research community.[9] Guided by some of the country's top methodologists, it took a hard stand on the integrity of systematic reviews, using the requirements of meta-analysis and the importance of experimental design to cull studies for inclusion. Consequently, in the education domain very few studies met the methodological criteria. For example, for a systematic review of the impact of after-school programs, only five studies out of 88 considered made the cut.

Unlike the WWC, however, the Campbell Collaboration confronted the fact that too rigorous a methodological filter would eliminate too much research and make the process of knowledge consolidation considerably less meaningful. Efforts to study and figure out how to accommodate quasi-experimental studies were much more proactive from the inception of the organization. Unfortunately, the education domain's limited number of experimental or quasi-experimental studies, shifts in education group leadership and funding challenges, as well as lack of incentives to researchers to commit time to executing reviews contributed to the fact that only five education reviews were completed as of late 2007, as opposed to ten from Campbell's law and justice group and 17 from its social welfare effort.

Ultimately, the WWC, the BEE, and the Campbell Collaboration took somewhat different approaches to the problem of how to identify (and ultimately encourage) high-quality research that is useful to policymakers and practitioners, but all of their efforts were hampered by conflations of quality construed as fidelity to particular research design principles. Looking back on these attempts to cull and synthesize education research to identify successful or promising educational interventions and approaches, one cannot help but feel a deep sense of frustration. We are still far away from being able to confidently rely on high standards of research evidence to make judgments about best practices, largely because there is a dearth of that evidence. We seem caught in the dilemma that Carol Weiss identified in 2002 of figuring out "what to do until the random assigner comes" (Weiss 2002:198).

Clearly, there are mechanisms that can accelerate the flow of usable research on effectiveness. More incentives to researchers in the field to pursue the intensive and time-consuming task of producing reviews that suit the WWC, BEE, and Campbell Collaboration's standards are needed. Commercial sponsors of curricula will also have to be given incentives to test the effectiveness of their products and share those results publicly. Finally, an accepted means of judging the rigor of a larger category of research incorporating a broader range of quasi-experimental methods would certainly contribute to a richer and more useful pipeline of research on effective education interventions.

It will be some time before we know if the attempts by the U.S. Department of Education to compel researchers to focus on highly applied and rigorous research are blossoming. Along with the knowledge sorting/output aspect of the WWC and the BEE, the Department seems to be pursuing a multipronged strategy including establishing a recognized location in the academy for "education scientists" pursuing causal research. It is unclear if the aim is to forge either a distinct field or a subdiscipline around "education science."[10] What does seem clear from the chronicle of these three attempts to build knowledge-sorting mechanisms is a stunning lack of patience and flexibility on the part of those who have the ability to create and fund research infrastructure. The impulse was well-meaning and compelled by a sense of urgency about demanding guidance from education research, but, ironically, all these efforts were and are burdened with rigid (albeit rigorous) decisions about how to extract useful findings from the research. Coupled with few incentives for researchers and commercial sponsors to buy in and feed those new frameworks, the result has been a low volume of strikingly unhelpful analysis.

Moreover, the fact remains that even with a proliferation of appropriately trained researchers, a larger flow of such studies and broader vendor participation, persistent dissemination and translation will be required if these analyses are to be utilized, which raises another thorny issue of authority: who is in a position to authoritatively and legitimately translate on behalf of the research community, much less with a view to the needs of policy and practitioner communities? In the rush to build capacity and enforce rigor, federal authorities have tacitly assumed that role but with insufficient participation and feedback from the education research enterprise and key market players.

Codification of what is known is an admirable goal and vital to the health of any field. It is also a pathway to greater transparency and connection to the general public—a consumer-oriented approach to utility. What seemed to be so difficult about getting on that pathway, as demonstrated by the WWC, the BEE and the Campbell Collaboration, was the determination of both rigorous and fair decision rules that provided a wide enough window to accommodate the range of existing research on interventions and a lack of attention to building the social press to get researchers and commercial sponsors to buy in.

The messy accumulation of knowledge presented by education research and practice should not be considered intractable, but reordering and sorting it requires a great deal more thoughtfulness about what kind of infrastructure and mechanisms are worthy of time and investment. Also worthy of rethinking is who or what serves as the appropriate and legitimate authority to adjudicate the utility of existing and new knowledge.

Does Utility Remain a Resonant Problematic for Education Research?

The period 1998–2004 may or may not rightfully be considered to be a cathartic moment of self-examination for education research, but it certainly was a period in time when a confluence of ideas around research quality and usefulness were coming together in dramatic fashion. These notions were debated within broader contexts: a rejection of the authority of intellectual inquiry in American life in political and public discourse, and soul searching within the academy over how it could better negotiate its relationship with the public sphere. During this period, public discourse around government budget priorities and general lack of faith in scholarship were rife; charges of low impact were not limited to education research. Public and political views about experts and the authoritativeness of their findings were not in place in the same fashion as in the first decades of postwar America. Those who argued for higher standards of quality and utility in education research were responding to these broader social challenges.

There has been much controversy over the proposed efforts to improve the quality of education research and acrimony over the definition of what may be considered science and scientific about the enterprise, but relatively little attention has been paid to the resonant problematic of utility that so elegantly and compellingly provided the basis for the proposed reforms of the practice of education research and the narrowing of its approaches, scope, and content.

Even as the education research debates deal with what stands worthy of being called science, there has also been a tussle over what kind of research could rise above the clamor and noise of translators and claim the imprimatur of independent objective research. However, there are real questions around who or what provides legitimacy to research findings since there is a multiplicity of actors both inside and outside the academy taking on that duty alongside the persistent differences of opinion about what constitutes good science that we have been documenting (Brown 2006). The U.S. Department of Education and the field itself have attempted to build new locations of legitimization and quality control, but have done so with frameworks so tight that the better part of the knowledge base was squeezed out of consideration. And the range of questions about the education enterprise that were deemed worthy of investigation was severely truncated in the process.

My personal response to notions of priorities for investment and education research utility is that we must indeed shore up and utilize our education knowledge base as well as clarify and tighten the linkages between knowledge production and knowledge use. We must acknowledge that the research enterprise can inform and direct us toward improvements in our education system. Whatever the source of the dollars to support it, education research must be considered a public investment and resource. That means we must be proactive about engaging the various constituencies and be both smarter and expeditious about how to rethink the enterprise. There is a "value proposition" to be made concerning enhancing the quality and utility of education research that implicates both the supply of and the demand for knowledge. Clearly, new mechanisms will be required to achieve a new national approach to education research, and a particular kind of political/scientific détente and a reengineering of existing resources will have to take place.

To get started we need a national conversation that can help the field, federal authorities, foundations, and education leadership confront the challenges of volume, diffusion, and out-and-out messiness presented by the field's current output. In my opinion this is an opportunity for federal authorities to take on the role of conveners rather than adjudicators. The agenda would be ambitious. We need to determine how to:

- spend the time and dollars to look back with intent to clarify what our education knowledge base can tell us and do so with an intentionally open view to what knowledge is. The WWC and the Campbell Collaboration were start-up attempts in politically fraught territory, but their goals were fundamentally right. If federal authorities seek to continue to play the role of infrastructure builder and quality screen they must reconfigure the screening apparatus and incorporate incentives for intervention originators/owners to opt in;
- explore more systematic and applied approaches to solutions, measures, and tools incorporating a research and development approach with a looser but still rigorous presumption of appropriate methodologies and standards for findings. Problem specification is very important but the intellectual exercise and training required to pursue solutions is a challenge that the scholarly community should not back away from. We must accept the risk that a solution orientation will in the short term not only focus but also possibly narrow the scope of inquiry in education research as researchers chase available research dollars;

- consider whether there are new fields or subfields to be identified and nurtured in light of the challenges to progress we face now. Causal studies are being promoted as one such candidate, but surely the reinvigoration of older subfields like educational history and the creation of new multidisciplinary fields of inquiry around instruction and learning are of equal importance to invigorating the education research community. It is through careful attention to this middle stratum of inquiry that a rush to build out education science or any other particular subfield can be better digested by the education research enterprise;
- figure out how best to encourage the kinds of cross-disciplinary, cross-methodology conversations that ignite creative new approaches to education research. Breaking down the silos means breaking down barriers to cross-fertilization within and outside of the education research community. The education research community should take the lead in forging those conversations, partnering with federal authorities and foundations;
- identify locations in the pipeline preparing researchers where new skill sets or interdisciplinary approaches can be learned that support these goals. Thoughtful field building means integrated and rigorous training programs, mentorship, and career placement in multiple locations within education research;
- nurture and celebrate out-of-the-box thinking—new alliances, locations for cross-sector collaboration between foundations, universities, business, and government—which can help us think through how best to build new research capacity.

In sum, if a corrective second wave following the education research debates can be initiated, it will have to include the range of interested parties and present a new platform addressing the three features that have alienated so many: provide broader definitions of what deep understanding entails, allow for a wider spectrum of methods to model and test possible remedies, and be disciplined but more open to the range of questions queued up for priority inquiry.

This last point deserves more elucidation. A call for a unified if broad-based approach to knowledge building should only be pursued if it is animated by an urgent and specific inquiry agenda in education research. My own personal checklist of top research priorities follows. In the spirit of placing the ultimate consumer of education research first, all my suggestions focus on how we can make progress in what is arguably the core function of schooling: promoting student learning.

- We need to know much more about how individuals learn and about when progressions in learning accelerate and stall out throughout the lifecourse.

- We need to be able to make determinations about both the immediate and the long-term effects of interventions in early childhood.
- We need to know how to identify effective instruction and train teachers accordingly, which will require a much deeper and more systematic understanding of the complexities of the classroom.
- We have to more fully understand how technology and information use is shifting the expectations and needs of students and leverage that understanding to develop new and more effective environments for teaching and learning.
- We need measures developed that will chart the accumulation of academic content and skills that students need to succeed in school and life. In the process, we need more clarity about the complicated mix of factors that allow individuals to persist, sustain, and succeed in the education system.

Complex and challenging to address? Absolutely. There are substantial competing theories that undergird these questions that will have to be sorted through. Specifying and testing a meaningful research question elicited by these concerns will be a substantial intellectual hurdle. Data availability, the ingenuity required for rigorous research design, time requirements to execute an appropriate inquiry, and higher costs are just a few of the operational elements that will make breakthroughs on these questions difficult. However, the potential contribution of research around these issues is indisputable and highly worthy of deep and sustained attention on the part of funders, researchers, policymakers, and practitioners.

There are also a number of examples of second-wave research that should give us the courage and inspiration to pursue this path. Although there are not many multidisciplinary, theoretically driven, but highly applied experimental research projects, there are at least three notable ones. The Tennessee STAR experiment randomly assigned almost 12,000 students to various sizes of classroom and was designed to evaluate the impact of class size on student outcomes. Also a randomized assignment design, the ongoing multipronged Moving to Opportunity (MTO) study takes a longitudinal look at the range of social and economic impacts on urban families provided with the chance to upgrade their housing and their neighborhood. More recently, and once again using an experimental design, researchers are teaming with a national tax preparation service to determine whether assistance with federal financial-aid forms and financial-aid information distributed by tax professionals directly to families as they fill out their tax forms can make a difference in postsecondary outcomes for low-income youth. This effort is being piloted in Ohio and North Carolina in 2008 and will touch as many as 40,000 families. All of these studies were conducted by academic researchers, informed by multidisciplinary perspectives, animated by theory, driven by program evaluation needs, and responded to real questions about innovative policy and practice.

There are also new nodes of important utility-focused knowledge creation tightly intertwined with real-world policy concerns, schools, and schooling. These field a variety of research designs and approaches. To name just a few, the Consortium on Chicago School Research at the University of Chicago works to provide analyses on student and school outcomes that the Chicago public school system can use to improve teaching and learning at the district, school, and classroom levels. The Human Services Policy Center at the University of Washington has forged close ties with state policymakers in Ohio and Tennessee in order to develop new approaches to state-school finance policies. SERP in its latest incarnation has initiated a researcher-run literacy intervention for middle schools in Boston that has had highly encouraging results in district classrooms. Finally, the Johns Hopkins University Center for Social Organization of Schools has provided a stream of studies and tools about high-school transition and curricular remediation drawn from a research-based school model of its invention that has grown into a national network of rejuvenated high schools.[11]

Tracing the rise of the research utility resonant problematic and unpacking the key issues involved exposes core questions that we simply do not have definitive answers to. Must the quality of research be judged primarily by its utility? Must we prioritize our resources and favor research that searches for what works? The answer in my opinion is no to the first and yes to the second. Education research needs to focus on both the upper and the lower right-hand corner of Pasteur's Quadrant, inclusive of both use-inspired and applied research. Broader inquiry, such as work in history and the philosophy of education, must be supported, but all stages of research, problem identification, specification, and the modeling and testing of solutions require keen attention and nurturing. As Kathleen Brown has stated, "Education research in the public interest is more of a service and a process . . . rather than a particular type of research project or end goal" (Brown 2006). Just so. The point is that field building is a matter of "and," not "or," when it comes to ensuring the health and meaningfulness of the education research enterprise now and in the future.

Our society urgently needs a responsive and rigorous research capacity and agenda and must initiate the public conversations that will allow those to flourish. We must pursue the resonant problematic and elevate education research's utility, but more generously and synthetically think about what we need to know to be able to achieve the progress we seek in both understanding and executing stronger systems of teaching and learning.

Notes

* * The positions and opinions expressed here are solely those of the author and do not represent a statement of the views or opinions of the Bill & Melinda Gates Foundation. Moreover, any errors or misrepresentations are the responsibility of the author alone.
* 1 For additional insight on the nuanced politics that infiltrate determinations of scholarly quality see Brenneis (1994).

2   The National Research Council, Division of Behavioral and Social Sciences and Education established a project entitled "Evidence for Use: Improving the Quality and Utility of Social Science Research" in spring 2007 to respond to questions about evidence, the best means to measure quality and promote research improvement, how research evidence can contribute to improved policy and practice decisions, what policies are most amenable to what types of research, and how research results are best communicated to decisionmakers.
3   For a particularly poignant example of these tensions playing out, consider debates within the U.S. area studies community during the 1990s around membership, mission, and orientation as chronicled by Worcester (2004) and as discussed by Featherman (1991) in the Social Science Research Council's quarterly publication *Items*.
4   For analyses of the more dire consequences of field diffusion see also Carnine (2004), Hess (2008), Labaree (1998), and Schoenfeld (1999).
5   A discussion of the interaction (or lack thereof) between education research and policy/practice is beyond the scope of this chapter, but some impassioned analysis about this can be found in Carnine (2004), Hess (2008), Labaree (1998), and Wolk (2007).
6   Level of analysis problems, misclassification of the purpose of the intervention, and other charges were made. See Schoenfield (2006) and Confrey (2006) for complaints made about WWC attempts to review curricular effectiveness.
7   See www.bestevidence.org.
8   See www.cddre.org/Resources/InterventionSelectionRubrics.pdf.
9   It is also important to note that from 2002 the Campbell Collaboration was a close partner in collaboration with the research firm American Institutes for Research to construct the What Works Clearinghouse on behalf of IES. Many of the founders and leaders of the Campbell Collaboration were called in to spearhead the WWC effort.
10 Along with the WWC and BEE, IES financed the creation of a new education research organization, the Society for Research on Educational Effectiveness, in 2004, as well as organizing grant-making priorities and fellowship competitions around RCT design (see Walters, Chapter 1). More recently IES has created a new "National Center on Response to Intervention" (2007) and a series of public forums on "Scientific Evidence in Education" (2007).
11 See for Consortium on Chicago School Research www.ccsr.uchicago.edu; for Human Services Policy Center www.hspc.org; for SERP http://www.serpinstitute.org/content/page.php?cat=4&content_id=17; and for the Center for Social Organization of Schools www.csos.jhu.edu.

References

Brenneis, Donald. 1994. "Discourse and Discipline at the National Research Council: A Bureaucratic *Bildungsroman*." *Cultural Anthropology* 9:23–36.
Brown, Kathleen M. 2006. Book review of *Education Research in the Public Interest: Social Justice, Action and Policy*. *Teachers College Record* (online edition). Retrieved August 17, 2006 (http://www.tc record.org).
Calhoun, Craig. 2005. "The Promise of Public Sociology." *British Journal of Sociology* 56:355–363.
Carnine, Douglas. 2004. "Why Education Experts Resist Effective Practices (and What It Would Take to Make Education More Like Medicine)." Washington, DC: The Thomas B. Fordham Foundation. Retrieved February 18, 2008 (http://www.edexcellence.net/doc/carnine.pdf).
Cohen, David K. and Carol A. Barnes. 1999. "Research and the Purposes of Education." Pp. 17–42 in *Issues in Education Research: Problems and Possibilities*, edited by Ellen Condliffe Lagemann and Lee S. Shulman. San Francisco, CA: Jossey-Bass.
Confrey, Jere. 2006. "Comparing and Contrasting the NRC Report on Evaluating Curricular Effectiveness with the What Works Clearinghouse Approach." *Educational Evaluation and Policy Analysis* 28:195–213.
Dewey, John. [1916] 1976. "Democracy and Education." *The Middle Works of John Dewey*, Volume 9, 1899–1924: *Democracy and Education, 1916 (Collected Works of John Dewey)*, by John Dewey (author), Jo Ann Boydston (editor), Sidney Hook (Introduction). Carbondale, IL: Southern Illinois University Press.
——. [1927] 1988. *The Public and Its Problems*. Athens, OH: Ohio University Press.
Featherman, David L. 1991. "Mission-Oriented Basic Research." *Items* 45:75–77.
Goldhaber, Dan and Dominic Brewer. 2008. "What Gets Studied and Why: Examining the Incentives That Drive Education Research." Pp. 197–217 in *When Research Matters: How Scholarship Influences Education Policy*, edited by Frederick M. Hess. Cambridge, MA: Harvard Education Press.

Hess, Frederick M. (ed.). 2008. *When Research Matters: How Scholarship Influences Education Policy.* Cambridge, MA: Harvard University Press.

Labaree, David. 1998. "Educational Researchers: Living with a Lesser Form of Knowledge." *Educational Researcher* 27:4–12.

Louie, Vivian. 2007. "Who Makes the Transition to College? Why We Should Care, What We Know, and What We Need to Do." *Teachers College Record* 109:2222–2251.

Price, Derek. 2005. "Summary of 'Fifth Sector' Reports on the Transition from High School to College: 1998–2004 Synopsis." New York: Social Science Research Council.

Ranis, Sheri H. and Pamela Barnhouse Walters. 2004. "Education Research as a Contested Enterprise: The Deliberations of the SSRC-NAE Joint Committee on Education Research." *European Educational Research Journal* 3:795–806.

Schoenfeld, Alan H. 1999. "The Core, the Canon, and the Development of Research Skills: Isssues in the Preparation of Education Researchers." Pp. 166–202 in *Issues in Education Research: Problems and Possibilities*, edited by Ellen Condliffe Lagemann and Lee S. Shulman. San Francisco, CA: Jossey-Bass.

——. 2006. "What Doesn't Work: The Challenge and Failure of the What Works Clearinghouse to Conduct Meaningful Review of Studies of Mathematics Curricula." *Educational Researcher* 35:13–21.

Shaughnessy, Michael F. 2008. "Interview with Reid Lyon: Reading First Is the Largest Concerted Reading Intervention Program in the History of the Civilized World." *EdNews*, May 4. Retrieved May 5, 2008 (http://ednews.org/articles).

Shavelson, Richard J. and Lisa Towne (eds.). 2002. *Scientific Research in Education.* Committee on Scientific Principles for Educational Research, National Research Council. Washington, DC: National Academy Press.

Slavin, Robert. 2007. "The What Works Clearinghouse: Time for a Fresh Start." *Education Week* 27(16):36.

Steinmetz, George (ed.). 2005. *The Politics of Method in the Human Sciences.* Durham, NC: Duke University Press.

Stokes, Donald E. 1997. *Pasteur's Quadrant: Basic Science and Technological Innovation.* Washington, DC: Brookings Institution Press.

Viadero, Debra. 2004. "Researchers Question Clearinghouse Choices." *Education Week* 23(44):30–32.

Weiss, Carol. 2002. "What to Do until the Random Assigner Comes." Pp. 198–224 in *Evidence Matters: Randomized Trials in Education Research*, edited by Frederick Mosteller and Robert Boruch. Washington, DC: Brookings Institution Press.

Wolk, Ronald. 2007. "Education Research Could Improve Schools, but Probably Won't." *Education Week* 26(44):38–39.

Worcester, Kenton W. 2004. "Social Science Research Council 1923–1998." Retrieved February 18, 2008 (http://publications.ssrc.org/about_the_ssrc/SSRC_History.pdf).

PART III
Toward a More Comprehensive Understanding of Science and Policy

CHAPTER 6

Narrow Questions, Narrow Answers: The Limited Value of Randomized Controlled Trials for Education Research

ANNETTE LAREAU*

With their emphasis on "scientific rigor" and references to a "gold standard," recent federal guidelines leave little room for debate about the importance of randomized controlled trials for education research.[1] In this chapter I offer a critical assessment of this position. I suggest that randomized controlled trials, although useful in selective research situations, are not a helpful research method for the field as a whole. The most important questions in education simply cannot be answered with this approach. I argue that the medical research model has been misunderstood by advocates of randomized controlled trials in education and misapplied to the field of education research.

The limited value of randomized controlled trials in education, and in various areas of medicine, has many sources. I focus on three. One problem is that the research questions that can be asked using this method are relatively narrow and thus cannot accommodate the complexity of the educational process. The method seeks to control all features except for one important variable or "treatment" effect. Yet, as I argue below, educational institutions are multifaceted organizations; there are constant changes in many of the "independent" variables that have an impact on the "dependent" or outcome variables. A further aspect of the complexity problem is that it involves questions of meaning. Randomized controlled trials cannot address this type of "variable." Understanding organizational processes and the meanings participants assign to events is crucial to the development of a rich picture of educational institutions; the effects of educational treatments or variables depend in critical ways on what they mean to students, parents, and teachers, among others. Important research questions—such as the mechanisms through which the position of parents transmits advantages, the processes through which some principals are more effective than others, or the micro-interactional strategies that build trust among principals and teachers—thus fall outside the methodological realm of randomized controlled trials.

Second, randomized controlled trials pose formidable problems of execution. It is common for researchers to have difficulty selecting a control group that truly acts as a control. In education, even studies blessed with talented staff and generous resources have encountered difficult problems. Researchers cannot sustain core elements of the method, including the expectation that treatment groups are delivered the treatment and control groups do not receive it. Also, randomized controlled trials are based on the assumption that the control group is deprived of the potentially valuable treatment. In a population of schoolchildren, this traditional assumption raises complex ethical concerns. Researchers promoting randomized controlled trials are guilty of a naive hopefulness that these problems in execution will not overwhelm the research. Yet previous studies (some of which I discuss in this chapter) have not been promising in terms of the ability of researchers to execute core elements of the design.

Third, in their enthusiastic embrace of randomized controlled trials as an education research method, policy analysts have not paid sufficient attention to the crucial issue of implementing research results. Decades of research in education clearly demonstrate that it is not possible for policymakers to mandate the successful adoption of an educational policy. Rather, successful reform requires that educators "buy into" the new policy. In medicine, too, "buy-in" significantly affects the likelihood of achieving change. Even when medical research demonstrates that many lives and millions of dollars can be saved by a relatively simple innovation, the necessary change may be resisted if it runs counter to the logic and culture of the organization. Moreover, as I discuss below, in both education and medicine, promising reforms may be difficult or impossible to implement or "scale up" beyond the initial research setting.

In sum, there are formidable limits to the randomized control approach—limits which the proponents of this methodology have not sufficiently recognized. To achieve "rigor" in education research, we need to adopt a more realistic grasp of the problems that plague attempts to implement research results as well as a greater openness to other approaches that offer crucial insights into social processes in organizations. For these purposes, qualitative methods, including participant observation and in-depth interviews, are likely to be the most promising.

What Kinds of Questions Can Be Answered?

Randomized controlled trials involve the random assignment of participants to different experiences or "treatments," with all other components of the experience "held constant" (Mosteller and Boruch 2002). A close cousin to a randomized control trial is a study that compares individuals who received a "treatment" with individuals who sought the same treatment but remained on the waiting list. As the materials in the appendices to this volume clearly demonstrate, randomized controlled trials have skyrocketed in popularity in recent years. The authorizing legislation for No Child Left Behind emphasizes the importance of using "scientifically based research" methods (see Appendix A). Cook and Payne (2002:177) provide a ringing endorsement:

> The superiority of random assignment for drawing inferences about the consequences of planned change attempts is routinely acknowledged in philosophy, medicine, public health, agriculture, statistics, micro-economics, psychology, criminology, prevention research, early childhood education, marketing and those parts of political science and sociology concerned with improving opinion surveys.... This article does not argue that correct causal conclusions come only from experiments. It does argue, though, that experiments provide a better warrant for such conclusions than any other method. So, if experiments can be conducted in schools, they should be. Not to use them requires a very strong justification.

It is relatively rare that social scientists successfully carry out a randomized controlled trial in a high-quality, thoughtful, and well-executed study. But when they do, the results can be crisp, clear, and causally irrefutable. Indeed, when a trial is appropriately designed and conducted, and when its purpose is specifically to evaluate the effect of an intervention or treatment, the results can be stunningly appealing. One example is an evaluation of the Big Brother/Big Sister program in Philadelphia, conducted by the non-profit group Public/Private Ventures (Tierney, Grossman, and Resch 2000). The study compared those on the waiting list for a Big Brother/Big Sister with those involved in the program. The researchers found that program participants had less drug use compared to those on the waiting list. Since the problem of self-selection has been effectively handled in this design, the results are convincing: The program has a positive impact. Similarly, in a series of thoughtful studies the Moving to Opportunity and New Hope reforms used a random assignment of services for low-income families to rent an apartment with a combined quantitative and ethnographic research approach (Duncan, Huston, and Weisner 2007; Kling, Liebeman, and Katz 2007). This random-assignment study clearly showed that the housing service that placed families in less economically depressed neighborhoods improved mothers' mental health by reducing their rates of depression. The housing service also had an impact on participants' obesity, but not on other measures of physical health. The neighborhood context did not raise adults' income, however, and the results for children's school performance were mixed: generally quite positive for girls but quite negative for boys (Kling et al. 2007). Importantly for my purposes here, the randomized controlled trial itself could not shed light on *why* effects differed for girls and boys. For insights into why gender might have had an impact, the study team turned, appropriately, to ethnographic research (Clampet-Lundquist et al. 2006).

Even when conducted in tandem with qualitative investigations that are better suited to answering why and how questions, random-assignment studies have formidable built-in constraints. They must isolate one dependent variable and control all other factors except the "treatment." Examination of interaction effects (i.e., where the results are contingent upon one set of circumstances but not another) is possible, but cumbersome, as Cook and Payne (2002:152) acknowledge:

> At their most comprehensive, [random-assignment] experiments can responsibly test only a modest number of the possible interactions between treatments. So, experiments are best when a causal question involves few variables, is sharply focused, and is easily justified.

The models also presume that during the study period, conditions are static, not dynamic. Educational institutions do not conform to these basic assumptions. Schools are complex organizations with many different levels, including the classroom (and student groupings within the classroom), the school, and the district. Many of these levels are in flux, particularly in a climate of educational reform (Hubbard, Stein, and Mehan 2006; Sunderman, Kim, and Orfield 2005). Dynamics in classroom learning are shaped by many factors; it is difficult to delineate sharply one causal question.

Randomized controlled trials focus on factors that can be manipulated via policy intervention. But crucial aspects of social life that affect education cannot be manipulated this way. For example, there is an extensive body of research on the friendship networks of youth and the influence of peers on educational aspirations, homework patterns, and other aspects of schooling (Hallinan 2006). Students cannot be assigned to different friendship networks by a research study, let alone be assigned randomly to peer groups by researchers. Similarly, social-class differences in child rearing, in parents' knowledge about educational institutions, and in the flexibility parents have for attending school events during work hours are not readily subjected to manipulation (Entwisle, Alexander, and Olson 1997; Lareau 2000, 2003). Arguably, many classic studies in education would never have been undertaken in the current research climate, since the topics these studies have addressed—peer networks, physical attractiveness, immigrant status, and students' aspirations—would not be amenable to a randomized controlled trial approach. Further, decades of research on educational achievement have shown that it is the elements least open to external manipulation (especially family background and peer networks) that are the most important influences on student learning (Hallinan 2006). In randomized controlled trials the scope of questions that can be studied is narrowed considerably, leaving unstudied precisely the factors that prior research has identified as key influences on educational outcomes.[2]

The "narrow questions/narrow answers" problem is also found in medicine. For example, drug trials with a double-blind design, a placebo, and controlled conditions have yielded many important insights about which drugs are most effective.[3] But randomized controlled trials have not provided insight into arguably the most important questions in medicine today. For example, a critical problem is that many patients are non-compliant in the taking of drugs (Haynes, McDonald, and Garg 2002; National Council on Patient Information and Education 2007). Research suggests that approximately one-half of the time patients are non-compliant (or non-adherent) in taking pills or other medical treatments at the time(s) specified.[4] Non-compliance rates are particularly high for psychological disorders (e.g., an 80% rate of non-compliance among patients with manic depression) (Osterberg and Blaschke 2005). Doctor–patient communication problems and patients' failure to grasp the nature of their medical problem also are ubiquitous (National Council on Patient Information and Education 2007). The high cost of medical insurance for employers, the difficulty individuals with chronic health problems have purchasing affordable insurance, and the relatively large medical costs U.S. residents shoulder compared to their Western European counterparts are among today's most important policy issues, yet they cannot be addressed through research based on the method of random assignment (Furman and Rubin 2007).

Nor is random assignment useful in understanding health crises that occur as a result of malfunction in several institutions at the same time, as is often the case with natural disasters. For example, in his analysis of the hundreds of heat-related deaths in Chicago during one week in 1995, Eric Klinenberg (2002) found that multiple social institutional factors contributed to the high rates of death of the elderly: the para-military organization of the emergency health services, the social isolation of the elderly, lack of cooling facilities in the apartments and buildings housing the elderly, and the slow identification of the health-care crisis by political organizations and the media. Many of these patterns resurfaced in the Hurricane Katrina disaster. These disasters' rare nature as well as the multiple institutions involved in shaping the (ineffectual) response do not permit study via the method of random assignment (Ericksen 1978; Klinenberg 2002). Similarly, schooling is a complicated process that is affected by multiple institutions, of which only *one* is schools themselves.

Moreover, the randomized control trial gives short shrift to the *meaning* of events in the lives of individuals. Take, for example, the vast amount of research that has been done on parent involvement in schooling—research that identifies parent involvement as an important influence on children's achievement. There is little doubt that teachers value parent involvement highly (Epstein 2002). They call for "partnerships" in education with parents. Most surveys also reveal that parents want to take an active, helpful role in their children's schooling.[5] There have been interventions to increase parent involvement in schooling; parent involvement was promoted in the What Works Clearinghouse (U.S.

Department of Education 2006). But these studies do not sufficiently recognize that social class appears to influence what parents *mean* by the term "parent involvement." For example, in selecting schools, middle-class parents appear to collect very detailed information about educators, and these parents oversee their children's educational lives closely (Diamond and Gomez 2004; Lareau 2000). Working-class parents, on the other hand, also see themselves as heavily involved in schooling, but they often interpret involvement to mean preparing children to go to school and deferring to the educational professional expertise of educators (Lareau 2000, 2003).

It is important to remember that the study of what people do is only one piece of the puzzle. Complex social processes undergird educational reform. Small, intensive, non-random case studies are crucial for identifying these processes and shedding light on the conditions associated with successful reform initiatives.

Barriers to Randomized Controlled Trials

In practice, the emphasis on "rigor" incorporated into No Child Left Behind has come to be equated with a commitment to and reliance on randomized controlled trials (see the appendices to this volume). Indeed, Institute of Education Sciences Director Grover "Russ" Whitehurst has termed randomized controlled trials the "gold standard." The approach has many advocates. Yet despite the desire of researchers to implement a medical model, there are problems. One is difficulty in selecting and sustaining control groups.

When Is a Control a Control?

Sustaining the quality and quantity of the control group is challenging, as the authors of a review of diabetes research note (Montori et al. 2006):

> In conducting systematic reviews of RCTs [randomized controlled trials] in diabetes we have noticed that researchers seem to pay little attention . . . to methodological safeguards that limit the introduction of bias into RCTs. As a result, these potentially biased RCTs could mislead clinicians. . . . When reports leave out critical information about methodological safeguards against bias, readers cannot ascertain if these safeguards were present.
>
> (p. 1833)

The authors reviewed RCTs published in general medical journals (e.g., the *New England Journal of Medicine*), in those that specialize in diabetes research (e.g., *Diabetes*), and in those that address metabolics and nutrition (e.g., *American Journal of Clinical Nutrition*). They described their evaluation criteria this way:

> We considered trials to be of low methodological quality when they had three or more of these criteria: inadequate (or not reported)

allocation concealment, inadequate (or not reported) blinding of patients and caregivers, failure to adhere to the intention-to-treat principle, or a reporting >10% (or did not report information to calculate) of loss to follow-up.

(p. 1834)

The authors judged 53% of the 199 trials they evaluated to be of "low quality." That figure is itself a cause for concern, but the authors suggest that it may be an underestimate. They focused only on work published in "top journals"; a review of studies across a broader sample of scientific journals would likely show a higher rate of low-quality studies (Montori et al. 2006).

Similar quality-related problems have surfaced in education studies. Indeed, among the most basic assumptions of any randomized trial are that the control group and the experimental/treatment group are highly similar before the start of the study, that the experimental group will receive a full course of treatment, while the control group will not receive *any* exposure to the treatment, and that the treatment "dosage" will be delivered consistently over time. In school settings these assumptions are difficult or impossible to meet, as researchers who have attempted to use randomized controlled trials have discovered.

When educational reforms prove successful in specific settings, they often are implemented elsewhere. For example, James Comer's complex reform for promoting education of at-risk youth was adopted in Chicago. The program sought to improve education through community involvement, intensive parent involvement programs, and community programs. The introduction of this highly regarded reform into the Chicago public schools was subject to an unusually elaborate array of randomized controls and program evaluation. Implementing a study based on randomized control methodology is exceptionally difficult in a tumultuous organizational environment, however. At the start of the reform effort, the Chicago public school system was just such an environment. It was experiencing high rates of teacher turnover, changing district politics, changes in administrator leadership, and turnover in the student population.

Thomas Cook was among those studying the reform. In published papers reporting the results of this research, he and his colleagues (to their credit) explicitly acknowledge some of the barriers they faced trying to use a randomized control approach to evaluating the impact of the Comer school development program:

> Unfortunately 5 of the 24 schools dropped out of the study at different times for various reasons. . . . In two cases, a new principal was appointed who did not want the program; in the third, the principal did not want the quantitative research component (although his school stayed in the program and the ethnographic component continued). Of the Phase II schools, only one dropped out, [but it was]

almost immediately after learning it had been assigned to control status....

(Cook, Murphy, and Hunt 2000: 544)

Such selective attrition vitiates the randomized experiment because more Comer than control schools dropped out and because the treatment is clearly confounded with principal turnover.

(pp. 544–545)

That "a new principal ... did not want the program" and that one-fifth of the schools dropped out of the study for periods of time are critical problems. Other difficulties Cook and his co-authors do not mention include researchers' lack of control over subject turnover (in addition to student and teacher turnover, top leadership at participating schools can change); and researchers' limited power either to shore up principals' flagging interest in participating in a study or to overcome their initial resistance to such participation. As a result, randomized controlled trials that focus on longitudinal change in schools face daunting, and arguably insurmountable, challenges.

Of even greater concern is the fact that the double-blind character of the medical model, made possible by a clinical environment in which a treatment pill and a "sugar pill" look identical, has no counterpart in education. In the social and political world of schools, there is no way to create a double-blind reform. School reforms are discussed by teachers, principals, district leaders, and, in some schools, by parents and students as well. These parties do not live in a vacuum, and educators in the "control" and the "experimental" schools have social and professional relations. As a result, studies are easily contaminated: In a real-world educational setting, it is not possible for researchers to prevent the control group from being exposed to the treatment. As Cook et al. (1999) acknowledge in the Chicago Comer reform study:

Three comparison schools borrowed some program elements: In one case, a husband and wife worked in different schools, one with and one without the program, in another case the daughter of a senior New Haven program central staff member worked as an administrator at a control school; and, in the last case, a comparison group principal liked the program, studied it for himself, and discussed it with principals from program schools. And further diffusion between program and control schools probably occurred during district-wide in-service training sessions conducted by the county program coordinator.

(p. 584)

The fact that a principal in a "control" school liked the program and the program was diffused in district-wide training sessions is a sign of the social character of education. Still, Cook and his co-authors discount the impact of this source of contamination on their results:

> But we judge the degree of diffusion from these sources to have been relatively minor. The three schools in question did not have access to the major program elements that build and sustain the program in a school, namely the in-school facilitator, local program in-service training sessions, and training sessions in New Haven. Moreover, reclassifying these three control schools made no difference in analysis of student effects.
>
> (p. 584)

But it is clear that the most basic element of the design, notably that there would be a distinctly different experience for "control" and "experimental" groups, was not adequately met. Nor could researchers be confident that the "treatment" would be consistently delivered to the treatment group:

> Midway through the study the political context changed. The mayor and his appointees . . . reduced the power of local school councils. . . . The new emphasis made test scores the dominant criterion for judging school effectiveness (rather than success in creating decentralized management). Because of their low test scores, one sixth of all city schools were put on probation.
>
> (Cook et al. 2000: 541)

Hence, the vigor with which *basic elements* of the reform were enacted differed across time. This pattern has been found in many other studies.

In sum, medical research shows that it is difficult to sustain trials where subjects in "treatment" and "control" groups have radically different experiences. Large numbers of subjects are frequently non-compliant. School settings are vastly more complex and "noisy" than medical studies. Indeed, the Cook evaluation had an ethnographic component which offered a powerful critique: "[Before the end of the study] the ethnographers were not willing to classify any of the programs as faithfully following all of the program guidelines although some were very close" (Cook et al. 2000: 564). If the programs are not being faithfully followed, then it is difficult to accurately evaluate their effectiveness.

Translating Legislation into Practice: The Problem of Implementation

Finally, it is worrisome that the proponents of randomized controlled studies of educational reform have paid so little attention to the nature of the policy intervention. There is ample evidence that the road between the passage of policy and its implementation is long and rocky (Hubbard, Stein, and Mehan 2006; McLaughlin 1987). As Milbrey McLaughlin (1987: 172) has pointed out:

> [T]he overarching, obvious conclusion running through empirical research on policy implementation is that it is incredibly hard to make something happen.... It's hard to make something happen primarily because policymakers can't mandate what matters. We have learned that policy success depends critically on two broad factors: local capacity and will.... But will, or the attitudes, motivation, and beliefs that underlie an implementer's response to a policy's goals or strategies, is less amendable to policy intervention.

"Will" cannot be mandated but it plays a crucial role in implementation. Yet advocates of randomized controlled trials have failed to come to terms with the fact that the factors that can easily be manipulated experimentally, and thus whose effects can be studied in a randomized controlled trial, may be precisely those elements that matter the least in the grand scheme of schooling and learning.

Literature on implementation of public policy also suggests that local context significantly shapes implementation. For example, in the randomized trial evaluation of the Comer School Development Program researchers were unable to achieve a standardized implementation. Instead, the reform varied to "maximize the fit to local circumstances" in Chicago. Cook explains:

> Elements of the implementation of [Comer's] SDP [School Development Program] vary by both district and school in order to maximize the fit to local circumstances. The Chicago program is unique in many ways. It was introduced in the middle of a citywide educational reform initiated by local politicians, businesses and philanthropies.... At first, the reform emphasized local school councils; ... councils were encouraged to set their own school goals and establish their own instructional designs ... [although this pattern] ... did not arise in practice.
>
> (Cook et al. 2000: 541)

If policy implementation is not standardized, then the validity of an assessment of its impact using a randomized controlled trial is compromised.

Several studies suggest that principals play a critical role in policy implementation. One study of "teacher accountability" in California reported:

> Our research revealed that principals often played a pivotal role in how teachers experienced accountability policies. Principals either acted as a "buffer," shielding teachers from test-score pressures, or as an added source of pressure for teachers, emphasizing the need to raise test scores and the school's ranking.
>
> (PACE 2006: 8)

The role of principals appeared to be key in understanding how teachers experienced a reform:

> Principals' attitudes towards accountability and their leadership styles also influenced teachers' experiences with district and state mandates. Principals' emphasis on or avoidance of certain district and state instructional reforms, for example, were reflected in teachers' acceptance or critiques.
>
> (PACE 2006: 8)

The authors of this study also note that rather than simply looking at schools, we need to look more directly at the mediating role of districts:

> Currently, accountability policy assumes that individual schools are the primary locus of reform. While school-based reform is essential, our research shows that districts, through various programs and policies, have the power to facilitate or hinder school improvement. The state must recognize district influence in the implementation of accountability policy.
>
> (PACE 2006: 9)

The message is clear: There are many mediating factors that shape the implementation of educational policy. This is why it is crucial that reform initiatives incorporate procedures and "feedback loops" so that during the implementation, mandated changes can be modified to accommodate institutional constraints.

The more fundamental issue, however, is the degree to which institutions will respond to results produced by randomized controlled trials if the implementation process is not closely monitored. Here too, the evidence from medicine is not encouraging. Consider, for example, the surprisingly large numbers of hospital patients who are exposed to an infection from germs on the hands of doctors and/or nurses. Research by Sean Berenholtz and colleagues (2004) and reporting by Atul Gawande (2007) indicate that contamination of "lines" (such as a line for a catheter) from the germs on caregivers' hands can lead to infection. In intensive care units, patients who have a line in for more than ten days have an infection rate of 4%. Fatalities from line infections range from 5% to 28%, depending on how sick patients are when they become infected. Those who survive line infections spend more days in intensive care. Thus such infections clearly are a serious problem. They result in more deaths, more days in the hospital, more dollars spent on medical costs, and more days of missed work.

Johns Hopkins researcher and physician Peter Provonost and his colleagues designed a policy intervention focused on the steps that health practitioners take when putting in a line: they wash their hands with soap, clean the patient's skin with an antiseptic, put sterile drapes over the patient's entire body, wear a sterile mask, hat, gown, and gloves, and put a sterile dressing over the catheter site once the line is in. The researchers discovered that about one-third of the time, the clinicians skipped one of these essential steps (Berenholtz et al. 2004; Gawande 2007). Eventually, Dr. Provonost's team developed a checklist for a new protocol that empowered nurses to stop doctors to question them if they missed a step. Infection rates plummeted. Compared to an earlier period, the ten-day line infection rate went from 11% to 0%. In a 15-month period, there were only two line infections. Thus, adhering to the new protocol probably prevented 43 infections and eight deaths, and saved $2 million in costs (Berenholtz et al. 2004).[6]

Yet when hospital administrators attempted to "scale up" this new model and implement it widely, the policy intervention was resisted rather than embraced (Bernholtz and Pronovost 2003; Gawande 2007). This happened, in part, because, as in schools, the intervention required a change in organizational processes. The hierarchy of authority in medicine has been weakened due to changes in insurance and managed care. Nevertheless, doctors have considerable power; nurses have lower professional status and autonomy compared to doctors. The checklist required that nurses or technicians stop the procedure (in hectic, often understaffed intensive care units) to ask, "Doctor, have you washed your hands?" This reversal of the usual hierarchy of authority was difficult to implement. In addition, many hospitals and clinics have been subject to severe budget cuts and staffing reductions, both of which make routine procedures more rushed and thus undermine attempts to add even a simple new safeguard to the standard repertoire.

How long it will be before the average doctor or nurse is apt to routinely use a checklist? Peter Pronovost is not optimistic: "We could get I.C.U. checklists in use throughout the United States in two years, if the country wanted it, [but] ... [A]t the current rate, it will never happen" (quoted in Gawande 2007: 8). The resistance is rooted not in science or technology but in social and institutional factors:

> If someone found a new drug that could wipe out infections with anything remotely like the effectiveness of Pronovost's lists, there would be television ads with Robert Jarvik extolling its virtues, detail men offering free lunches to get doctors to make it part of their practice, government programs to research it, and competitors jumping in to make a newer, better version. That's what happened when manufacturers marketed central-line catheters coated with silver or other antimicrobials: they cost a third more, and reduced infections slightly—and hospital[s] have spent tens of millions of dollars on them. But with a checklist, what we have is Peter Pronovost trying to

see if maybe, in the next year or two, hospitals in Rhode Island and
New Jersey will give his idea a try.

(Gawande 2007: 7)

It is rare that a policy intervention is as clearly effective as the checklist. Thus the resistance to its implementation is a particularly important cautionary tale for educational researchers. It is hard to implement research results. Valid findings are not enough; teachers, parents, students, and administrators need to be "brought along," to be helped to "buy into" the proposed change. Any other approach is naive.

Concluding Thoughts

There are variations in how strident researchers are in insisting on the need for randomized controlled trials. But, as Pamela Barnhouse Walters has noted in Chapter 1, the use of this methodology in education research has made headway. Increasingly, funding priorities for research grants and for professional training resources privilege random assignment; journal reviews, grant reviews, and academic career assessments consider this criterion in evaluating the "quality" of education research. The term "gold standard" is common.

This trend would be less alarming if federal department of education decisionmakers acknowledged that there are many varied research questions in education, and that different questions call for different methods. From this perspective,[7] randomized controlled trials would be one, and only one, approach among many in the repertoire available to social science researchers. It also would be a less troubling movement if advocates of randomized controlled trials offered a more clear-eyed assessment of the problems associated with carrying out randomized controlled trials. Thus what is problematic is the combination of a narrow vision and the belief, signaled by the frequent reference to RCTs as a "gold standard," that all other methods are, in crucial ways, inferior. That such sweeping claims are made despite the flawed and structurally limited opportunities schools offer for carrying out randomized controlled trials is of great concern. Educational institutions are not ideal places to do research. The conditions of the "laboratory" change frequently, and sometimes dramatically.

It is also troubling that advocates of RCTs do not sufficiently acknowledge that, even if conditions could be made ideal, the range of questions this methodology can accommodate is narrow. Many important questions in education research, as in medicine, are not amenable to a random assignment approach. Key factors in education research are difficult to manipulate, but this does not make them any less important. Studying the meaning and social processes of educational delivery systems is crucial, and it is an area advocates of a random assignment approach do not sufficiently acknowledge.

The current movement toward the use of randomized controlled trials in education research fails to offer an umbrella sufficiently broad to both welcome and respect diverse methodological approaches. This narrowness of spirit is not only a tactical mistake. Its short-sightedness will, in the end, impede random assignment advocates from realizing the educational reform goals they hold most dear.

Notes

*   The author is grateful to Dana Burke, Aaron Pallas, Pamela Barnhouse Walters, and the anonymous reviewers for helpful comments on an earlier version of this chapter. All errors, of course, are the responsibility of the author.
1. For example, at the top of the home page of the U.S. Department of Education, Institute of Education Sciences, National Center for Education Research is the statement: "The National Center for Education Research (NCER) supports rigorous research that addresses the nation's most pressing education needs, from early childhood to adult education." Under "What's New," an announcement for a summer research institute on cluster-randomized trials explains, "The purpose of the Summer Research Training Institute on Cluster-Randomized Trials is to increase the national capacity of researchers to develop and conduct rigorous evaluations of the effectiveness of education interventions." Retrieved December 18, 2007 from http://www.nces.ed.gov and http://wes.ed.gov/whatsnew/conferences/?id=310&cid=5. See also U.S. Department of Education (2003a, 2003b) and Lewis (2003).
2. Given the evidence that exists about the effectiveness of policy interventions of the last 40 years, it is foolhardy to search for a single policy intervention or "silver bullet" to improve the educational achievement for all American children in all schools all of the time. There are also likely to be interactions. Doris Entwisle and Karl Alexander at the Johns Hopkins University, for example, showed that teachers who themselves had low socioeconomic origins did particularly well in producing achievement from students with low socioeconomic origins; these teachers from low socioeconomic origins outperformed teachers who had been raised in more prosperous families (Entwisle, Alexander, and Olson 1997). Thus the impact of policies that are universally implemented is not universal in the student population. Some students benefit more than others.
3. In the development of clinical trials for drugs, neither the physician nor the patient knew if the patient was in the subgroup that was receiving a "placebo" or "sugar pill" or if he/she was actually receiving the treatment, hence the term "double-blind." In this research tradition, every effort is made to select individuals who are so similar to one another that any difference in their outcomes could be attributed to the treatment. It is this approach that has been adopted for schools.
4. Compliance is higher for acute illnesses than for chronic conditions. In clinical trials, patients tend to be more dutiful due to the follow-up, but even under these conditions medication adherence rates are reported to be only in the range of 43% to 78% (see Osterberg and Blaschke 2005).
5. Some teachers are more effective in promoting parent involvement than others; see Becker and Epstein's work (1982) on teacher leaders.
6. Provonost and colleagues stress the importance of retaining professional expertise rather than dictating a complex set of procedures. They explain: "We reduced our rate of [infection] using relatively simple and inexpensive interventions, as opposed to implementing more expensive interventions, such as antibiotic/antiseptic catheters. For interventions to work in the busy world of clinical practice, they should be simple to implement. By changing systems rather than exhorting providers to comply with guidelines, we can help ensure that patients receive effective therapies. For example, it was difficult to write a detailed guideline regarding the need for a central venous catheter; there are too many decisions to account for. It is unlikely that detailed guidelines would be practical for complex decisions, such as ICU admission and discharge, extubation, and use of catheters. Rather, we simply asked physicians to consider daily whether central catheters could be removed, highlighting the risk of catheters yet allowing physicians to use their clinical judgment" (Berenholtz et al. 2004: 2020).
7. A perspective that most first-year graduate students in the social sciences and in education encounter in their beginning research methods courses, by the way: that the trick is to match the research method to the question the researcher wants to investigate, not to find one one-size-fits-all "best" method.

References and Further Reading

Anyon, Jean. 2005. *Radical Possibilities: Public Policy, Urban Education, and a New Social Movement.* New York: Teachers College Press.

Becker, H. and J. Epstein. 1982. "Parent Involvement: A Survey of Teacher Practices." *The Elementary School Journal* 83(2):85–102.

Berenholtz, Sean M., Peter J. Pronovost, Pamela A. Lipsett, Deborah Hobson, Karen Earsing, Jason E.Farley, Shelley Milanovich, Elizabeth Garrett-Mayer, Bradford Winters, Haya R. Rubin, Todd Dorman, and Trish M. Perl. 2004. "Eliminating Catheter-Related Bloodstream Infections in the Intensive Care Unit." *Critical Care Medicine* 32:2014–2020.

Berenholtz, Sean M. and Peter J. Pronovost 2003. "Barriers to Translating Evidence into Practice." *Current Opinion Critical Care* 9:321–325.

Burton, Linda M., Townsand Price-Spratlen, and Margaret Beale Spencer. 1997. "On Ways of Thinking about Measuring Neighborhoods: Implications for Studying Context and Developmental Outcomes for Children." Pp. 132–144 in *Neighborhood Poverty: Policy Implications in Studying Neighborhoods*, edited by Jeanne Brooks-Gunn, Greg J. Duncan, and J. Lawrence Aber. New York: Russell Sage.

Chronicle of Higher Education. 2008. "Education Dept. to End Controversial Study of Upward Bound." March 7, 2008. http://chronicle.com/weekly/v54/;26/26a02001.htm. Accessed September 22, 2008.

Clampet-Lundquist, Susan, Katheryn Edin, Jeffrey B. Kling, and Greg J. Duncan. 2006. "Moving At-Risk Youth out of High-Risk Neighborhoods: Why Do Girls Fare Better than Boys?" Working Paper, Industrial Relations Section, Princeton University.

Comer, James P. 1995. *School Power.* New York: Free Press.

Comer, James P. and Norris M. Haynes. 1999. "The Dynamics of School Change: Response to the Article 'Comer's School Development Program in Prince George's County, Maryland: A Theory-Based Evaluation' by Thomas D. Cook et al." *American Educational Research Journal* 36(3):599–607.

Conrad, Clifton F. and Ronald C. Serlin (eds.) 2005. *The SAGE Handbook for Research in Education: Engaging Ideas and Enriching Inquiry.* Thousand Oaks, CA: Sage Publications.

Cook, Thomas D. and Monique Payne. 2002. "Objecting to the Objections to Using Randomized Assignment in Educational Research." Pp. 150–179 in *Evidence Matters: Randomized Trials in Education Research*, edited by F. Mosteller and R. Boruch. Washington, DC: Brookings Institution Press.

Cook, Thomas D., Robert F. Murphy, and H. David Hunt. 2000. "Comer's School Development Program in Chicago: A Theory-Based Evaluation." *American Educational Research Journal* 37(2):535–597.

Cook, Thomas D., Farah-Naaz Habib, Meredith Phillips, Richard A. Settersten, Shobha C. Shagle, and Serdar M. Degirmencioglu. 1999. "Comer's School Development Program in Prince George's County, Maryland: A Theory-Based Evaluation." *American Educational Research Journal* 36(3):543–597.

DeParle, Jason 2004. *American Dream: Three Women, Ten Kids, and a Nation's Drive to End Welfare.* New York: Viking.

Diamond, John B. and Kimberley Gomez. 2004. "African-American Parents' Orientations towards Schools: The Implications of Social Class and Parents' Perceptions of Schools." *Education and Urban Society* 36:383–427.

Duncan, Greg J., Aletha C. Huston, and Thomas S. Weisner. 2007. *Higher Ground: New Hope for the Working Poor and Their Families.* New York: Russell Sage Foundation.

Edin, Kathryn and Laura Lein. 1997. *Making Ends Meet: How Single Mothers Survive Welfare and Low-Wage Work.* New York: Russell Sage.

Educational Researcher. 2002. Theme issue on *Scientific Research and Education.* 31:3–29.

Entwisle, Doris R. and Karl L. Alexander. 1992. "Summer Setback." *American Sociological Review* 57:72–84.

Entwisle, Doris R., Karl L. Alexander, and Linda Steffel Olson. 1997. *Children, Schools, and Inequality.* Boulder, CO: Westview Press.

Epstein, Joyce Levy. 2002. *School, Family, and Community Partnership: Your Handbook for Action.* New York: Corwin Press.

Ericksen, Kai 1978. *Everything in Its Path.* New York: Simon and Schuster.

Erickson, Frederick and Kris Gutierrez. 2002. "'Science' Rejects Postmodernism." *Educational Researcher* 31(8):21–24.

Furman, Jason and Robert E. Rubin. 2007. *Universal, Effective, and Affordable Health Insurance: An Economic Imperative.* Washington, DC: Brookings Institution Press.

Gawande, Atul 2007. "Annals of Medicine: The Checklist." *The New Yorker*. December 21, 2007. Retrieved January 2, 2008 (http://www.newyorker.com/reporting/2007/12/10/071210fa_fac_gawande?printable=true).
Hallinan, Maureen T. (ed.). 2006. *Handbook of the Sociology of Education*. New York: Springer.
Haynes, R. Brian, Heather B. McDonald, and Amit X. Garg. 2002. "Helping Patients Follow Prescribed Treatment." *Journal of the American Medical Association* (JAMA) 288:2880–2883. Retrieved December 11, 2002 (http://www.jama.com).
Howe, Kenneth and Margaret Eisenhart. 1990. "Standards for Qualitative (and Quantitative) Research: A Prolegomenon." *Educational Researcher* 19(4):2–9.
Hubbard, Lea and Hugh Mehan. 1999a. "Scaling Up an Un-tracking Program: A Co-constructed Process." *Journal of Education for Students Placed at Risk* 4(1):83–100.
Hubbard, Lea and Hugh Mehan. 1999b. "Race and Reform: Educational 'Niche Picking' in a Hostile Environment." *Journal of Negro Education* 68(2):213–226.
Hubbard, Lea, Mary Kay Stein, and Hugh Mehan. 2006. *Reform as Learning: When School Reform Collides with School Culture and Community Politics*. London: Routledge.
Iceland, John. 2005. "Measuring Poverty: Theoretical and Empirical Considerations." *Measurement* 3(4):207–243.
JESPAR (*Journal of Education for Students Placed at Risk*). 1998. "Changing Schools for Changing Times: The Comer School Development Program." Special issue of the *Journal of Education for Students Placed at Risk* (JESPAR). 3(1):3–19.
Kaestle, Carl F. 1993. "The Awful Reputation of Education Research." *Educational Researcher* 22(1):23, 26–31.
Kahne, Joseph and Kim Bailey. 1999. "The Role of Social Capital in Youth Development: The Case of 'I Have a Dream' Programs." *Educational Evaluation and Policy Analysis* 21(3):321–343.
Karabel, Jerome and A. H. Halsey (eds.). 1977. *Power and Ideology in Education*. Oxford: Oxford University Press.
Klinenberg, Eric 2002. *Everything in Its Path*. Chicago: University of Chicago Press.
Kling, Jeffrey R., Jeffrey B. Liebman, and Lawrence F. Katz. 2007. "Experimental Analysis of Neighborhood Effects." *Econometrica* 75:83–119.
Kozol, Jonathan. 1991. *Savage Inequalities: Children in America's Schools*. New York: Crown.
Labaree, David F. and Aaron M. Pallas. 1996. "Dire Straits: The Narrow Vision of the Holmes Group." *Educational Researcher* 25(4):25–28.
Lamont, Michele. 2005. "Criteria for Evaluation of Qualitative Research." Workshop on Interdisciplinary Standards for Systematic Qualitative Research. National Science Foundation Cultural Anthropology, Political Science, Sociology, and Law and Social Science Programs. May 19–20, 2005. Washington, DC. Retrieved December 15, 2007 (http://www.wjh.harvard.edu/nsfqual/).
Lareau, Annette. 2000. *Home Advantage: Social Class and Parental Intervention in Elementary Education*. Updated edition. Lanham, MD: Rowman and Littlefield.
———. 2003. *Unequal Childhoods: Class, Race, and Family Life*. Berkeley, CA: University of California Press.
Lareau, Annette and Jeffrey Shultz (eds.). 1999. *Journeys through Ethnography: Realistic Accounts of Fieldwork*. Boulder, CO: Westview.
Lewis, Anne C. 2003. "New Hope for Educational Research?" *Phi Delta Kappan* 84(5):339–340.
Lowes, Robert. 1998. "Patient-Centered Care for Better Patient Adherence." *Family Practice Management* 5(3). Retrieved December 10, 2007 (http://www.aafp.org/fpm/980300fm/patient.html).
McLaughlin, Milbrey Wallin 1987. "Learning from Experience: Lessons from Policy Implementation." *Educational Evaluation and Policy Analysis* 9(2):171–178.
Montori, Victor M., Yaqian Grace Wang, Pablo Alonso-Coello, and Sumit Bhagra 2006. "Systematic Evaluation of the Quality of Randomized Controlled Trials in Diabetes." *Diabetic Care* 29:1833–1838.
Mosteller, Frederick and Robert Boruch (eds.). 2002. *Evidence Matters: Randomized Trials in Education Research*. Washington, DC: Brookings Institution Press.
National Council on Patient Information and Education. 2007. *Enhancing Prescription Medicine Adherence: A National Action Plan*. Bethesda, MD: National Council on Patient Information and Education.
Osterberg, Lars and Terrence Blaschke 2005. "Adherence to Medication: Review Article." *New England Journal of Medicine* 353:5. Retrieved September 22, 2008 (http:// www.nejm.org).
PACE (Policy Analysis for California Education). 2006. *Voices from the Field: Educators Respond to Accountability*. Elisabeth Woody, Melissa Buttles, Judith Kafka, Sandra Park, and Jennifer Russell. University of California, Berkeley. Retrieved September 22, 2008 (http://pace.berkeley.edu/ERAP_Report-WEB.pdf).

Pierson, Paul. 2004. *Politics in Time: History, Institutions, and Social Analysis.* Princeton, NJ: Princeton University Press.

Ragin, Charles, Joane Nagel, and Patricia White. 2004. *Workshop on Scientific Foundations of Qualitative Research.* Sociology Program, National Science Foundation, July 11–12, 2003. Retrieved December 2, 2007 (http://www.nsf.gov/pubs/2004/nsf04219/nsf04219.pdf).

Rainwater, Lee and Timothy Smeeding. 2003. *Poor Kids in a Rich Country: America's Children in Comparative Perspective.* New York: Russell Sage.

Reich, Jennifer A. 2005. *Fixing Families: Parents, Power, and the Child Welfare System.* New York: Routledge.

Research for Action. 2005. "Children and Families First: An Evaluation of the Philadelphia Say Yes to Education Program." Philadelphia, PA, November. Retrieved November 20, 2007 (http://www.researchforaction.org).

Rumberger, Russell W. and Scott L. Thomas. 2000. "The Distribution of Dropout and Turnover Rates among Urban and Suburban High Schools." *Sociology of Education* 73(1):39–67.

Ryan, Gery W. 2005. "What Are Standards of Rigor for Qualitative Research?" Workshop on Interdisciplinary Standards for Systematic Qualitative Research. National Science Foundation Cultural Anthropology, Political Science, Sociology, and Law and Social Science Programs. May 19–20, 2005. Washington, DC. Retrieved September 22, 2008 (http://www.wjh.harvard.edu/nsfqual/).

Sunderman, Gail L., James S. Kim, and Gary Orfield. 2005. *NCLB Meets School Realities: Lessons from the Field.* Thousand Oaks, CA: Corwin Press.

Swanson, Christopher B. 2004. "The Real Truth about Low Graduation Rates: An Evidence-Based Commentary." Education Policy Center, The Urban Institute, Washington, DC. Retrieved September 22, 2008 (http://www.urban.org/UploadedPDF/411050_realtruth.pdf).

Teachers College Record. 2005. A Symposium on the Implications of the Scientific Research in Education Report for Qualitative Inquiry. 107:1–58.

Tierney, Joseph P., Jean Baldwin Grossman, with Nancy L. Resch. 2000. *Making a Difference: An Impact Study of Big Brothers/Big Sisters.* Philadelphia, PA: Public/Private Ventures. Retrieved November 28, 2007 (http://www.ppv.org).

U.S. Department of Education, Institute of Education Sciences, National Center for Education Evaluation and Regional Assistance. 2003a. *Identifying and Implementing Educational Practices Supported by Rigorous Evidence: A User Friendly Guide.* Washington, DC: U.S. Government Printing Office.

U.S. Department of Education, Office of the Secretary, Office of Public Affairs. 2003b. *No Child Left Behind: A Parents Guide.* Washington, DC: U.S. Government Printing Office.

U.S. Department of Education, Institute of Education Sciences. 2006. *What Works Clearinghouse: A Trusted Source of Scientific Evidence of What Works in Education.* Washington, DC. Retrieved December 12, 2007 (http://www.whatworks.ed.gov/).

U.S. Department of Education, 2007. *The Condition of Education.* Washington, DC: U.S. Government Printing Office.

Whitehurst, Grover "Russ." 2002. "Evidence-Based Education." Presentation at the Student Achievement and Student Accountability Conference. U.S. Department of Education, Institute for Education Sciences. Washington, DC, October 8, 2002.

CHAPTER 7

A Quixotic Quest? Philosophical Issues in Assessing the Quality of Education Research

D. C. PHILLIPS

Introduction: Diagnoses of Disease

It appears that the research enterprise in education suffers from a mysterious disease or, more than likely, from several mysterious diseases that might or might not be interrelated. Disparaging remarks about its health have come often enough from those outside the research community—from members of federal and state legislatures, from senior civil servants, and from education administrators and practitioners. As historian Carl Kaestle (1993:26) noted, education research has had an "awful reputation," one that developed over many apparently sickly years during which it failed (or appeared to have failed) to live up to the expectation that it would contribute to advances or improvements in educational practice. Almost 40 years ago, Ralph Tyler (1965), referring even further back into the past, when a number of bureaus of education research had been formed, commented that

> [m]ost of those active in founding these bureaus believed that educational research would quickly provide valid answers to educational problems and that teaching and administration would soon be professions based on research findings as engineering is based on the natural sciences and mathematics. This belief proved untenable.
> (p. 1)

Members of the educational community outside these bureaus were, presumably, as disappointed as the individuals laboring within them; education research must be ill if, despite the complexities it was revealing about educational phenomena, it could not produce usable findings. More than a decade after Tyler wrote, Jacob W. Getzels (1978:477) opined that the "skepticism of educators about the bearing of research—and particularly of basic or theory-oriented research—on the operation of schools is quite extraordinary." But, he added, even "more extraordinary is the skepticism of the researchers themselves" (p. 477).

It is significant that a second and rather different concern about the health of research has come from "insiders," that is, those actively engaged in research. While of course assuming that their own work is healthy, individual researchers frequently have pointed a diagnostic finger at the work of others. The disease they identify is not lack of relevance but—depending upon who is doing the pointing—either lack of rigor, or misplaced rigor. This mutual finger pointing is one way to interpret reactions to the National Research Council (NRC) report *Scientific Research in Education* (Shavelson and Towne 2002), in which a panel of reputably healthy individuals (including the present author) prescribed a modest lifestyle change for their supposedly less-healthy (because less-rigorous) research colleagues. It is noteworthy that not all those who were diagnosed as being ill have acknowledged their diseased condition, and instead have tried to turn the tables. They have accused their would-be benefactors of themselves suffering from a pernicious degenerative condition, or at least from tunnel vision, and also of attempting to force a universal methodological "cure-all" ("the gold standard" method of randomized controlled experimentation) on all researchers who do not currently use it. This welter of diagnoses and counter-diagnoses is not likely to disappear in the foreseeable future.[1]

The concern with rigor also has a considerable history. A few years after Tyler made the comment cited above, the Committee on Educational Research of the National Academy of Education (NAE) issued its findings. The report's editors, committee members Lee J. Cronbach and Patrick Suppes, took care not to point an accusatory finger at the research community and instead opted for exhortation. This approach, however, only thinly disguised the concern about ill health:

> Anyone undertaking educational research can hold himself [sic] to the highest standards of careful observation and systematic reasoning ... given sufficient effort, talent, and self-discipline, systematic inquiry can be expected to give a far more dependable explanation than will come from casual reflection upon casual observations.
> (Cronbach and Suppes 1969: 18)[2]

Not only has research been lacking in rigor, it has suffered from yet another internal defect: It has been the wrong kind of research. Too much emphasis, critics charged, has been given to applied research with the chimerical goal of immediate pay-off, whereas genuine salvation lies in the direction of rigorous basic research. This theme was developed, to select a representative figure, by Fred Kerlinger in his presidential address to the American Educational Research

Association (Kerlinger 1977). But to add insult to injury, others have seen theory-oriented or basic research as too "ivory tower" and remote from pressing day-to-day problems. Perhaps trying to keep a foot in each of these rival camps, Ellen Lagemann and Lee Shulman, editors of a 1999 NAE report, remarked that "one must also ponder the downside to the more local, small-scale, case-focused styles of research that have become more popular recently. Will we lose all bases for generalization?" (Lagemann and Shulman 1999: xvii).

It is clear that over the years these different, complex, sometimes conflicting diagnoses—lack of practical impact, lack of rigor, and incorrect focus—often have been run together under the general label *lack of quality*. In the NAE report, Lagemann and Shulman stated, on behalf of the writing panel, that their first concern was "how to safeguard the quality of the research being carried out" (pp. xiii–xiv). The volume in which the present chapter is located continues the general concern with quality. But for many decades, from left, right, and center, and from inside and out, education research has been criticized for being "ivory tower"; "trivial" or "telling us what we all knew anyway"; "producing too little too late"; "focused on the wrong issues"; "lacking in rigor" or even "unscientific" or "methodologically flawed"; "based upon an outmoded positivist or modernist paradigm" or, what often amounts to the same charge, "scientistic"; "lacking the means to ensure quality because of adherence to postmodernist ideas," or, perhaps, "relativistic." In short, charges that mix together the main sources of concern distinguished above.

At the risk of making an already complex story even more so, still another point needs to be added. Some commentators stress that research in education must be recognized as having as its focus phenomena that are quite different from those that are the focus in the natural sciences, and the expectations about what can be achieved by educational inquiry need to be correspondingly modest. Education is a field of social activity, shaped in large part by political, value, and ideological factors. Thus there is a limit to what "professional social inquiry" can achieve—or at the very least what it *can* achieve needs to be inquired into (Lindblom and Cohen 1979). As David Labaree (1998) put it (in a paper with the provocative title "Educational Researchers: Living with a Lesser Form of Knowledge"), unlike the "hard sciences" such as physics, education research is a "soft knowledge" field. This means that researchers are faced with two difficult problems:

> One is that, unlike workers in hard knowledge fields, they must generally deal with some aspect of human behavior. This means that cause only becomes effect through the medium of willful human action, which introduces a large and unruly error term into any predictive equation. These billiard balls are likely to change direction between the cue ball and the corner pocket. The other is that research projects in behavioral fields have embedded within them the values and the purposes not only of the researchers (like hard fields) but also

of the actors under study. The result is a messy interaction of the researcher and the research subject.[3]

(p. 5)

The discussion that follows will survey this complex and conflicted scene, bringing to bear a degree of philosophical detachment that aims to provide a series of modest clarifications, as opposed to a definitive diagnosis or a plan for major remedial intervention. Taking seriously the insights offered by Lindblom, Cohen, Labaree, and others suggests that the maladies afflicting education research are not as serious as commonly supposed. Indeed, those who pass negative judgments on the quality of education research might do better to take as their model the judging of competitive diving, where the execution of the dive is graded, but so is the dive's degree of difficulty. (Executing the hardest type of dive, even with some flaws, is a major achievement that can generate a winning score!)

Before we begin the main discussion, several preliminary clarifications must be made.

1. The first clarification is a terminological one. The expression "education (or educational) researcher" covers more territory than one it is commonly compared with, namely "medical researcher." The former includes (among others) historians and philosophers, economists, those who study curriculum and instruction with a humanistic or political theory orientation, and those who study policy and institutional structures, as well as empirical researchers with orientations derived from disciplines such as experimental or measurement psychology, sociology, anthropology, or linguistics. The term "medical researcher" usually is applied much more narrowly; historians and philosophers and others might do work that is welcome, but their fields are identified as "history of medicine," "medical education," and the like. Neither they nor their white-jacketed colleagues mistake these investigators for "medical researchers." The point is that when diagnosticians speak of the health of education research, especially its lack of rigor ("quality"), their diagnoses are made much more difficult by the diversity of types of inquiry that are pursued within education research and the concomitant array of disciplinary criteria and norms to which these inquiries—to be rigorous—must conform. There are very few, if any, diagnosticians who are qualified to pass judgments about work in all of these fields. Thus the careless suggestion that *all* educational researchers need to be rigorous in "the scientific sense" (to cite one cavalier dictum that has arisen in the wake of too rapid a reading of the NRC report [Shavelson and Towne 2002]) causes many researchers representing respectable scholarly disciplines to take umbrage. To add further complexity, some scholars working in

education argue that thinking of any serious educational inquiry in terms of "science" is a mistake.

This cause of strain can easily be eliminated by, for instance, following the lead of Lindblom and Cohen (1979:7) and using the all-embracing label "practitioners of professional social inquiry" (pPSI). Another route would be to identify two fields—a narrower one of "educational researchers," and a more inclusive one of "scholars of education" who engage in "educational inquiry" (a category which would include historians, philosophers, curriculum theorists, postmodern theorists, neo-Marxist cultural critics, etc.). The current practice, however, is to modify the term "research" with terms like "empirical" or "scientific," and it is this modified label that serves both to exclude the likes of historians and philosophers and other humanistic types and to include the territory in which the diseases mentioned above have been identified as lurking.

There is a "sting in the tail" of this terminological issue that is largely responsible for the vituperative nature of many recent debates, namely the notion that public funding of research in education should be restricted to *rigorous scientific research.* Sloppy research is in no one's interest. On the other hand, it is shortsighted at best to eliminate research funding for many categories of scholars who regard themselves as meeting relevant disciplinary standards as they pursue research aimed at a better understanding of the complexities of educational problems. At the very least, such a restrictive policy places a heavy responsibility on those who control the purse strings (and also on those who advise them) to put their understanding of "science" on a firm and defensible base. This, as will be seen, is not an easy responsibility to meet.

2. The second clarification regards the focus of the discussion to follow. In broad terms, this will be the state of scientific or empirical research on educational phenomena, leaving the border of this terrain a little fuzzy. The precise focal point will be the complexities surrounding the assessment of rigor and/or quality in education research. The diagnoses of serious illness generally have not included the work of those identified above as educational scholars; of course, there is some work of dubious scholarly quality done by historians, philosophers, and others who are not working within anything remotely resembling a traditional scientific framework, and the work of postmodernist scholars remains highly controversial in many quarters. But there is much "educational inquiry" that is solid and stands in good repute among scholars both inside and outside of education. For example, there is currently an expanding body of work by philosophers of education, and by philosophers who write about education, that is highly regarded in the domains of political theory and political

philosophy and that at the same time illuminates issues of citizenship and multiculturalism in liberal pluralistic democracies. Names to conjure with here include Harry Brighouse (2000), Eamonn Callan (1997), Amy Gutmann (1987), Meira Levinson (1999), and Rob Reich (2002). This less problematic domain largely disappears from view in the remainder of this chapter.

3. The final preliminary clarification addresses the nature of the conflicts over quality that occur between insiders within the broad field of education research. There are at least three situations that it is helpful to recognize. (a) Researchers within one theoretical or methodological framework sometimes take to task those who work within another. Adherents of randomized controlled studies can be dismissive of those who pursue qualitative case studies (and vice versa), just as, in the fifties and sixties, those who favored behaviorism frequently leveled criticisms at those who were Freudians (who responded in kind). Resolution of such inter-paradigmatic disputes—to use the Kuhnian term in its now-common loose sense—is difficult if not impossible, at least in the short term. Here, the much-touted "remedy" of peer review is likely to be of no help, for the reviewer might well be the peer of one disputant but not the peer of the rival. (b) Researchers within the same framework or "paradigm" do not always agree, and there can be shoddy or rigorous work internal to the frame, about which there can be vituperative exchanges. This is the kind of quality dispute where peer review is at its best. (c) Criticism also can come from scholars who reject all traditional "modernist" research frameworks, and who instead offer postmodernist arguments that, in some quarters,

> are often taken as good reasons for abandoning certain research strategies in the social sciences. Apparently these arguments, or ones like it [sic], are given as "justifications" for dismissing the collection of data, for dismissing certain heuristic guides for theory, for abandoning quantitative techniques, or dismissing attempts at formulating covering-law explanations.
> (D'Amico 1992:142)

These radical attacks on the traditional research enterprise, from individuals who often still regard themselves as researchers but who wish to reformulate the enterprise on what they argue is a more valid footing, perhaps are the greatest challenge to pinning down the nature of quality in education research, although the problem outlined under (a) is also a significant barrier.

The distinctions made above also illuminate the suggestion that the only workable way to increase the quality of research is to encourage the disciplines to police themselves. While this is appealing in that, if taken seriously, it would dampen any tendency on the part of outsiders to interfere in "internal" scholarly matters, it runs into trouble on two counts. First, if internal dissension is strong enough, the discipline might not be able to police itself, or it might simply disintegrate.[4] Second, the advice ignores significant "outside" institutional pressures that encourage publication of pabulum or worse.[5]

Relevance and Quality: A Tenuous Link?

Despite the considerable historical precedent, there are grounds for being cautious in using the criterion of "resulting in improvement in educational practice" (or related locutions) for judging the quality, especially the rigor, of either an individual piece of education research or an entire research program. To put it most starkly, some highly estimable research has produced results useful to practice, while other equally laudable studies have failed to have an impact.[6] It is crucial to note, however, that some dubious pieces of work also have had an impact while other representatives of this genre have not. Quality of the research, qua research, seems, prima facie, to be neither a necessary nor a sufficient condition for practical impact. Of course, there is an easy way out of this dilemma as well. "Quality" can be defined simply in terms of "having an impact"—but this would be a Pyrrhic victory that merely marks refusal to face up to the difficulty of the issues.

Why is the link between quality and impact so tenuous? There are numerous reasons, some deep and some rather trivial, and most are well known. In the first place, not all research is *intended* to have an impact. To use the distinction introduced by Cronbach and Suppes (1969), some work is theoretical or fundamental or "conclusion oriented" rather than "decision oriented." Such research might at some stage have practical implications, but that is not its point—any more than the study of black holes in astronomy is intended to influence the course of human history. In the words of Philip Jackson and Sara Kieslar (1977:13),

> There is no army of educational practitioners expectantly waiting to hear what the fundamental researchers have to say, nor is there a corresponding group of researchers. The truth is that most practitioners do not turn directly to researchers for advice, nor do most researchers offer it. The two groups talk more among themselves than they do to each other—and so they should if they are to do justice to their respective tasks.

Kerlinger (1977:6) was even more outspoken:

> Scientific research never has the purpose of solving human or social problems, making decisions, and taking action. The researcher is preoccupied with, and should be preoccupied with, variables and their relations. He should never be required to think about or to spell out the educational implications of what he is doing or has done.

This position is extreme, and it is not borne out by important cases from the history of science. Early work on the physics of gases was directly inspired by the need to understand why it was that water pumps failed to keep mine shafts clear of water when they were more than 32 feet in depth; and Stokes (1977) offered a convincing argument that important *theoretical* work in science has come in the wake of pursuing *practical* problems that lie in what he termed "Pasteur's Quadrant."[7] Nevertheless, the point remains that some research does not have practical implications because the researchers never aimed for it to have any. They were pursuing problems that did not arise from practice and were far removed from it.

Far more interesting for present purposes are cases where researchers do intend their work to be "decision oriented." (It is worth recalling that Cronbach and Suppes cautioned that their distinction was not an absolute or watertight one.) Why are the results of such work so often lacking in impact? An obvious contender is that the work in question may be so shoddy that its defects are discernable even to policymakers or practitioners unsophisticated about the world of research—very few individuals are cynical enough to make deliberate use of shoddy goods.

But what about cases where the work apparently was of high quality? One possibility is that the research was directed at the wrong issues—issues that might in principle be relevant to a key problem, policy, or program, but that were not of interest to the decisionmakers at the time. This often has been the fate of the results of methodologically competent evaluation research—an especially ironic twist, given that this is a field where there has been ever-growing sophistication about how information use is influenced by such things as stakeholder pressure (e.g., pressure from program operators, or district or state-level administrators, or from elected officials who have an eye on the whims of their electorates and who may fear recalls), financial exigencies, and unrealistic timelines.

There appears to be growing consensus that utilization of research or program evaluation information in the formation of policies is a *political*, not an academic/scientific, act (Phillips 2007). Decades ago, Cronbach et al. (1980: 3) warned that "a theory of evaluation must be as much a theory of political interaction as it is a theory of how to determine facts. . . . The evaluator's professional conclusions cannot substitute for the political process." And when Kaestle (1993:30) discussed the "awful reputation" of education research, he described the field of education (not just the field of evaluation) as "enmeshed in politics" and agreed with one of his informants, who stated that politicization "adds to the impression that education research is not scientific, that the facts can be manipulated." Labaree (1998:5) concurred:

> [E]ducational processes are fundamentally political, reflecting social purposes—such as democratic equality, social efficiency, and individual opportunity—that embed contradictory pressures within education

and provide conflicting criteria for evaluating educational success.... As a result, educational researchers are able at best to make tentative and highly contingent claims that are difficult to sustain in the face of alternative claims by other researchers.

Doubtless there are cases where some pressing educational or social need legitimately trumps even unequivocal research findings, so that some policy or program might be introduced despite what research has to say about it. For example, to promote social equity, or to avoid civil or sectarian strife, it might be necessary to mount some program despite the failings that researchers have detected in it. It also seems possible that critics of education research's lack of impact might be underrating the importance of cases where a prospective hypothesis or nascent idea for an intervention has been squashed by solid research that reached a negative or disconfirming conclusion. Many ideas that once seemed promising are stillborn as their defects become apparent. For example, formative evaluation at the early stage of development of a program often functions as much negatively as it does positively—"feature X ought to be dropped, but feature Y is promising and could be expanded upon in manner Z." The policy community is apt to overlook this kind of beneficial (but negative) impact of research.[8]

A well-known point from philosophy of science can illuminate another common problem that arises in attempts to utilize research results, namely that sometimes a promising and apparently relevant research finding leads to dismal failure in practice, leading in turn to a negative reevaluation of the original research. ("It failed in practice, so it must have been low-quality research.") It is useful to bear in mind that even in physics, where there are laws and theories that have survived severe tests and that repeatedly have proven their worth for engineering purposes or for the making of predictions, there is a dark side: These generalizations, of purportedly universal applicability, always have associated with them so-called ceteris paribus clauses. For the law or theory to hold true, *other things need to be equal.* Boyle's Law holds that the relation between the pressure and volume of a gas is (nearly) constant—but the validity of this law requires that the temperature and the mass of the gas must not alter. If other things are *not* equal, if these basic conditions (and, indeed, certain others) are not met, the law will not hold and any predictions based upon it will fail.

Generalizations from education research come with a resounding CETERIS PARIBUS! This is what sometimes underlies the observation that these findings are "soft."[9] Another way of putting this is that the results of education research are heavily *contextualized,* as are many of the findings across the social sciences (Flyvbjerg 2001).[10] A wide array of situational factors can turn a positive research finding into a dud in practice: the setting typically is a different school, often in a different geographical or socioeconomic locale; the teachers and students are different (and may have different values or purposes from those individuals who were in the original research study); and the time of day when the application is utilized may deviate from that in the original study. Sometimes, perhaps because they lack an understanding of the ramifications of this contextualization of research findings—or worse, because they do not understand the nature of education as a normative and policy-impregnated field—decisionmakers and members of the general public hold researchers culpable when well-attested research findings fail to hold up in new settings. (No such fate befell Robert Boyle in settings where "other things" were not held equal—and a sample of gas is simple in comparison to education!) In *Reliable Knowledge*, first published in 1945, Harold Larrabee (1964) referred to the "multiple relativity" of social science research, and then continued with this observation:

> [A]ll statements to the effect that something is reliably known should, strictly speaking, be made only with extensive qualifications indicating the degree of reliability claimed, on what evidence, for what knowers, and in what contexts. In actual practice, this would load conversation and writing with an intolerable burden of qualifying clauses. To save time, breath, and inked paper, [we] ... are likely to go right on with our broad, sweeping, abstract generalizations about what we claim to know.
>
> (p. 6)

He went on, noting that, unfortunately, "not all audiences" are sophisticated enough to add the provisos that are necessary. Little increase in sophistication seems to have occurred in the ensuing 65 years.

The points raised in the paragraphs above lead directly to the issue of generalizability or external validity, and also to complex issues concerning the nature of causation in the domains covered by education research and the social sciences. But before turning to these topics, there are other fish to fry.

Methodology and Quality: Another Tenuous Connection?

It is natural, when seeking a way to judge the elusive dimension of "quality," to turn to an examination of the methodology the study employed. The reasoning is straightforward: *The more adequate and rigorous the methodology (the more appropriate the methodology was for the problem that was being investigated, and the more care with which it was applied) then the higher the quality of the research.* While no doubt it is no great compliment to remark with philosopher of science Abraham Kaplan (1964:24) that a "pervasive trait of American culture is manifested in the overemphasis on what methodology can achieve," there nevertheless is much to be said on behalf of the simple line of reasoning adumbrated above. There also are downsides that need to be highlighted, the main one of which is suggested by the question "better or more adequate or appropriate in the judgment of whom?"

Kaplan is not as negative as the sociologist David Riesman, whom he reports as saying that methodological preoccupation is "congenitally self-defeating" (quoted in Kaplan 1964:25). Kaplan's concern is with the excessive normative respect that can be paid to methodological precepts, a concern he expressed in memorable language:

> What I am protesting is the conception of the methodologist as baseball commissioner, writing the rules; or at any rate as umpire, with power to thumb an offending player out of the game. He is at best only a coach, and the merit of his recommendations rests entirely on what the play of the game shows to be effective.
>
> (p. 25)

Kaplan introduces three issues here that merit discussion.

First, different branches or subfields of research have their own norms or standards or central methods, so in appealing to a methodologist to judge the adequacy of a research study the allegiance of this particular umpire is of crucial importance. Asking a baseball umpire to officiate at a soccer match may be more than inappropriate; it might well be disastrous, for a person expert at one sport may have a low opinion of other sports. Similarly, an adherent of hermeneutically oriented case studies might make a different judgment about a piece of research than would a neo-behaviorist. The former believes that human actors are impelled by such things as reasons, motives, and ideals, while the latter holds that the only causes that can be entertained are publicly observable and measurable ones. And as what counts as a cause is different in the two cases, so there are concomitant differences in the respective research methods.

To this it might be replied that theorists, and perhaps even researchers, have allegiances or commitments that color their judgments, but methodologists are pristine and are able to take what philosopher Thomas Nagel (1986) called "the view from nowhere," and are thus unimpaired in their ability to serve as neutral (unbiased) and authoritative umpires. This is simply a professional conceit, the very one that Kaplan was objecting to in the passage quoted above; even in baseball an umpire is located *somewhere* that colors his view. As Thomas Kuhn (1962) pointed out, no judgments can be made outside of some paradigm or framework, for it is the foothold in a framework that provides the underlying assumptions, definitions, and other criteria on the basis of which judgments are made. To move out of one paradigm or framework is to move into another. It is worth stressing, however, that to say all this is not a surreptitious way of making the point that all decisions are suspect. An umpire located at home plate may sometimes make questionable calls because of the limitations in perspective imposed by his position, but often as not, he makes good (even the "right") decisions.

Sometimes, in a vain attempt to avoid the exercise of judgment, a checklist approach to research appraisal is advocated, along the lines of "rate on a five-point scale each of the following: was the sample size adequate, were the individuals in the sample randomly assigned to treatment and control groups or was there some other way of assuring that the groups were equivalent at the outset, was attrition from both groups kept to acceptable levels, was the integrity of the treatment maintained?" But rating the items inevitably involves judgment, as did the initial selection of items for the rating scheme.

The second general issue arising from Kaplan's wonderful (negative) analogy of the methodologist as baseball umpire is that appealing to methodology is the scientific equivalent of appealing to the established canon in literature. It is an essentially conservative gambit, equivalent to appealing to the currently dominant (Kuhnian) paradigm. As Kaplan (1964:25) put it, the "irony is that methodology itself may make for conformism—conformity to its own favored reconstructions." We all are familiar with stories of an author who suffered through numerous rejections of what turned out to be a major novel because reviewers felt the work failed to observe canonical precepts. Similarly, the scientific community's reluctance to accept the relevance of data and arguments regarding continental drift delayed acceptance of that phenomenon for decades (the notion that coastlines and their geological strata might fit together like pieces of a jigsaw puzzle was an affront to the conservative scientific mind).

As an antidote to the conservatism of "methodolatry," Kaplan (1964:27) cites the refreshing remark of Nobel laureate Percy Bridgman that "the scientist has no other method than doing his damnedest." Doing one's damnedest, however, might not be appreciated by an umpire who is firmly rooted in the unyielding soil of traditional methodological precepts, soil that does not include "damnedest" among its basic nutrients. The philosopher Paul Feyerabend was a tad more radical, saying that in science the basic rule is "anything goes." He cited with approval Einstein's remark that the scientist must be an "unscrupulous opportunist" (see Motterlini 1999:116). There is the additional complication that methods regarded as valid at one time are revised or reversed later. Even the grandest method of them all—the so-called "scientific method"—has not been static. It alters as later generations profit from their forebears having done "their damnedest," or as later generations profit from questioning the metaphysical or epistemological assumptions underlying earlier views about the nature of scientific inquiry.[11]

The third issue related to Kaplan's vivid analogy is that there is at least one rival position that can be put forward. The methodologist may be cast as "inspirational figure" or perhaps "coach," as Kaplan (1964) termed his own preferred vision. The advocate of this alterative who comes to mind most readily is John Dewey ([1948] 1971:96), who wrote of science as *the method of reflective or experimental intelligence*, which

> projects a better future and assists man in its realization. And its operation is always subject to test in experience. The plans which are formed, the principles which man projects as guides of

reconstructive action, are not dogmas. They are hypotheses ... to be rejected, corrected and expanded as they fail or succeed in giving our present experience the guidance it requires.

Dewey—his heart beating at one with Kaplan—summarily rejects the view that scientists "form a sacred priesthood" (p. xxxv). Elsewhere, he departed a little from such "inspirational" prose and described the methods of science in more specific terms, but still in a way that cannot serve as an effective rulebook for a field umpire, but which can serve to provide a general orientation (see Dewey [1933] 1971: chs. XI–XIII). The analysis of scientific method given in the 2002 NRC report similarly is not specific enough to be used widely as an umpire's handbook, although possibly it could serve as the basis for sending a few strikingly aberrant players along for remedial coaching. This point serves as a segue to the next section.

Science and Scientism

The scientific revolution was a watershed in human intellectual and social history not just for the advances that were made in the understanding of the physical and biological (and later the social) realms, but also for the development of trustworthy and fruitful intellectual methods. In the terminology of the founder of pragmatism, C. S. Peirce ([1877] 1982), the scientific method became *the* way of "fixing belief," replacing the method of tenacity, the method of authority, and the a priori method, which each had dominated in some earlier epoch. But the scientific method, in its turn, ran the risk of becoming the new "authority." The term "scientistic" evolved to cover cases where there was exaggerated respect for, and a narrow and illiberal account of, the "scientific method." Several points need to be made here.

Science as the Method of Intelligence

John Dewey, as a successor of Peirce, had a huge respect for science but arguably was not scientistic because—as sketched above—he understood the scientific method very broadly as effective and reflective thinking that is disciplined by experience; reason is "experimental intelligence, conceived after the pattern of science," whose products are tested in practice. The artist struggling with the composition of a painting, or the "man-in-the-street" who is late for an appointment across town, use "the method of intelligence" no less than the laboratory scientist (Dewey [1948] 1971:96). As he explained,

> in doing their specific jobs scientific men worked out a method of inquiry so inclusive in range and so penetrating, so pervasive and so universal. ... It is a method of knowing that is self-corrective in operation; that learns from failures as from successes. The heart of the method is the discovery of the identity of inquiry with discovery.
> (pp. xxix–xxx)

Furthermore, in *Logic: The Theory of Inquiry* ([1938] 1966), Dewey made the point that the methods that work in science and other realms of inquiry have been discovered empirically (and not by some abstract a priori reasoning), a position that implies that if defects are discovered then a method can be modified or discarded.

> We know that some methods of inquiry are better than others in just the same way in which we know that some methods of surgery, farming, road-making, navigation, or what-not are better than others. It does not follow in any of these cases that the "better" methods are ideally perfect.
>
> (p. 104)

Dewey's position is antithetical to those that identify the essence of science as being located in one specific and unchanging method (or in a small number of methods) whose usefulness has been established once and for all.

Postpositivist Views of Science

During the twentieth century a new view (or family of views) of the nature of science slowly evolved, as the positivist account of science and its methods withered (see Phillips and Burbules [2000] for an outline). The emerging broad "postpositivist" view was inspired, in part, by the work of philosophers such as Dewey, Popper, Kuhn, Lakatos, Feyerabend, Scheffler, Laudan, and dozens of others. Detailed investigations of real (as opposed to artificially constructed or highly compacted) examples of scientific research undertaken by historians of science and sociologists of science, as well as philosophers, also were important stimuli. It would be absurd to claim that there has been unanimity concerning the details of the emerging picture—unanimity is not to be expected between (and even within) lively scholarly communities, especially when philosophers are involved. But the new accounts have homed in on several features of science: there are no ultimate, potentially unchallengeable sources of knowledge (epistemology must be non-foundationalist), and consequently the conclusions reached by scientists are *hypothetical* in the sense that these, too, are never absolutely established and are not insulated completely from the possibility of future challenge.

It also appears that skeptics such as Kaplan were right. The overemphasis on methodology as the unitary criterion detracts from the main question at hand, which is this: *Has the overall case made by the scientist been established to a degree that warrants tentative acceptance of the theoretical or empirical claims that were made?* Making a case for tentative belief is, in essence, the culmination of scientific inquiry. The methodology used in a particular study is an important consideration, but it should not be accepted as an "authoritative umpire" that rules in or out of play the various diverse considerations the scientist puts forward in developing his/her case. A weakness here might be compensated for by a strong argument or relevant piece of evidence there, but a methodological purist might exert a negative or at least an unnecessarily restraining influence because some of the relevant considerations have escaped mention in his/her rulebook.[12] So, to repeat: What needs to be judged is the overall case the scientist has made. To use Dewey's felicitous expression, has a *warrant justifying the assertion of the claim* under consideration been established?

The attitude towards research being canvassed here is that it should be recognized as being an exercise in rhetoric, in the classic and not the modern sense in which the term almost becomes synonymous with "spinning" or "non-rational persuasion." Although this feature of research is most apparent in published reports, it is equally true of day-to-day activity in the lab, or in the field, or in the library. In each instance the goal is to construct a convincing case. In *The Craft of Research*, Wayne Booth and his colleagues (2003:114, emphasis in original) offer this succinct summary: "In a research report you make a *claim*, back it with *reasons* based on *evidence*, *acknowledge* and *respond* to other views, and sometimes explain your *principles* of reasoning. There's nothing arcane in any of this." Another way of putting this is that scientific research can be regarded as parallel to the work of a trial lawyer—what is crucial is the way the case is built up, how evidence or arguments are marshaled to fill in the "holes," how the final argument hangs together, including whether it can stand up to the critical scrutiny of peers (trial lawyers working for the other side) and the independent jurors who need to be convinced "beyond all reasonable doubt." Unquestionably, assessing a complex piece of rhetoric that purports to warrant a claim can be an extremely difficult task, and it is one that many critics of the quality of education research abrogate. Making such an assessment by way of a checklist of methodological precepts simply will not suffice, although it might be part of an adequate assessment.

Consider as an example the complex multimethod case that William Harvey developed to convince his scientific peers that blood circulates in arteries and veins, and that it is pumped by the heart. What overall conclusion would a checklist of predetermined methodological precepts have generated for this case? It is not unreasonable to suppose that it would have been judged quite badly (in historical fact, it took several decades for the case to be widely accepted). Harvey made dissections of human bodies and of animals; he watched the way blood spurted from severed blood vessels in animals; he made observations of comparative anatomy (organisms with two-, three-, and four-chambered hearts); and he performed simple (uncontrolled but repeatable) "demonstrations," such as applying pressure to the vessels in his own limbs to see on what side of the obstruction the blood accumulated. There was no "methodological cookbook" for judging the case, any more than there was a standard for making it convincing. Later generations recognized the genius of Harvey's work and the persuasiveness of his rhetoric.[13]

Viewing science as a rhetorical case-making activity, along the lines sketched above, throws into relief the problematic nature of judging the quality of *research proposals* as opposed to assessing the *final product*. In the latter situation, the entire case, with its arguments and observations and experimental evidence, is available for evaluation, but in the former all one has to go on is a set of promises and hopes. A proposal to work on a problem the resolution of which is not yet known (and the accurate formulation of which might also not be apparent)—and where even the most fruitful strategy for reaching a solution also is not yet known—must of necessity be vague. Rather than being a virtue, undue precision here suggests something is amiss. Harvey could not have been precise at the outset of his work, and neither could Pasteur, or Galileo, and countless other groundbreaking researchers. It is for this reason that proposals to undertake so-called "design research" in education are difficult to rate in terms of research quality. In this type of work, research activities are deliberately responsive to issues and problems that arise in the course of the design process. Most if not all of these issues cannot be delineated at the outset.

The Context of Scientific Discovery

As the examples above illustrate, a narrow view of the nature of science, and crucially of its methods, is fostered if too much attention is paid to what the philosopher Hans Reichenbach termed "the context of justification" and too little notice is given to the vitally important "context of discovery". This distinction is heuristically valuable, but it is too crude to be taken as marking an absolute dichotomy. In practice, ideas often are tested as they are formulated, leading to many of them quickly being discarded as unworthy. There are not two temporally distinct processes occurring, as a crude understanding of Reichenbach's distinction might suggest, but one complex one in which probing, hypothesis formation, critiquing, and testing are intermingled, as the case of William Harvey amply illustrates.[14]

Crude as it is, however, the discovery/justification distinction is extremely helpful when applied to the recent debates concerning the use of the so-called "gold standard" in education research. Thus, those who insist that *the* criterion to use in identifying scientifically rigorous education research is whether or not the study in question used randomized controlled field trials or experiments (RFTs), or quasi-experimental designs that approximate them, are guilty of focusing on only one half of Reichenbach's categorization of the logic of science. RFT methodology is well suited to throw light only on the *justificatory* issue—that is, on whether or not it can be claimed that a treatment actually caused (produced) a desired effect. This focus is, of course, an important one, but taken by itself (and it is often put forward by itself) it egregiously misrepresents the nature of scientific inquiry. For what is omitted is the vital steps leading up to the *initial discovery or production* of the treatment (or program or hypothesis) whose claim to effectiveness is being subjected to justificatory investigation by means of the RFT. It often is this "phase" of discovery where scientists get to display their creative genius, their range and depth of background knowledge, their "opportunism," their ability to "do their damnedest." And it is this that is being ignored so cavalierly when "scientific method" is identified with a particular method of hypothesis testing. Furthermore, the careful case building that occurs in the early stages of research often obviates the need for a final RFT (assuming that one is even possible), for the case that finally emerges can be so sound that a final grand "test" is not required (as, again, the case of William Harvey shows).

Another way to put this emerges from the analysis of the steps in scientific problem solving advanced by Karl Popper, and the independent but surprisingly similar analysis of "reflective thinking" (which includes problem solving in science) given by John Dewey.[15] To use the latter's account, five logically (but not necessarily temporally) distinct steps can be distinguished: first, a felt difficulty; second, its location and definition; third, a suggestion of a possible solution;[16] fourth, development by reasoning of the bearings of the suggestion; and fifth, further observation and experimental testing leading to an acceptance or rejection of the suggestion (see Phillips 1992:85; Dewey [1933] 1971:107ff.). According to both Dewey and Popper, then, the RFT is a logical latecomer to the scientific process. There is a prima facie case that we should sit up and pay heed when three philosophers of note—one a positivist (Reichenbach), one a pragmatist (Dewey), and one a critical rationalist (Popper)—are in such close agreement that the testing of a hypothesis is the end of a scientific cycle, *and is not its entirety*. All three would have been staggered at the enormity of the historically unfounded suggestion that testing is the only aspect of research or inquiry that is worthy of public funding, or with the suggestion that the RFT and some related but "weaker" designs are the only methods of science that can serve as markers of "quality."

The foregoing discussion does not undermine the contention that the RFT is one of the major weapons in the armamentarium of the educational researcher, one that is peerless for determining that a program or intervention that is supposed to produce beneficial effects actually does so (or fails to do so). Clearly beliefs or suppositions are not enough (for they can be *false* beliefs), even when they arise as the consequence of a process involving careful analysis, problem identification, and creative (and usually theory-driven) formulation of tentative hypotheses or solutions. This is why Reichenbach, Dewey, and Popper all included rigorous testing as part of their analyses of scientific method.

To reiterate, what is of utmost importance is the strength of the often complex case that scientists produce to warrant the claims that they make. Although the RFT and quasi-experiments or regression discontinuity designs can be part of such a case (occasionally they may even make up the entire case), their use is not the *only* way that such a warranting case can be made. There are many other valuable methods—and not just the ones that are mentioned, usually *sotto voce*, by adherents of the "gold standard" when it is not possible to randomly assign or to intervene in a situation that is being studied. This leads directly to a discussion of the so-called quantitative–qualitative divide, but before heading to that topic, a final issue, one that concerns the importance of establishing causation in science, and more particularly in education research, must be addressed.

Causation and the Purposes of Education Research

The point was made earlier that the label "education research" covers an extremely large and diverse domain; philosophers would say that the term does not denote a "natural kind." It is a category made by us, and does not emanate from some preordained Platonic realm. The diversity of the contents of this category is such that it is quixotic to suppose that one purpose can be identified that all the forms of research encompassed by the category have in common. (And this, of course, is one of the main reasons that formulating criteria of quality that have some punch is not a trivial endeavor.)

This being acknowledged, it is clear that at least one of the major purposes of research is descriptive. This can be seen, for example, when researchers aim to determine differential graduation rates from high school or college (between, say, males and females), or aim to catalogue events that took place during the monitoring of a field trial, or aim to depict what "life is like" in certain types of classrooms or schools or communities, or aim to elucidate what Clifford Geertz called the "webs of meaning" that help constitute the cultural settings within which individuals live and act, or aim, as Jonathan Kozol has, to expose gross inequities in the provision of schooling. Rigorous descriptive work is an important part of science (it *dominated* some sciences—botany and astronomy, for example—for much of their history), but in the current "context of justification," with its nearly exclusive focus on the design and execution of experimental and quasi-experimental interventions, descriptive work is undervalued.

Judging the quality of a piece of descriptive research is often far from easy, but at least it seems straightforward and relatively uncontroversial in principle: Is the description accurate (would other describers reach more or less the same conclusion)? Is it biased in the descriptive language being used? Has there been selection bias at work in deciding the site to be studied? Did the observer note only what he/she *wanted* to see or *hoped* to see before the observations began? Were other "threats to the validity" of the observational study guarded against? Does the description uncover events or phenomena occurring in the settings or programs being described that are worthy of others' attention or that have previously passed unnoticed?

There is no denying the fact, however, that another major purpose of education research is to establish causation or, relatedly, to illuminate the precise nature of the causal processes or mechanisms that are at work in producing some effect or result relevant to policy or classroom practice. This purpose is partly disguised by the practice of using euphemisms—instead of saying "X caused Y," a researcher's locution can be that "X influenced Y," "X produced or partially produced Y," "X resulted in Y," "X led to Y," "X set up or helped to establish a climate in which Y came about," "X increased the likelihood that Y would be found." But Shakespeare had it right—a rose by any other name . . . Even a policy statement is a causal claim; essentially it is a recipe, and a recipe embodies causal knowledge (or what is supposed to be causal knowledge). Use these ingredients, combine them in such-and-such a way, and (other things being equal) the result will be the product you desired. Educational researchers have made (and disputed) many causal claims, including ones about the efficacy of teaching machines, about frequent use of classroom questions, about phonics in the early teaching of reading, about the benefits of including the study of science or Latin in the curriculum, about reduction of class size, about streaming, about "constructivist" methods of teaching, and about parental involvement in schools.

Many issues need to be teased apart here. First, in order for a scientist to assert authoritatively that "X causes Y," he/she will need to put forward a warranting case. It is important to note that no warrant is ever immune to the possibility of revocation.[17] The warrant for asserting that there are 48 chromosomes in human somatic cells (an example from this author's youth) was revoked in the late fifties and a new warrant was issued on behalf of the claim that there are only 46; the warrant for the claim that noxious vapors are the causal agent in cases of deadly puerperal fever (which caused the death of large numbers of women who contracted it during childbirth) was withdrawn around 1848, after Ignaz Semmelweis developed a much stronger case for blood poisoning as the causal agent.[18] Very few things in science are established with absolute certainty. Cronbach (1975) argued that we live in an "interactive universe" in which generalizations "decay"—a descriptive or even a causal statement applicable to a population at a particular time might not hold true at some later time. In all, a degree of modesty seems advisable, not only when asserting beliefs or claims, but also in the degree of trust placed in the cases that currently support these claims.

Second, although using a randomized controlled experiment can produce a strong case for the causal efficacy (or lack of it) of some treatment, it is not an *unassailable* case. It is a strong method because it is an instantiation of one of John Stuart Mill's ([1843] 1874) "principles of logic"—if two groups that are identical except for one factor end up differing, the cause of the difference must be the one factor with respect to which they differed. In an RFT, the groups are formed by randomization, which is designed to remove any systematic difference between them, and then one group is given the experimental treatment or program while the other group is designated as the control, so that the treatment *must* have been the cause of any resulting difference between the two groups.[19] This is a strong but not *absolutely* strong research method. The following caveats apply: The treatment can be held to have had a causal effect, *provided* that other things were equal and that the study did not fall victim to any of the well-known threats to validity (which is why the experiment needs to be monitored), and *provided* that the resulting difference is statistically significant (with the further proviso that statistics serve only as a guide, since they address probabilities and not certainties), and *provided* that some as yet unknown causal factor is not at work, or, if it is, then *provided* that it is distributed evenly between the treatment and control groups.[20]

Third, there are other ways to make a case that is strong enough to warrant acceptance of a causal claim, providing that the message of the discussion above is taken to heart and it is recognized that acceptance of scientific claims always should be tentative. Consider the following three possibilities for case building. First, if after sufficient exploratory activity and observation a hypothetical causal model can be developed, then a situation might be devised wherein the proposed mechanism is disrupted to determine if the consequences that occur are the ones to be expected in the light of the model. This, essentially, was William Harvey's procedure. He reasoned that if the heart was pumping blood away through the arteries and the veins were returning it, then if he closed an artery it should distend on the "upstream" side but not on the "downstream" side, whereas a closed vein should distend on the side of the obstruction furthest from the heart.

A second somewhat similar technique is what Michael Scriven (1974:68–84) dubbed the modus operandi (MO) method, which offers a non-experimental means of deciding between causal possibilities in situations where some background information is known. He is suitably cautious, recommending its use only when the "usually more desirable" approaches are not possible. But he points out that by using MO reasoning, "we are thus able to get plausible conclusions from incredibly weak and commonly available premises" (Scriven 1974:74). The MO method is familiar from police work, where evidence collected at a crime scene points to a method of action associated with a known suspect. Scriven develops the logic of the MO method with some sophistication, focusing on its use in program evaluation to eliminate unlikely causes of program effects and to illuminate the likely factor.

The third case-building alternative to the randomized controlled trial is—simply—observation, which on occasion can be the grounding for a causal claim. In some complex situations, unaided observation is deficient, for the causal relations might not be distinguishable from the non-causal ones. But this difficulty does not always arise; observer testimony can convict a suspect of having caused a murder, and an observant umpire can reliably rule that a baseball bounced before it was caught by an outfielder. All of us, from early in life, are accustomed to making reliable causal judgments (in physical as well as social or cultural settings) on the basis of what we observe. The fact that sometimes our judgments are wrong is no slight on the reputation of the general method, any more than the fact that statistics sometimes "lie" undermines statistical reasoning as a general technique. Observation is often a reliable guide—and sometimes it is the only guide available.

A further point concerning the use of the RFT in building a case is that although the randomized study is a strong method for determining that

"X caused Y," the role of context introduces an important proviso: An RFT can establish that X caused Y only in the particular setting in which the study took place, with the various background conditions that were then in existence, with the particular group of subjects involved, and with that particular method of delivering the program or experimental treatment. It often happens, however, that what is of interest to practitioners, policymakers, or even researchers is the degree of generalizability of the finding that "X causes Y." Unfortunately, as is well known, the aspects of an experimental study that promote its internal validity (what Donald Campbell and Julian Stanley [1963] called the *sine qua non*, the feature that determines the worth of the study as a trustworthy experiment) often are in tension with factors that influence its external validity or generalizability (e.g., the applicability of its findings to new sites, new populations, etc.; see Cronbach [1982]). In order to maximize external validity while also preserving a high degree of internal validity, appropriate features need to be built into the design before the experiment begins, adding to the complexity and cost of the study.[21]

Fifth, establishing that "X caused Y" by true experimental or any other means needs to be distinguished from the very important task of establishing the *causal mechanism or process* by virtue of which X achieved its causal effect. Forming two groups by random assignment, delivering X to one of the groups but not to both, monitoring the experiment to ensure that no threats to validity are operative, and then determining that the group that received X exhibits Y and the control group does not, can make the case that in this particular context "X caused Y," but it does nothing by itself to establish why or how X was able to produce this result. Sometimes supporters of the use of the RFT as the "gold standard" for judging the quality of education research downplay the need to establish the mechanism. Occasionally, they are right to do so—but as a general stance, their position has very little to recommend it. Science advances largely through the discovery of mechanisms, of causal processes, and the mode of operation of causal factors, and here a diversity of methods (including "doing one's damnedest") are useful. Furthermore, it should not be overlooked that knowledge of causal mechanisms is often of great relevance to members of the policy community, and of course it facilitates generalizing.

Thus the physicist Wilhelm Conrad Roentgen was not content to discover that photographic plates in his laboratory were exposed when his "vacuum tube" had a current passing through it—he was not content merely to label the unknown causal agent as "X radiation." Over the course of several months he pressed on to discover as much as he could about the nature of this mysterious radiation. Understanding why an observed relationship occurs can be as important as establishing the fact of the relationship. It might be a reliable finding that (on average) students learn more in high schools of medium size than they do in very small or very large schools, but this effect is mere magic if the mechanism producing the impact on learning is not known. It would be sad if the contemporary advocates of the "gold standard" turned out, in essence, to be supporters of the dark arts because of their refusal to countenance the search for underlying causal mechanisms as an important (even an indispensable) part of the scientific enterprise!

Sixth, there is the complex question of the nature of the causal factors that it is appropriate to countenance in social science and education research. The behaviorists (and their kin, the positivists) would allow only factors that were observable (what counts as being "observable" is another complex issue that, mercifully, need not be pursued here). They deemed as outside the domain of genuine science the "inner variables" that "folk psychology" treats as causal agents (e.g., motives, ideas, beliefs, values).[22] This is the point at which the discussion must turn to the so-called "quantitative versus qualitative divide," and the validity or otherwise of hermeneutical or interpretive methods.

Natural versus Social Science, and the Role of Qualitative and Interpretive Methods

During the closing decades of the twentieth century, the field of education research was enlivened by "paradigm wars"; the issue at stake was whether or not qualitative research methods were compatible with (and could be used alongside) quantitative methods, or whether they represented contrasting or incompatible paradigms. If the latter interpretation had triumphed, it would have doomed many forms of "multi or mixed method research." Kenneth Howe (2003:29), a regular contributor to the debates on this general issue, provided this helpful summary:

> The incompatibility thesis permits *disjunctive* combinations of quantitative and qualitative methods within the same study, in which different methods are applied to different questions but in which the study as a whole presupposes different epistemological paradigms. The incompatibility thesis bars *conjunctive* combinations of methods, in which different methods may be applied to the same questions and in which the study as a whole presupposes the same epistemological paradigm.

Howe supports the compatibilist view, according to which thorough integration of methods is both logically acceptable and often advisable.

With the birth of the new millennium the debate largely has died down. There is widespread although not universal consensus that quantitative and most qualitative approaches are not paradigms in anything like the Kuhnian sense; it may not even be possible to clearly demarcate one from the other, and certainly there is no theoretical reason why they cannot be used as part of the same research program. It is now regarded almost as a truism that "mixed methods research" is scientifically respectable.

However, there are several important complexities that deserve comment. First, just as it would be simplistic to claim that there is one set quantitative method, or even one closely related family of quantitative methods, so it is simplistic to think of qualitative methods as forming a closely related set. There are a large number of qualitative methods, and some of these are underwritten by theoretical positions (or "paradigms") that make them sit uneasily with each other—witness studies that use predetermined observational checklists, ethnographies, educational criticisms derived from the exercise of connoisseurship, and various types of narrativist studies.[23] Support for the compatibilist position needs to be tempered with caution.

Nevertheless, there are certain epistemological commonalities across many of the quantitative (including experimental) and qualitative methods. None produce results that are, in principle, immune from overthrow (see discussion above); and the cases or warrants that are produced by the use of any of them (separately or in conjunction), although fallible, are always much stronger if threats to validity have been guarded against. The threats to true and quasi-experimental studies are well known from the work of Campbell and Stanley (1963) and Cook and Campbell (1979), but the notion is also fruitful when applied to qualitative work.[24]

Further, interpretive or hermeneutical methods are a special class of qualitative methods, and many scholars have argued that their use not only serves to distinguish the social sciences from the natural sciences but also marks the former as *not being sciences* at all. In brief, the argument is that in the natural sciences, events or phenomena are explained by showing that they result from the operation of causal mechanisms or laws within the relevant portion of nature, together with the relevant "initial conditions." In explaining the voluntary behavior of a human, however, there is quite a different procedure—there are no laws of "voluntary human action." Instead, explanations are given in terms of the person's motives, beliefs, values, background knowledge, and so forth.[25] To explain why Bob went into the store, his need for a particular item and his belief that the store stocked that item might be cited. Bob could be asked to explain what he did and why he did it, but it would be possible also to observe his action in precise detail and then, using the background of cultural knowledge that we share with him, to offer a justifiable interpretation that makes clear the meaning of his behavior.

According to the interpretivist or hermeneutical framework, to identify an action or to have determined its meaning is, under most circumstances, also to have explained it. Bob does something that calls for explanation (he is wandering the streets with a puzzled expression on his face); determining that he is "searching for the supermarket" both identifies his action (its meaning is now known) and explains it (he does not know where the store is located, but he wants to find it because he intends to purchase something). Of course, as often happens in science, an explanation may open up other issues for which further explanations are required (such as why had Bob forgotten the location of the store). This indeed seems markedly different from what happens in the natural sciences, but it still does not seal the case that the social sciences are not sciences in the same sense that the natural sciences are. And it is crucial to note that, like all explanations across the sciences, interpretations can be examined for their reasonableness, for the way in which they stand up to critical scrutiny. An interpretation does not have to be taken on faith, and a case that supports a particular interpretation over other possible explanations needs to be available.

Nevertheless, if "science" is defined narrowly in terms of the possession and use of specific *types* of explanatory concepts (e.g., ones that pertain to "matter in motion," and that are directly accessible to observation, such as those used in classic physics or by the behaviorists), then by definition the social sciences are not sciences—but then (arguably) neither are fields such as "string theory" in physics and portions of cognitive psychology. To take this definitional route is to overlook the fact that it is stultifying and ultimately fatal to all sciences to pronounce at the outset the type of concepts that an inquiry in a specialist field must not use. Throughout history, scientists have introduced not only novel, but novel *types* of concepts as their inquiries pushed into domains where new ideas were necessary for headway to be made. For example, Newton introduced the then-shocking concept of "action at a distance"; quantum physicists introduced notions of chance into discussions of the fundamental structure of matter that offended some, including Einstein, who objected that the Deity "did not play dice"; and some behaviorists in psychology who had long insisted that explanatory variables needed to be publicly observable to be acceptable eventually relented and permitted the use of "inner variables." So the fact that some students of human action require concepts like "motives" or "beliefs" is not an argument that their work is "unscientific," provided that *there are means available both to check (at least indirectly) the claims that are made and to convince others that these claims are worthy of assent.* Problems arise only when there is no way in principle to check on a researcher's claims, for then the work has left the domain of science and has entered the realm of metaphysics.[26] The basic point may be summarized as follows:

> A case can be made . . . that for the purpose of social science, meanings and intentions can be investigated using traditional scientific methods. That is, it can be argued that there is no epistemological difference in kind between gaining knowledge about the other objects of science and gaining knowledge about meanings and intentions. Many branches of science can provide cases in which the objects of interest are not directly observable or measurable, but in which their presence (and their nature) is inferred from what is observable. This process is hypothetical, and it is not guaranteed to be successful; but it is self-corrective—by a bootstrapping process involving testing and elimination of errors (which is itself a tentative business), the warrants

for the claims that are made about such objects become stronger ... hermeneuticists can—and *do*—use the hypothetico-deductive method that is common in the natural sciences.

(Phillips 2000:38–39)

In short, those who believe that interpretive methods are not the kind of methods that can be used in high-quality research, because they are not scientific methods at all, are being cavalier (if not worse). They are operating with a severely narrow or truncated view (i) of the nature of science that, ultimately, is not borne out by the history of the natural sciences themselves;[27] and (ii) of the nature of human beings, for in essence they are refusing to acknowledge that people are so constituted that they act for reasons and that their actions are influenced by their beliefs and knowledge. This second truncated view is a challenge to the very enterprise of education itself—for why bother to educate children at all if it is supposed that their ensuing knowledge is not causally efficacious?

There is one matter, however, on which one can fault those who support the view that the social sciences are hermeneutical or interpretive in nature. Their framework often embodies the questionable assumption that the social sciences are *dominated* by a concern with voluntary human action. While this is an important focus, to hold that it is the *only* one (or that it is the predominant one) is to ignore the many "group-level" phenomena that are of interest and which require rigorous investigation.[28] Thus, macro-sociology and macro-economics are examples of fields where the hermeneutical understanding of the actions of individuals is of no professional concern, for the focus is on group-level phenomena; and, to give another generic example, a researcher interested in the relationship between socioeconomic status or ethnic group membership on enrollment in higher education can carry out this work without necessarily delving into the motives and beliefs of individuals.

The Postmodern Challenge to Research

The occasional flashes of energy in the debate across the qualitative–quantitative divide fade into insignificance when contrasted with the vituperative nature of some of the exchanges across what might be termed the "chasm" between positivists and postpositivists on the one hand and postmodernists on the other hand.[29]

Postmodernism, perhaps appropriately for a position that rejects both the possibility of making wide-sweeping generalizations and the normative claim of rationality, is difficult to pin down and even more difficult to write about in a clear way. Sometimes its supporters even stress (unplayfully) that "the postmodern" is actually part of "the modern," and they rightly object to the use of "it" by pointing out that there are a multitude of postmodernisms rather than a unitary position; and all—experts and novices alike—attest to the fact that most forms are not describable in any simple way.[30]

The aspect of postmodernism that is relevant here is the critique of the scientific enterprise, and the related analysis (deconstruction?) of scientific rationality. In one of the key early sources, *The Postmodern Condition: A Report on Knowledge*, Jean-François Lyotard ([1979] 1984: xxiv) famously argued for an attitude of "incredulity towards metanarratives." By this he meant that we ought to be suspicious of the justificatory "grand narratives" that are put forward to underwrite or establish as valid the major intellectual, moral, and aesthetic enterprises of the modern world, such as the quest for truth—for objective knowledge about nature—that characterizes modern science. This postmodern challenge to the use of reason in science was described well by a critic of it, Harvey Siegel (2003:315–316):

> According to at least one version of this challenge, the cultivation of reason depends on a "totalizing" or "universalizing" conception of reason which both illicitly presupposes the perspective of dominant groups and denies the particularity of those who are members of other groups, thereby marginalizing and oppressing them. Accordingly, "reason" must be seen not as a universal form or criterion of proper thought, but instead merely the form in use, and favored, by dominant groups, whose power is enhanced by imposing it upon dominated others. Reason, that is, is not any sort of ultimate authority or arbiter, but is simply one ideology among others, which must be recognized as a source of unjust power and privilege rather than a legitimate source of epistemic authority.

This postmodernist critique of scientific reason bore (bitter) fruit in the form of the "science wars" that erupted in the closing years of the twentieth century. In these debates, in place of the traditional view that the claims of science were justified in terms of the evidence and arguments presented by researchers, the postmodernists (with the support of some radical sociologists of knowledge) argued, in effect, that scientists were deluded, and that the forms taken by their knowledge claims were shaped causally by socioeconomic forces. The elimination of scientific rationality from the case-building process discussed earlier was made abundantly clear in influential work in the nascent field of science studies. In *Laboratory Life*, Bruno Latour and Steve Woolgar (1986:237) asserted that "there is little to be gained by maintaining the distinction between the 'politics' of science and its 'truth'. . . . The same 'political' qualities are necessary both to make a point and to out-manoeuvre a competitor."[31]

Undoubtedly the adherents of scientific education research should take seriously the critiques of the postmodernists and the radical sociologists of knowledge. Education research is based on (or warranted by) suppositions about rationality, objectivity, and the centrality of evidence and rational argumentation in the building of cases to support knowledge claims. To ignore challenges to these suppositions is to be unscientific, for an important aspect of science is the delivery and acceptance of strong criticism. Furthermore, postmodernists are right to stress that research is a social activity, and so like all social activities it is bound to be impinged upon by economic factors, by religious and political ideologies, and by the exercise of power and personal interests. The issue is to what degree such factors do or should encroach upon the practice of scientific inquiry.[32] But it also seems pertinent to note that when the scientific community identifies a study as having been unduly influenced by so-called external, non-epistemic factors, it reacts strongly to enforce its traditional norms and to minimize as far as possible the influence of these forces (Phillips 2000:Ch. 13).

In the end it is evident that postmodernists are not offering friendly amendments to traditional (modernist) accounts of science and its methods; although they present what purport to be arguments in support of their position, this position is self-refuting—for they claim (or assume) that their arguments against scientific reason are *reasonable* ones.[33] And paradoxically—for some of them claim to be scientists—they apparently want to do away with the game of science, or to change its underlying rules and procedures. It is unclear what they have to offer in its place, however; nor does it seem consistent of them to acknowledge (and desire) the positive fruits that society gains from modern science (see, e.g., St. Pierre 2002).

Having considered the postmodern challenge, it is now time to briefly examine the 2002 NRC report and its attempt to characterize the features that ought to be present in a piece of rigorous scientific research in education. In doing so, the discussion in this final section serves as well as a summary of the foregoing material.

Conclusion: The NRC Report and Its Modest View of Scientific Rigor

Around the turn of the millennium, when the National Research Council established a panel to report, inter alia, on "What are the principles of scientific quality in education research?" the climate in Washington was marked by skepticism and concern about the quality of education research, especially when it was compared with other domains of research that have input into policy discussions (such as medical and health-related research). The US Congress seemed to be on the verge of restricting research funds in education to scientifically rigorous research, as *defined by Congress itself*.[34] So the research community was keen to have an independent group jump the congressional gun and offer a reasoned account of what it was to be rigorously scientific. Members of the committee established by the NRC to undertake this task were clear among themselves that they were not defining rigorous education research, *simpliciter*, for they recognized that there was much valuable educational inquiry that fell outside the domain of science.[35] Their task was much more restricted: What are the desiderata for those types of research that purport to be "scientific," and the findings of which are often taken to offer concrete guidance for policymakers? In addition, some members of the committee had the aim of strengthening education research so that the guidance stemming from it would be as reliable as (or stronger than) that which the medical research community offers on health-related matters. These committee members believed, further, that adherence to the principles of scientific method was key to the reliability of findings. Some members also were committed to the view that any reasonable list of scientific principles or desiderata would need to be such that academically respectable but non-experimental research fields such as anthropology and ethnography would be included under the mantle of "science."[36]

It is important to bear in mind that it was no part of the committee's charge to question the wisdom of the effort to establish these desiderata, or to criticize the wisdom of the course upon which Congress appeared to be setting out (although individual members of the committee harbored serious misgivings about this); the internal monitoring procedures of the NRC ensured that there was adherence to the charge.

The list of criteria delineating scientific research in education, and the supporting arguments and examples, were settled upon after a number of public hearings, and after much back-and-forth in the committee room about examples from the history of the sciences, and about examples of education research (some of which were drawn from members' own work). Draft sections of the report were circulated for emendation and eventual approval, and the aim was to have enough of a spirit of compromise to allow unanimous assent to the final report.[37]

The final criteria were formulated as six "guiding principles" for a "healthy community" of scientific researchers. Although these criteria are common-sensical and do not all need to be met by any one particular piece of research, they have generated controversy in many quarters.[38] Because most of the criteria have appeared in somewhat different form in the preceding discussion, they will be presented here in short summaries without nuance or supporting rhetoric.[39]

1. Scientific research should pose significant questions that can be investigated empirically (the questions and the designs developed to address them should, of course, reflect relevant theoretical and methodological understanding).
2. Research should be linked, explicitly or implicitly, to some overarching theory or conceptual framework.
3. Methods should be judged in terms of their appropriateness for addressing a specific question; often, multiple-method designs will be appropriate.

4. A piece of scientific research will provide a coherent and explicit chain of reasoning—one that addresses limitations and biases, that counters alternative explanations, and that is compelling to the skeptic.
5. Findings should be replicated, and generalized (via new studies) beyond the narrow settings and populations where they were initially carried out.
6. Research studies should be opened up to wide professional scrutiny and critique—this strengthens the work and ensures as far as possible its objectivity.

It should be evident that these six principles do not prohibit the use of qualitative or hermeneutical methods; indeed, the report itself makes clear that it was a mistake for researchers in the past to adopt too narrow a view of the nature of human action, and it refers in critical tone to the "physics envy" that has often driven research in the human sciences. Nor is there blind advocacy in the report for the use of randomized controlled experimentation, although the committee certainly was supportive of the use of this methodology in contexts where it is appropriate.

What needs to be added as postscript to the NRC report? In the light of the earlier argument, the report could have been clearer about the difference between judging a proposal and assessing a completed piece of work; it could have been clearer about the fact that there is no algorithm either for pursuing problems in the "context of discovery" or for judging the final claims that are advanced in a completed research paper; it could have been acknowledged that some of the criteria do not apply well to work done within the (vaguely demarcated) "context of discovery"; it could have stressed even more that the quality of each study needs to be judged in the light of the case that eventually is made to warrant acceptance of its claims, and that this assessment needs to be made with an open (but also somewhat skeptical) mind; it could have been even more nuanced in its analysis of educational phenomena, stressing more than it did that education is a normative and policy-oriented field and that this poses severe problems for the researcher; and, although it acknowledged that humans act within a sociocultural matrix, and are impelled by motives, beliefs, values, and the like, there perhaps was not sufficient discussion of the specific methodological issues that arise in the course of research that takes these factors seriously. But these reservations arise with the benefit of hindsight. Overall it can be argued that the report points to a path through the jungle, a path that leads in the direction of a defensible, modest view of rigorous research that—if developed with more nuance, and then widely put into practice—will lead to the restoration of the health of education research, or at least to those branches of it that aspire to be described as "scientific."

Notes

1. For a sample of the diverse readings of, and reactions to, the NRC report, see the special symposia in *Educational Researcher* (2002), *Educational Theory* (2005), *Qualitative Inquiry* (2004), and *Teachers College Record* (2005).
2. A similar concern was expressed in the U.K. about a decade later, in a collection of essays by British researchers. One of the editors remarked that his "major concern is with the evidence of breakdown which is internal to educational research itself" (Dockrell 1980: 12).
3. David Berliner (2002) captures this sentiment pithily with his paper title, "Educational Research: The Hardest Science of All."
4. Arguably, this is what happened when the American Psychological Association (APA) underwent division in the wake of disputes between scientifically oriented researchers and clinicians. In 1998, those committed to what they saw as scientifically oriented psychology split from the APA to found the American Psychological Society (now the Association for Psychological Science).
5. Given current practices, there is a real need to have numerous, easily accessible venues for publishing and presenting papers in order to facilitate dossier building prior to tenure review.
6. A late-seventies NAE report (Suppes 1978) provides numerous past examples of practical contributions; and the What Works Clearinghouse is attempting to collate present-day examples of rigorous experimental and quasi-experimental research that *ought* to influence practice. Retrieved September 15, 2007 (www.W-W-C.org).
7. This is a reference to the fact that many of Pasteur's major theoretical contributions resulted from his pursuit of practical problems, such as why wine or milk spoils.
8. This general point roughly parallels a past controversy over the problem of "bias" in research journals, whereby editors were cast as being seduced by submissions that find a statistically significant result, but tend to ignore the majority of studies that fail to find a significant effect, even though these negative findings might be of great policy relevance and might show the significant findings to be statistical artifacts. See Morrison and Henkel (1970).
9. For a different perspective, see the nuanced account of "softness" in Labaree (1998).
10. See also the excellent critical exposition in Hammersley (1990), especially Chapter 1.
11. See Tiles (1993) for changes in the view of experimentation as intervention in nature.
12. For example, methodological rulebooks do not usually stress the importance of knowing a great deal about the field or problem-space being investigated. Yet the compelling case Darwin made in 1859 depended crucially upon the extraordinary wealth of knowledge of biological details that he built up over many years following the conclusion of his voyage on the *Beagle*.
13. Butterfield (1957:Ch. 3) provides a helpful discussion of Harvey's investigations. Gower (1997: 63–64) discusses Descartes' analysis of the lacunae in Harvey's case—a critique that focused on the functions of the heart and the changes in blood as it circulates.
14. Supporters of "design experiments" in education might cite such work as examples of this kind of intermingling of processes. See the symposium in *Educational Researcher* (January 2003).
15. These two views are compared in Phillips (1992). See especially pp. 84–85.
16. Popper referred to this as the formation of a "tentative theory" or hypothesis, which he stressed was an act of creativity about which the *logic* of scientific method necessarily remains mute.
17. Indeed, it is likely that part of Dewey's point in using the expression "warrant for assertion" (or "warranted assertibility") is that a warrant can be withdrawn as circumstances change.
18. This example is developed brilliantly in Hempel (1966: Ch. 2).
19. See Mosteller and Boruch (2002) for a discussion of randomized field trials, including their virtues and the criticisms and politics of their use, written chiefly by advocates.
20. An interesting critical discussion by two philosophers of science of the justifications put forward for randomization touches on some of these caveats. See Howson and Urbach (1989: 146–154).
21. The checklist developed by the What Works Clearinghouse to rate experiments, to its credit, takes this issue into account.
22. Skinner's work serves as a fine cautionary tale. His account of the nature of science—based on early twentieth-century logical positivism—carried a heavy burden; it determined what concepts he allowed to enter into his psychology. See Phillips (1996).
23. For a helpful discussion of the diversity within the field of qualitative methodology, see the essays in Denzin and Lincoln (1998).
24. See Phillips (2000:153–155). See also Miles and Huberman (1994:Ch. 10), where a detailed discussion of means of guarding against such threats proceeds without the term actually being used!
25. For discussions of the details of this argument, see Phillips (2000:Ch. 2) and Phillips and Burbules (2000:Ch. 4).

26 This caveat, of course, reflects Karl Popper's "criterion of demarcation." See Phillips (2000: Ch. 8).
27 Campbell (1978) has argued convincingly that even physics is built upon a foundation of "qualitative knowing."
28 See Phillips (2000:Ch. 2) and Phillips and Burbules (2000:Ch. 4) for more detailed discussion.
29 Positivism and postpositivism are both "modernist" positions, but there is little that unites them except that both have been the object of postmodernist contumely.
30 See Cooper (2003) for a rare, admirably lucid short account.
31 The science wars reached a climax in the "Sokal Affair." Physicist Alan Sokal wrote a spoof account of his field of quantum gravity that he deliberately packed with a nonsensical collocation of postmodernist jargon. The essay was accepted and published by an influential postmodernist journal which took it to be a serious piece of scholarship. This affair and numerous other examples are discussed in Phillips (2000:Ch. 11).
32 Kitcher (2001) makes a philosophically able case that science should be to some degree responsive to input from a democratic polity.
33 See Siegel (2003) for a strong formulation of this flaw in postmodernism.
34 Various attempts to legislate scientific rigor are detailed in Eisenhart and Towne (2003).
35 It should be noted that the present author was a member of the committee whose work resulted in the final 2002 report.
36 Discussions of the structure of a federal research organization also took place but are excluded from the present account.
37 In practice this meant that individual committee members eventually assented to sections that they, personally, might have phrased differently, or slightly more guardedly, or perhaps even more strongly!
38 For a range of reactions, see the symposia referred to in note 1.
39 For the executive summary of these principles, see Shavelson and Towne (2002:2–6). The report's third chapter provides a more extensive presentation.

References

Berliner, David C. 2002. "Educational Research: The Hardest Science of All." *Educational Researcher* 31(8):18–20.
Booth, Wayne G., Gregory G. Colomb, and Joseph M. Williams. 2003. *The Craft of Research*. 2nd ed. Chicago, IL: University of Chicago Press.
Brighouse, Harry. 2000. *Social Justice and School Choice*. Oxford, U.K.: Oxford University Press.
Butterfield, Herbert. 1957. *The Origins of Modern Science*. London: G. Bell and Sons.
Callan, Eamonn. 1997. *Creating Citizens: Political Education and Liberal Democracy*. Oxford, U.K.: Oxford University Press.
Campbell, Donald T. 1978. "Qualitative Knowing in Action Research." Pp. 184–209 in *The Social Contexts of Method*, edited by M. Brenner, P. Marsh, and M. Brenner. London: Croom Helm.
Campbell, Donald T. and Julian C. Stanley. 1963. "Experimental and Quasi-experimental Designs for Research on Teaching." Pp. 171–246 in *Handbook of Research on Teaching*, edited by Nathaniel Gage. Chicago, IL: Rand McNally.
Cook, Thomas D. and Donald T. Campbell. 1979. *Quasi-experimentation: Design and Analysis Issues for Field Settings*. Chicago, IL: Rand McNally.
Cooper, David E. 2003. "Postmodernism." Pp. 206–218 in *A Companion to the Philosophy of Education*, edited by Randall R. Curren. Malden, MA: Blackwell Publishing.
Cronbach, Lee J. 1975. "Beyond the Two Disciplines of Scientific Psychology." *American Psychologist* 30:116–127.
———. 1982. *Designing Evaluations of Educational and Social Programs*. San Francisco, CA: Jossey-Bass.
Cronbach, Lee J. and Associates. 1980. *Toward Reform of Program Evaluation*. San Francisco, CA: Jossey-Bass.
Cronbach, Lee J. and Patrick Suppes (eds.). 1969. *Research for Tomorrow's Schools: Disciplined Inquiry for Education*. New York: Macmillan.
D'Amico, Robert. 1992. "Defending Social Science against the Postmodern Doubt." Pp. 137–155 in *Postmodernism and Social Theory*, edited by Steven Seidman and David Wagner. Cambridge, MA: Basil Blackwell.
Denzin, Norman K. and Yvonna S. Lincoln (eds.). 1998. *The Landscape of Qualitative Research: Theories and Issues*. Thousand Oaks, CA: Sage Publications.

Dewey, John. [1933] 1971. *How We Think*. New ed. Chicago, IL: Henry Regnery.
———. [1938] 1966. *Logic: The Theory of Inquiry*. New York: Holt, Rinehart, and Winston.
———. [1948] 1971. *Reconstruction in Philosophy*. Enlarged ed. Boston, MA: Beacon Press.
Dockrell, William Bryan. 1980. "The Contribution of Research to Knowledge and Practice: Truth—What Is That?". Pp. 11–22 in *Rethinking Educational Research*, edited by William Bryan Dockrell and David Hamilton. London: Hodder and Stoughton.
Educational Researcher. 2002. Theme issue on *Scientific Research in Education*. 31(8):3–29.
Educational Researcher. 2003. Theme issue on *The Role of Design in Educational Research*. 32:3–37.
Educational Theory. 2005. The Education Science Question: A Symposium. 55:235–322.
Eisenhart, Margaret and Lisa Towne. 2003. "Contestation and Change in National Policy on 'Scientifically Based' Education Research." *Educational Researcher* 32(7):31–38.
Flyvbjerg, Bent. 2001. *Making Social Science Matter: Why Social Inquiry Fails and How It Can Succeed Again*. Cambridge, U.K.: Cambridge University Press.
Getzels, Jacob W. 1978. "Paradigm and Practice: On the Impact of Basic Research in Education." Pp. 477–521 in *Impact of Research on Education: Some Case Studies*, edited by Patrick Suppes. Washington, DC: National Academy of Education.
Gower, Barry. 1997. *Scientific Method: An Historical and Philosophical Introduction*. London: Routledge.
Gutmann, Amy. 1987. *Democratic Education*. Princeton, NJ: Princeton University Press.
Hammersley, Martyn. 1990. *Reading Ethnographic Research: A Critical Guide*. New York: Longman Publishing Group.
Hempel, Carl G. 1966. *Philosophy of Natural Science*. Englewood Cliffs, NJ: Prentice-Hall.
Howe, Kenneth R. 2003. *Closing Methodological Divides: Toward Democratic Educational Research*. Dordrecht, NL: Kluwer Academic Publishers.
Howson, Colin and Peter Urbach. 1989. *Scientific Reasoning: The Bayesian Approach*. Peru, IL: Open Court Publishing.
Jackson, Philip and Sara B. Kiesler. 1977. "Fundamental Research and Education." *Educational Researcher* 6(6):13–18.
Kaestle, Carl F. 1993. "The Awful Reputation of Education Research." *Educational Researcher* 22(1):26–31.
Kaplan, Abraham. 1964. *The Conduct of Inquiry: Methodology for Behavioral Science*. San Francisco, CA: Chandler Publishing Company.
Kerlinger, Fred N. 1977. "The Influence of Research on Education Practice." *Educational Researcher* 6(8):5–12.
Kitcher, Philip. 2001. *Science, Truth, and Democracy*. Oxford, U.K.: Oxford University Press.
Kuhn, Thomas S. 1962. *The Structure of Scientific Revolutions*. Chicago, IL: University of Chicago Press.
Labaree, David F. 1998. "Educational Researchers: Living with a Lesser Form of Knowledge." *Educational Researcher* 27(8):4–12.
Lagemann, Ellen Condliffe and Lee S. Shulman (eds.). 1999. *Issues in Education Research: Problems and Possibilities*. San Francisco, CA: Jossey-Bass.
Larrabee, Harold Atkins. 1964. *Reliable Knowledge: Scientific Methods in the Social Studies*. Revised ed. Boston, MA: Houghton Mifflin.
Latour, Bruno and Steve Woolgar. 1986. *Laboratory Life: The Construction of Scientific Facts*. Princeton, NJ: Princeton University Press.
Levinson, Meira. 1999. *The Demands of Liberal Education*. Oxford, U.K.: Oxford University Press.
Lindblom, Charles E. and David K. Cohen. 1979. *Usable Knowledge: Social Science and Social Problem Solving*. New Haven, CT: Yale University Press.
Lyotard, Jean-François. [1979] 1984. *The Postmodern Condition: A Report on Knowledge*. Translated by Geoff Bennington and Brian Massumi. Minneapolis, MN: University of Minnesota Press.
Miles, Matthew B. and A. Michael Huberman, A. M. 1994. *Qualitative Data Analysis: An Expanded Sourcebook*. 2nd ed. Thousand Oaks, CA: Sage Publications.
Mill, John Stuart. [1843] 1874. *A System of Logic*. New York: Harper and Brothers.
Morrison, Denton E. and Ramon E. Henkel. 1970. *The Significance Test Controversy: A Reader*. Piscataway, NJ: Aldine Transaction.
Mosteller, Frederick and Robert F. Boruch (eds.). 2002. *Evidence Matters: Randomized Trials in Education Research*. Washington, DC: Brookings Institution Press.
Motterlini, Matteo. 1999. *For and against Method: Imre Lakatos and Paul Feyerabend*. Chicago, IL: University of Chicago Press.
Nagel, Thomas. 1986. *The View from Nowhere*. Oxford, U.K.: Oxford University Press.
Peirce, Charles Sanders. 1982. "The Fixation of Belief." Pp. 61–78 in *Pragmatism: The Classic Writings*, edited by H. Standish Thayer. Indianapolis, IN: Hackett.

Phillips, D. C. 1992. *The Social Scientist's Bestiary: A Guide to Fabled Threats to, and Defenses of, Naturalistic Social Science.* Oxford, U.K.: Pergamon Press.
———. 1996. "Philosophical Perspectives." Pp. 1005–1019 in *Handbook of Educational Psychology,* edited by David C. Berliner and Robert C. Calfee. New York: Macmillan Reference Books.
———. 2000. *The Expanded Social Scientist's Bestiary: A Guide to Fabled Threats to, and Defenses of, Naturalistic Social Science.* Lanham, MD: Rowman and Littlefield.
———. 2007. "Adding Complexity: Philosophical Perspectives on the Relationship between Evidence and Policy." Pp. 374–402 in *Evidence and Decision Making.* 106th yearbook of the NSSE, edited by Pamela A. Moss. Malden, MA: Blackwell Publishing.
Phillips, D. C. and Nicholas Burbules. 2000. *Postpositivism and Educational Research.* Lanham, MD: Rowman and Littlefield.
Qualitative Inquiry. 2004. "Symposium on Scientific Education Research." 10:5–129.
Reich, Robert. 2002. *Bridging Liberalism and Multiculturalism in American Education.* Chicago, IL: University of Chicago Press..
Scriven, Michael. 1974. "Maximizing the Power of Causal Investigations: The Modus Operandi Method." Pp. 68–84 in *Evaluation in Education: Current Applications,* edited by W. James Popham. Berkeley, CA: McCutchan Publishing.
Shavelson, Richard J. and Lisa Towne (eds.). 2002. *Scientific Research in Education.* Committee on Scientific Principles for Educational Research, National Research Council. Washington, DC: National Academy Press.
Siegel, Harvey. 2003. "Cultivating Reason." Pp. 305–319 in *A Companion to the Philosophy of Education,* edited by Randall R. Curren. Malden, MA: Blackwell Publishing.
Stokes, Donald E. 1997. *Pasteur's Quadrant: Basic Science and Technological Innovation.* Washington, DC: Brookings Institution Press.
St. Pierre, Elizabeth Adams. 2002. "'Science' Rejects Postmodernism." *Educational Researcher,* 31(8):25–27.
Suppes, Patrick (ed.). 1978. *Impact of Research on Education: Some Case Studies.* Washington, DC: National Academy of Education.
Teachers College Record. 2005. "A Symposium on the Implications of the Scientific Research in Education Report for Qualitative Inquiry." 107:1–58.
Tiles, James E. 1993. "Experiment as Intervention." *British Journal for the Philosophy of Science* 44:463–475.
Tyler, Ralph W. 1965. "The Field of Educational Research." Pp. 1–12 in *The Training and Nurture of Educational Researchers,* edited by Egon C. Guba and Stanley Elam. Bloomington, IN: Phi Delta Kappa.

CHAPTER 8

Education Research That Matters: Influence, Scientific Rigor, and Policymaking

PAMELA BARNHOUSE WALTERS AND ANNETTE LAREAU

Vociferous criticism of education research as "shoddy," "not scientific," and "low quality" has prompted a debate.[1] Some have rushed to repair the field of education research[2] and others have rushed to defend it. For both sides, the primary focus has been whether critics are right when they charge that education research is not of sufficiently high quality. Lost in this dispute is the opportunity to move the field of education research forward by building on the strengths of the past. We suggest that taking up the question of what the field has done well is a useful complement to the debate over what it has (or has not) done poorly.

Thus in this chapter we look backward in order to look forward. We ask broad questions: What have been the main advances in educational theory and research? Which studies have been widely honored and recognized as being influential? To be clear, this line of questioning speaks explicitly to only one of the two main criticisms that critics have leveled against the field in recent years—that it fails to meet commonly accepted standards for the conduct of good science. The second main criticism—that the education research community has hindered policymaking by failing to provide the research findings policymakers need to make good decisions—is a separate matter. We will turn to it after addressing the question of the studies that have done the most to move the research field forward.

As we will explain in more detail below, it is possible to identify a set of studies that are widely viewed as highly influential, and that have had a lasting impact. And it is also possible to identify a group of researchers whose work is considered exemplary. There is wide consensus, for instance, that Albert Bandura's (1977a, 1977b, 1986, 1997, 2001) work on self-efficacy and social cognition, Carol Gilligan's (1982) findings concerning gender differences in moral development, James Coleman's (1964, 1966, 1990) studies of school effects, Lee Shulman's (1998, 1999, 2004) models of teacher education, Shirley Brice Heath's (1983) research on cultural differences in language and learning, John Dewey's (1916, 1938, 1959) theories of active learning, and Benjamin Bloom's (1956, 1976) taxonomy of cognitive skills are responsible for significant advances in the field of education research.[3] However, as we will also show, these highly influential studies (and others like them) generally have had a limited *direct* impact on policy development, particularly at the federal level. Nonetheless, we find that what Sheri Ranis (in Chapter 5) terms the low-utility charge is overstated: Some studies held in high regard by the research community have shaped policy development, albeit in fairly diffuse ways that have gone relatively unrecognized in the current attempts to "rehabilitate" education research. Some of Coleman's research, for example, changed the very terms of public discussion about what is wrong with schools and how best to fix them.

Our analysis reveals that the studies held in high regard by education policy experts include few random-assignment experiments. The lauded studies are empirically rigorous but, in general, are more broadly focused and theoretically informed than those that conform to contemporary standards of "scientific rigor." Studies that use the random-assignment model currently being promoted for education research in order to identify effective treatments and interventions typically address narrowly-framed questions of "what works" in education. The two random-assignment experiments most widely considered to have significantly shaped educational policy, the Tennessee class-size experiment (Word et al. 1990) and the evaluation of the Perry Preschool Project (Weikart, Bond, and McNeil 1978), were large-scale organizational transformations, not narrowly focused treatments; and the research on their effects shed light on complex educational questions and processes.

From the perspective of many critics of the field of education research, the whole point of the efforts to rehabilitate it is to put education policy and practice on a firm scientific footing—that is, to make the vast system of schooling in the United States into an "evidence-based field." Thus we conclude the chapter by considering whether this is a reasonable assumption: We review what research on policy development has to say about the typical conditions under which research findings influence policymakers' decisions. We find the model of policy development that implicitly informs recent attempts to turn education into an evidence-based field is based on an assumption that decisions are made primarily on politically neutral grounds; that policymakers reach rational decisions about policy and practice after carefully weighing available technical information about what works and does not work in education. This rational-technical, and thus neutral, model is, we show, simplistic. Most notably, it fails to account for the fundamentally *political* nature of policy development.

Highly Influential Research

One problem with identifying the most influential studies and scholars within the field of education research is that the field is large and diverse. The research that has been most influential in, say, educational psychology will likely not be the same as the research that has been most influential in, say, educational leadership and administration. But the most significant research, we contend, has an influence that *transcends* subfields. Thus we focus on those studies and lines of inquiry that have helped set the research agenda in multiple subfields, and whose questions and findings it is reasonable to expect are familiar to most scholars across the field as a whole.[4]

To minimize the biases likely to characterize personal assessments, we base our discussion on two different and complementary institutionalized systems for assessing educational researchers' impact on the discipline. First, we consulted citation indices—counts of numbers of times an individual study or an individual scholar is listed in bibliographies in articles published in a set of journals—to identify the most frequently cited studies and scholars. Citation analysis has limitations, including potential bias and incompleteness of data sources, an over-reliance on journals rather than books, and the fact that a citation is an imperfect measure of influence (because, for example, the counts do not distinguish between a study cited positively versus negatively). Nonetheless, it is the most common method in academia for gauging the influence of individual studies and lines of research, and it is a useful way to take stock of a field as a whole.

Second, we consulted the list of recipients of prizes for outstanding scholarship awarded by the leading scholarly association in the field, the American Educational Research Association (AERA). Since 1964 the AERA has given an annual award for Distinguished Contributions to Research in Education. This award is given to those who exemplify "educational research at its best." After considering the works that have been highly cited by researchers in the field and identified as exemplars by the field's leading scholarly association, we reflect on the elements they share, before turning to the separate question of what research has to date had the greatest influence on educational policy and practice.

Citation Analysis

In 2003 the National Academy of Education–Social Science Research Council (NAE-SSRC) committee on education research[5] contracted with Thomson Scientific (formerly the Institute for Scientific Information) to analyze citation patterns in education journals. As Barbara Schneider notes (in Chapter 3), Thomson Scientific's citations database is the one most commonly used to identify influential journals, studies, and researchers in a wide range of scholarly fields. We drew on this database to identify the major journals in the field of education (a set of 129), and examined the period 1981 to 2002. During that period those 129 journals contained 125,658 distinct source articles. Those articles, in turn, contained citations to over one million works (including many that had been published prior to 1981). The questions we explore here are which of these one million-plus items were cited most frequently, and which scholars were most frequently cited in the source articles.

Table 8.1 lists the titles and authors of the 14 individual pieces of scholarship—books, reports, and journal articles—that were most frequently cited. The first thing we note about these pieces is that few are examples of "research" as that term is generally understood within scientific fields—that is,

TABLE 8.1 Publications most frequently cited in source articles in 129 education journals, 1981–2002

Frequency of citation	Study
786	Wechsler, David. 1974. *Wechsler Intelligence Scale for Children – Revised.* New York: Psychological Corporation.
612	Glaser, Barney G. and Anselm L. Strauss. 1967. *The Discovery of Grounded Theory: Strategies for Qualitative Research.* Chicago: Aldine Publishing Company.
576	Lincoln, Yvonne S. and Egon G. Guba. 1985. *Naturalistic Inquiry.* Newbury Park, CA: Sage.
565	Cole, Michael, Vera John-Steiner, Sylvia Scribner, and Ellen Souberman (eds.). *L. S. Vygotsky, Mind in Society: The Development of Higher Processes.* 1978. Cambridge, MA: Harvard University Press.
518	Schön, Donald A. 1983. *The Reflective Practitioner: How Professionals Think in Action.* London: Temple Smith.
517	National Commission on Excellence in Education. 1983. *A Nation at Risk: The Imperative for Educational Reform.* Washington, DC: The Commission.
515	Gilligan, Carol. 1982. *In a Different Voice: Psychological Theory and Women's Development.* Cambridge, MA: Harvard University Press.
504	National Council of Teachers of Mathematics. 1989. *Curriculum and Evaluation Standards for School Mathematics.* Reston, VA: National Council of Teachers of Mathematics.
490	Heath, Shirley Brice. 1983. *Ways with Words: Language, Life and Work in Communities and Classrooms.* New York: Cambridge University Press.
485	Bandura, Albert. 1977. "Self-Efficacy: Toward a Unifying Theory of Behavioral Change." *Psychological Review* 84:191–215.
473	Kuhn, Thomas. 1970. *The Structure of Scientific Revolutions*, 2nd edition. Chicago: University of Chicago Press.
473	Palincsar, Annemarie S. and A. L. Brown. 1984. "Reciprocal Teaching of Comprehension-Fostering and Comprehension-Monitoring Activities." *Cognition and Instruction* 1:117–175.
469	American Psychiatric Association. 1994. *Diagnostic and Statistical Manual of Mental Disorders.* Arlington, VA: American Psychiatric Publishing.
445	Bowles, Samuel and Herbert Gintis. 1976. *Schooling in Capitalist America.* New York: Basic.

analyses and interpretations of original empirical findings from a particular study or a series of related studies. Two (*A Nation at Risk* and *Curriculum and Evaluation Standards for School Mathematics*) are committee or commission reports. Each draws in part on results of prior research as a basis for formulating recommendations for new directions in educational policy, but neither is itself a research study. Five of the most frequently cited pieces are philosophical or theoretical essays by scholars whose main focus was not education or schooling per se but whose ideas are often applied to questions about educational theory, research, or practice: L. S. Vygotskii on language and cognition, Donald Schön on professional learning, Carol Gilligan on moral development, Albert Bandura on self-efficacy, and Thomas Kuhn on the philosophy of science. Two (*Wechsler Intelligence Scale for Children* and *Diagnostic and Statistical Manual of Mental Disorders*) are handbooks related to tests, measurement, and assessment, reflecting the importance of diagnosis and testing for the educational enterprise. Two (*The Discovery of Grounded Theory* and *Naturalistic Inquiry*) are methodological guides that, significantly, focus on the conduct of qualitative research, perhaps reflecting the qualitative turn the field of education research took in the 1970s and 1980s (see Chapter 1).

Only three of the 14 pieces are studies based primarily on original empirical research: Shirley Brice Heath's (1983) ethnographic study of language use in two southern communities; an article reporting a pair of studies by Annemarie Palincsar and A. L. Brown on instruction of school-age children (Palincsar and Brown 1984); and Samuel Bowles and Herbert Gintis' (1976) historical study of the development of public education in the U.S. Apart from the commission/committee reports discussed above, these are the only frequently cited pieces in which the primary focus is education or schooling.

We turn next to individual authors. Table 8.2 lists the authors who were most frequently cited in the same source articles examined above. When we exclude the two organizations on the list (the American Psychological Association and the U.S. Department of Education), we are left with 11 highly-cited individuals. The strong tie between the field of education research and the discipline of psychology is evident here: all but one (French anthropologist/sociologist Pierre Bourdieu) of the 11 individuals is or was a psychologist or educational psychologist. Further, research on and theoretical expositions about cognitive development, intelligence, and teaching and learning are the main preoccupations of the vast majority of scholars in this influential group. This might seem to be in line with current calls to make education research more useful for improving learning and instruction, but these authors' primary focus is not assessment of the efficacy of new instructional approaches or interventions. Rather, they are chiefly interested in better understanding *how* children learn. This type of work may indeed have important implications for educational policy and practice, but not in the tightly-linked way envisioned by those who call for more rigorous research on "what works" in schools and classrooms.

TABLE 8.2 Authors most cited in source articles in 129 education journals, 1981–2002

Frequency of citation	Author/discipline/major contribution
3,816	Jean Piaget (psychologist; theoretical work on the stages of cognitive development in young children)
3,388	Albert Bandura (psychologist; social cognitive theory and self-efficacy)
2,847	John Dewey (philosopher, psychologist, and Progressive-era educational reformer; theoretical work on democracy and education)
2,481	Herbert W. Marsh (educational psychologist; research on self-concept and motivation)
2,239	David Wechsler (psychologist; developed Wechsler Intelligence Scale for Children)
2,157	American Psychological Association
1,984	Ann Leslie Brown (educational psychologist; conducted research on children's learning and proposed new teaching methods)
1,939	Jacob Cohen (statistician and psychologist; work on statistical power and meta-analysis)
1,910	Keith E. Stanovich (psychologist and cognitive scientist; research on reading)
1,710	Michael Pressley (educational psychologist; research on teaching and learning and development of models for effective teaching)
1,614	Pierre Bourdieu (anthropologist/sociologist; empirical and theoretical work on social class and cultural capital)
1,554	Robert J. Sternberg (psychologist and psychometrician; theories of intelligence and cognitive styles)
1,520	U.S. Department of Education

One thing these citation analyses highlight, then, is the high degree to which scholars of education draw on the theoretical and methodological contributions of other fields. Clearly, the dominance of psychology in the field of education research was not shaken by the "paradigm wars" that racked the field in the 1970s and 1980s. Our analyses also show that the bodies of work and the individual publications to which scholars of education most commonly turn are broad works of fairly general theoretical significance. In that respect, our findings are in line with the point frequently made by recent critics of the field of education research: Education scholars favor work of abstract theoretical significance over work of immediate practical significance. Some see this as a key reason why education research has little influence on policy. Others, however, argue that we cannot develop policies and practices that "work" without developing a theoretical understanding of the processes that produce the desired outcomes.

AERA Awards

Since 1964 the American Educational Research Association has made an annual award to a scholar who has made distinguished contributions to research in education. This award is for a scholar's body of work, not an individual piece of scholarship, and is intended to honor the field's exemplary researchers. Table 8.3 provides a list of the recipients, along with their major areas of research.

One thing that sets the individuals listed in Table 8.3 apart from the most frequently cited authors listed in Table 8.2 is that the bulk of the awardees' contributions were based on empirical research rather than the development of new theories. Many, but not most, of those who received the distinguished research contribution award focused on the technical core of education and schooling, as did virtually all of the most-cited authors: They posed questions about intellectual development, language development or use, learning, and instruction. Another large group of award recipients made their major contributions in the methodological subfields of statistics, measurement, testing, or research methods. Also well represented are those who focused on the organizational, rather than the technical/instructional, side of schooling, particularly on questions about school reform and the organization of teaching. Compared to the authors of the most highly-cited articles and the most highly-cited authors themselves, this group of scholars is more strongly rooted in the field of education. Only 15 of the 44 award recipients did not hold at least a partial appointment in a department, college, or school of education. Those with disciplinary affiliations other than professional schools of education were drawn overwhelmingly from psychology.

With respect to the current debates about the appropriateness of randomized controlled trials for education research, it is noteworthy that the scientists who have done the most to promote experimental research in education are past recipients of the AERA distinguished contributions award. In 1980 and 1981, awards were bestowed on Julian C. Stanley and Donald T. Campbell, respectively, the joint authors of the highly influential volume *Experimental and Quasi-experimental Designs for Research* (Campbell and Stanley 1963). No scholar who is primarily known for *conducting* random-assignment evaluation studies in education or other kinds of assessments of the efficacy of particular educational programs or interventions, however, has been honored with the AERA award. As we saw with the most frequently cited studies and most frequently cited authors, those who have received the AERA award for distinguished research contributions have asked quite broad questions about complex educational processes and outcomes.

In sum, one striking characteristic of the most important and influential studies is that, despite their considerable diversity, they have in common the defining nature of their research question. Generally, these studies' authors have not asked narrow technical questions disconnected from current intellectual debates. Instead, they have answered the "so what?" question, rooting their specific research concern in broader intellectual concerns. At times, they have framed a "big picture" question that zeroed in on a core issue. For example, Coleman's research explored questions about the relative significance of families

TABLE 8.3 American Educational Research Association (AERA) recipients of Distinguished Contributions to Research in Education Award

Year	Recipient
2007	Milbrey Wallin McLaughlin: school and instructional reform; teachers' work
2006	Stephen W. Raudenbush: measurement and statistics; analysis of student learning
2005	Gene V. Glass: meta-analysis
2004	Lorrie A. Shepard: psychometrics and testing
2003	Anthony S. Bryk: statistics and methods; school improvement and reform
2002	*Shirley Brice Heath (English):* language; learning; culture
2001	Robert LeVine: culture and child development
2000	Edmund Gordon: minority achievement
1999	David K. Cohen: teaching; school effects; school reform; research and policy
1998	*John Ogbu (anthropology):* minority identity and educational achievement
1997	Robert Linn: educational assessment and accountability
1996	David C. Berliner: educational psychology; teacher education; educational policy
1995	Maxine Greene: philosophy of education
1994	Richard C. Anderson: educational psychology; reading; vocabulary; thinking
1993	John I. Goodlad: educational reform; educational change; teacher education
1992	David Tyack: history of education
1991	Ann L. Brown: educational psychology; learning and instruction
1990	*Lauren Resnick (psychology):* educational psychology, cognitive science, learning, instruction
1989	Lee S. Shulman: educational psychology; teaching and teacher education
1988	N. L. Gage: educational psychology; teaching
1987	*Michael Cole (communications, psychology):* cultural psychology; children's intellectual and social development
1986	Courtney B. Cazden: language; development of oral and written abilities
1985	*Jerome S. Bruner (law, psychology):* cognitive learning theory
1984	*Eleanor Maccoby (psychology):* sex differences
1983	*Anne Anastasi (psychology):* intelligence theory; psychometrics; testing
1982	Jeanne S. Chall: reading; literacy; instruction
1981	*Donald T. Campbell (psychology):* experimental design
1980	*Julian C. Stanley (psychology):* psychometrics; experimental design; education of the gifted
1979	John Bissell Carroll: linguistics; psychometrics
1978	*B. F. Skinner (psychology):* behaviorism; operant conditioning – named most influential psychologist of 20th century
1977	Lee J. Cronbach: educational psychology; testing; measurement
1976	*Robert Glaser (psychology):* learning; instruction
1975	*Urie Bronfenbrenner (psychology):* human development; child development; early childhood education
1974	*James S. Coleman (sociology):* sociology of education; public policy; social capital
1973	Robert J. Havighurst: human development and education
1972	Robert M. Gagne: educational psychology; learning; instruction

TABLE 8.3 Continued

Year	Recipient
1971	*Patrick Suppes (philosophy):* educational technology
1970	Benjamin S. Bloom: educational psychology; mastery learning; talent development
1969	Lawrence A. Cremin: educational history
1968	*Jean Piaget (psychology):* developmental theorist; child development and cognitive development; and Barbel Inhelder: school psychology (collaborator of Piaget's)
1967	E. F. Lindquist: educational testing, measurement; psychometrics
1966	T. R. McConnell: higher education; college student development
1965	Ralph W. Tyler: education and evaluation; curriculum development
1964	Arthur I. Gates: educational psychology; teaching of reading

Source: Award listing on the American Educational Research Association website. Retrieved May 15, 2008 from http://www.aera.net/AboutAERA/Default.asdpx?menu_id=20&id=226. Additional information gathered from multiple sources and listings of published works.

Note: Those whose names are listed in italics held an academic appointment in a unit other than a department or college of education; the discipline is listed.

and schools in shaping educational achievement. Bandura's work offered an important corrective to existing psychological research by showing social-psychological dimensions previously underexamined. These are topics widely recognized as important. In other instances, researchers began with a relatively small issue, which they then used as a springboard to address a question of interest to a broader group. But regardless of their chosen approach, all of the AERA awardees made a connection between their own study and broader theoretical debates. They offered a critique of existing literature or they challenged educational researchers to think differently about an issue. They modified, challenged, or advanced the literature. They focused their question so that it was clear what they were studying and what they were not studying rather than blurring foreground with background. They did not try to study everything. Instead, they all sought to rethink one or more of the field's existing conceptual ideas. We believe that the way in which researchers frame a question and influence the course of future research is an important policy impact, and one that today often goes unaddressed. We return to this point at the end of the chapter.

Research That Has Influenced Policy

Many have complained about the limited value of education research for educational policy and practice. In this section we look at what education research has done right—that is, at studies that have been identified as having had a positive influence on educational policy and practice. To do so, we take advantage of two prior stocktaking enterprises. The first is a recent survey of policy experts. The second is a series of essays by key leaders in the field of education research, commissioned by the Spencer Foundation in 2006. As with our citations analyses, we focus on exemplars, their shared traits, and the degree to which they conform to the models of "scientific rigor" presently being promoted for education research.

In 2006 the Editorial Projects in Education (EPE) Research Center,[6] with funding from the Thomas B. Fordham Foundation, conducted a survey of experts in education research and education policy in order to identify the research studies that had had the greatest influence on educational policy during the prior decade (see Swanson and Barlage 2006). The investigators identified persons considered experts in education policy and then selected 888 individuals from this group to participate in the first phase of the survey, which asked respondents to nominate those "studies, organizations, people, and information sources that have most strongly influenced educational policy during the past decade" (Swanson and Barlage 2006:3). The response rate was somewhat low (12%), but in line with the typical response rate for surveys of experts. In a follow-up survey of 834 individuals, respondents were asked to rate the leading nominees that emerged in each category from the open-ended survey. The response rate for the rating survey was higher (21%). The expert ratings were supplemented by an analysis of citations in leading news sources (based on Lexis-Nexis) and in scholarly journals (based on EBSCO's Academic Search Premier data system).

Here, we focus on the 13 studies that emerged from the EPE Research Center's survey as having most influenced education policy in the last decade. (See Table 8.4, pp. 208–209) From our perspective, the most striking thing about this list is that it, like our list of the studies most cited in articles in major education journals (see Table 8.1), contains so few research studies. The two most influential studies—the National Assessment of Educational Progress (NAEP) and the Trends in International Mathematics and Science Study (TIMSS)—are not scholarly publications by any definition. They are datasets that provide baseline information on educational achievement. The achievement benchmarks revealed by these regularly collected data are widely reported in the news media and have provided the basis for a huge number of separate publications. Their most significant contribution to education policy is, in our view, that the baseline indicators of educational achievement they establish have been taken to indicate that American students' achievement levels are lagging. The anxiety generated by this interpretation of the benchmark data has contributed significantly to the turn in American education policy discussions toward a focus on poor performance of American education and worrisome achievement gaps between and among student groups. In other words, the greatest significance of the NAEP and TIMSS publications lies in naming an educational problem that begs for remediation, rather than in identifying effective remedies.

A number of the publications listed in Table 8.4 are not single studies but instead are lines of research by a single investigator or organization on a single topic; some are syntheses of research in a given area, published by multiple investigators or by investigating organizations. *Teaching Children to Read*, the National Reading Panel's synthesis of prior experimental and quasi-experimental research on reading, is a prominent example. Perceptions among policymakers that existing experimental research on reading had settled long-contentious issues regarding the best instructional practices for reading were an especially important catalyst for policymakers' calls to the education research community to more strongly embrace random-assignment experiments.

The only classic individual empirical study on the list of work viewed as significantly influencing education policy over the past decade is the Tennessee Student/Teacher Achievement Ratio (STAR) experiment. STAR was a large-scale random-assignment experiment on the effect on student achievement of smaller class sizes. The experts in education policy whose opinions are reflected in this assessment cited the experiment itself rather than any one of the multiple scholarly publications that analyzed or reported its findings. The results of the STAR study have clearly influenced educational policymaking. For example, the findings spurred various initiatives to reduce class size (not all of which have been successful, a problem that raises issues about scaling up the results of relatively small-scale random-assignment studies). The study's results also have clearly influenced the debates about the need for educational researchers to more broadly adopt random-assignment experimental methods. That is, STAR is widely touted as an exemplar of "rigorous" research that informs education policy and practice.

The under-representation of experimental studies on the list is telling. Besides the STAR experiment, only two other of the 13 highly influential publications have a strong experimental component. All of the studies reviewed in the National Reading Panel report are experimental or quasi-experimental; and some of the studies done by Peterson on vouchers and school choice use random assignment. Both have figured prominently in the often-contentious debates about whether educational researchers should more fully embrace random-assignment experimental methods. But their significance lies mostly in being examples of random-assignment experiments to which advocates of such methods can point, rather than being strong guides to new forms of educational policy or practice. Indeed, educational practitioners remain strongly divided over the best methods for teaching reading, and although the voucher studies have undoubtedly influenced education policy, they have done so in a way that departs from the model of scientific influence on which efforts to transform education into an evidence-based field are founded. First, the soundness of the results most widely reported from Peterson's voucher research remains hotly debated among scholars.[7] Second, there is little evidence that the findings of these studies have swayed policymakers' opinions about whether vouchers (or other forms of school choice) should be more widely

TABLE 8.4 Studies that most influenced education policy

Most influential overall	Most highly ranked by experts	Most highly cited in news sources	Most highly cited in scholarly journals
NAEP[1]	NAEP[1]	NAEP[1]	NAEP[1]
TIMSS[2]	TIMSS[2]	TIMSS[2]	TIMSS[2]
Teaching Children to Read[3]	Teaching Children to Read[3]	STAR[4]	Teaching Children to Read[3]
STAR[4]	STAR[4]	Teacher quality[7]	How People Learn[9]
Preventing Reading Difficulties[5]	Sanders, value added[6]	Peterson, vouchers[13]	Preventing Reading Difficulties[5]
Sanders, value added[6]	Teacher quality[7]	Greene, graduation[11]	Elmore, school reform[10]
Teacher quality[7]	What Matters Most[8]	Teaching Children to Read[3]	What Matters Most[8]
What Matters Most[8]	Preventing Reading Difficulties[5]	What Matters Most[8]	Peterson, vouchers[13]
How People Learn[9]	How People Learn[9]	Sanders, value added[6]	STAR[4]
Elmore, school reform[10]	High School Diploma[12]	Preventing Reading Difficulties[5]	Teacher quality[7]
Greene, graduation[11]	Elmore, school reform[10]	High School Diploma[12]	Sanders, value-added[6]
High School Diploma[12]	Greene, graduation[11]	Elmore, school reform[10]	Greene, graduation[11]
Peterson, vouchers[13]	Peterson, vouchers[13]	How People Learn[9]	High School Diploma[12]

1. National Center for Education Statistics. Various years. *National Assessment of Educational Progress: The Nation's Report Card*. U.S. Department of Education. A large-scale American data set collected at regular intervals.
2. National Center for Education Statistics. Various years. *Trends in International Mathematics and Science Study* (TIMSS). U.S. Department of Education, organized by the International Association for the Evaluation of Educational Achievement. A large-scale cross-national data set collected at regular intervals.
3. National Institute of Child Health and Human Development. 2000. *Report of the National Reading Panel. Teaching Children to Read: An Evidence-Based Assessment of the Scientific Research Literature on Reading and Its Implications for Reading Instruction* (NIH Publication No. 00-4769). Washington, DC: U.S. Government Printing Office. An identification of findings of prior research on reading that utilized experimental or quasi-experimental designs.
4. Tennessee Student/Teacher Achievement Ratio (STAR) experiment. A large-scale random-assignment experiment, the results of which have been widely analyzed by education scholars. See Swanson and Barlage (2006:39) for selected list of specific studies.

TABLE 8.4 Continued

5. Snow, Catherine E., M. Susan Burns, and Peg Griffin (eds.). 1998. *Preventing Reading Difficulties in Young Children*. Washington, DC: National Academy Press. A report on factors related to normal reading development, based on an extensive review of prior research.
6. William L. Sanders on value-added methodology and the Tennessee Value-Added Accountability System. A series of articles that introduces a new method for measuring student academic progress. See Swanson and Barlage (2006:41) for selected list of specific studies.
7. Education Trust on teacher quality. A series of reports on the issue of impact of good teachers on student achievement, based on evidence from prior research. See Swanson and Barlage (2006:42) for selected list of specific studies.
8. National Commission on Teaching and America's Future. 1996. *What Matters Most: Teaching for America's Future*. New York: National Commission on Teaching and America's Future. This report argues that teacher quality is the key to improving American education, and lays out a plan for providing every American student with high-quality teachers.
9. Bransford, John D., Ann L. Brown, and Rodney R. Cocking (eds.). 1999. *How People Learn: Brain, Mind, Experience, and School*. Washington, DC: National Academies Press. A report that synthesizes research evidence from a variety of scholarly fields on learning processes.
10. Richard F. Elmore on school reform. A series of studies evaluating the process of school reform. See Swanson and Barlage (2006:45) for selected list of specific studies.
11. Jay P. Greene on high-school graduation rates. A series of studies that use a new method for calculating high-school graduation rates and indicate that graduation rates are generally lower than the most commonly-reported statistical methods show. See Swanson and Barlage (2006:46) for selected list of specific studies.
12. American Diploma Project *Ready or Not: Creating a High School Diploma That Counts*. 2004. Retrieved May 14, 2008 (http://www.achieve.org/files/ADPreport_7.pdf). A forward-looking report that proposes new high-school graduation requirements.
13. Paul E. Peterson on school choice and vouchers. A series of studies, some of which are random-assignment experiments, on academic gains on the part of students in school choice and voucher programs. See Swanson and Barlage (2006:48) for selected list of specific studies.

Source: Compiled from Swanson and Barlage (2006, Exhibit 4 (p. 14) and Exhibit 3 (p. 12)).

implemented. The major impact of research studies on policymaking appears to be to legitimate existing policy preferences. As Susan H. Fuhrman (2001) said, "Research is often used to justify political positions already taken rather than to set a new direction for policy." It does not appear to have frequently led policymakers to abandon old policy preferences and embrace radically different ones, although it often serves to entrench or ratify preexisting preferences. And it does not necessarily have to have passed standard scientific muster to do so. We return to this point later in a discussion of the fundamentally political nature of policymaking.

The Spencer Foundation Essays

In 2006 the Spencer Foundation, a non-profit education research foundation, asked a group of prominent education scholars to take stock of the impact of education research on policy and practice. Each scholar was asked to provide "five examples of research . . . that have had an impact on practice and/or policy; a brief description of the impact (your interpretation) and why you think it had influence; [and] views on how you believe the influence evolved—further research by others in the academy, discussion and debate in the policy circles, use by practitioners."[8] Fifteen individuals provided essays in response.[9] Briefly, these essays provide a sense of the churning nature of debates about the relationship between education research and policy and practice. The essays by Amy Gutmann, Richard Rothstein, and Patricia Wasley highlight research showing that early intervention in children's lives is highly consequential for later outcomes, a point buttressed by the findings from an exemplar of random-assignment experimental research, the evaluation of the Perry Preschool Project.[10] Those findings have supported funding decisions in preschool and various early-intervention programs. Other scholars (Mike Rose, in particular, but see also the essays by Anne Haas Dyson, James Paul Gee, and Patricia Wasley) point to research on reading which had an impact on instruction, particularly the lively policy debate about whole language compared to phonetics. Susan Moore Johnson (along with Rothstein and others) discusses the Tennessee class-size "STAR" study, but this is a rare example of randomized experiments among the works cited by the essayists. Johnson notes that the STAR study affirmed established findings from other research: "For decades, teachers have reported in surveys and interview studies that smaller classes (15–20 students) enable them to meet the varied needs of their students and to provide more attention and response to their work. However, it wasn't until the STAR study in the late 1980s that the importance of class size was confirmed in a large-scale randomized experiment." Johnson goes on to note that although "subsequent reductions in K-3 classes in California in 1996 were correlated with improved student performance," the policy's unintended consequences—it created a teacher shortage and prompted the hiring of many unlicensed teachers—were significant.[11]

Maureen Hallinan views the research on ability grouping and tracking as having "focused attention on ways in which institutional and organization inequities exist in schools and how they can be eliminated." She suggests some educators responded by eliminating these practices, while others "implemented reforms to reduce or eliminate the inequitable aspects . . . of grouping by ability." Charles Payne concludes that the research on the negative consequences of retention "took most of the steam out of what seemed a few years earlier like a national movement around the ending of social promotion. They were methodologically sophisticated studies, on an issue that ordinary people know about and understand, [and] were well covered by the press and were timely." Thus a "national movement" to insist that children repeat a grade until they had achieved the requisite skills dissolved in light of evidence that showed long-term hardships for youth, particularly in the form of high levels of high-school dropout rates. Promotion to a next grade, regardless of the level of academic performance, is currently the norm. In short, the essays not only make clear that a number of important education studies have had an impact, but also show how and why they have made a difference to policy and practice.[12]

In sum, institutionalized rankings reveal that there are studies of "iconic" status that are widely seen as influential. As we have noted, educational experts have also documented studies that they believe have had an impact on public policy. Yet it is striking that, with a few notable exceptions, there is relatively little overlap between works cited as influential education research studies and studies that have had an impact on educational policy. We believe that this lack of overlap is linked to the differing characteristics of these two categories of studies. Table 8.5 summarizes the differences. Particularly striking is the difference in framing and theoretical significance of studies in each realm.[13] As we have noted, widely influential education research studies often ask theoretically important questions. They also often change the terms of the intellectual debate by asking questions that have not previously been posed. By contrast, the studies seen as having influenced policy tend to have a much narrower framework. Many assess the impact of an educational program.[14] It is very unlikely that the studies that have been seen as influencing policy would be hailed as award-winning studies that have advanced the profession. This distinction between the characteristics of studies that influence education research and those that influence policy generally has been ignored, however. The failure to recognize this distinction is unfortunate since it leads to unrealistic expectations for the role of research.

TABLE 8.5 What research has made a difference?

Widely-read education research that has had an impact on future research	Education research that has had an impact on policy
Broad: Asks "big picture" questions	Often very focused and narrow
Theoretically informed	Often atheoretical
Timing often dictated by theoretical developments in scholarly field	Timed to mesh with a new policy interest
Often disconnected from a political agenda	Consistent with the political agenda of existing interest groups
Widely seen as high quality	Sometimes seen as high quality and sometimes not
Example: Coleman report Bandura on social cognition	Example: Tennessee class-size study Peterson's studies of vouchers

Can Good Research Make Education an Evidence-Based Field?

The overarching goal of current attempts to transform education into an evidence-based field through greater use of randomized controlled trials is to identify "what works" in education. A key problem with this goal is that it presumes that improvements along these lines in the quality of education research will lead, ipso facto, to an improvement in the quality of educational policy. Although not fully articulated, the assumption seems to be that the main impediment to making well-informed decisions about educational policy and practice is the shortage of good research findings on which to base those decisions. Ironically, this assumption is at odds with a large body of research on the policy development process that shows that evidence, information, data, and the like play a very small role in policy development, except under highly unusual conditions. Policymaking is fundamentally a *political* process, shaped largely by basic political factors (Kelman 1988; Kingdon 2002; McDonnell 2007; Stone 2001), and the subfield of educational policymaking is no exception.

As summarized by Lorraine McDonnell (2007), the research shows that policy development in the U.S. is shaped by three broad categories of factors. The first is the structural relationship among political institutions. With respect to public education, the fragmented nature of governance of and control over public education makes coordinated decisionmaking difficult. It means, as well, that even when good scientific evidence is available as an input into policymaking, it is a daunting task to get that evidence into the hands of the vast number of far-flung decisionmakers who, in the aggregate, set our educational policy. The decision points are too numerous to be systematically reached by good research findings (Cohen 2007).

The second category of factors is political interests. Typically, these are expressed by organized social groups that have different and competing sets of preferences for how public schools should operate. With respect to education, the educational policies advocated by teachers, for example, are often different from the policies advocated by political leaders, which in turn often differ from what business groups want schools to do. Depending on the particular issue, other groups with yet other sets of interests may enter the fray. Supporters of market-based reforms in schooling, for example, implicitly acknowledge the tremendous power that teachers' unions have had in the educational policy development process, and see market reforms as a way to undermine that influence (see, e.g., Chubb and Moe 1990). When the educational interests of multiple groups coincide, on the other hand, significant educational reforms are more likely to be undertaken. For example, the accountability movements of the 1990s resulted from a convergence of attention on the part of federal and state policymakers, reformers, and business leaders to the problem of low academic outcomes (Cohen 2007).

The wide-ranging influence on policy of the Tennessee class-size experiment also illustrates both the pivotal role that special interest groups often play in policy development and how they sometimes use research findings strategically to support their position. It is likely that this study's impact on policy occurred in part because its findings bolstered long-standing demands from powerful teachers' groups for better working conditions. More generally, research varies in the degree to which it is compatible with the interests of special groups and in the amount of legitimacy it can offer for the advancement of their particular interests. Indeed, in her Spencer essay Johnson notes that "in order for research to have sustained, positive impact on student learning (broadly conceived), it must influence people making decisions at many levels: policymakers at the federal, state, and district levels; and practitioners at the district office, school site, and classroom. Thus, no single study is sufficient to inform all of these people, each of whom has a different piece of the action."

The third set of factors is ideas, only one small subset of which may be research evidence, even under the best of circumstances. The ideas that shape educational policy usually are broad, and generally are political values rather than empirical "facts" or research findings (also see Kelman 1988; Stone 2001; Weiss 2007; and for a detailed analysis of the crucial role of political values in educational policymaking in particular, see Hochschild and Scovronick 2003). For example, legal and public rejection of the doctrine of "separate but equal"—a significant shift in American political culture—led to arguably the most significant educational policy change of the twentieth century: attempts to racially desegregate American schools (McDonnell 2007).

What research on the process of policymaking strongly suggests, then, is that even if policymakers and practitioners had available to them an abundance of good evidence about "what works" in education, that evidence would likely play *at best* only a very small role in the decisions they make. As Carol Weiss (2007) puts it, "policymakers at federal, state, and local levels have not displayed concerted eagerness to be guided by research" (p. 284), especially when the research findings "are out of sync with prevailing values and accepted knowledge" (p. 286). In short, policy development is seldom a knowledge-driven process guided by rational decisionmaking of any sort, including the application of scientific reasoning or analysis of empirical data (McDonnell 1988; Stone 2001). Even the most valid and compelling research evidence "becomes just one more resource policymakers can use as they attempt to balance among competing interests in an essentially political environment" (McDonnell 1988:91).[15]

There are numerous examples of good research findings being ignored when the findings are at odds with the preferences already in place among powerful policymakers. Reading instruction, often held up as a model of evidence-based practice in education, is an illustrative case. Dyson, drawing on her expertise in reading instruction, notes in her Spencer essay that "If I think about the current state of guidelines for language and literacy education among young children stimulated by the political climate, then it seems as if the last 40 years of language-based research has been thrown out of the window."

There are, on the other hand, conditions under which research *does* influence policy development in education. But here the primary factor is not the quality of the research per se; rather, it is the consistency of the research findings with prevailing political concerns, with prevailing understandings of what is wrong with schools and schooling, and with already-formed policy preferences of powerful social groups. As Weiss (2007:285) succinctly puts it, "when research supports the position favored by other pressures in the system, it is more likely to make headway." Similarly, in his Spencer essay, Chester Finn argues that scholarly research shapes educational policymaking when "advocates, policymakers, and journalists . . . [are] able to use these studies to devise, justify, or sustain a reform agenda. Thus the research is less a source of change and more an 'arsenal' for those already fighting the policy wars." Further, a set of what Michael Mintrom (1997) calls "policy entrepreneurs" needs to be in place to distill the research findings and take them to the key political decisionmakers, or to those David Cohen (2007) calls "influential agents," who are themselves not typically in a position to make independent judgments about the scientific quality or validity of these data. In other words, absent a political pathway from the research community to the policy community, good research will not inform policymaking.

An examination of the studies or lines of research that have influenced educational policy development shows something else of great importance: that *timing is everything*. Take, for example, the famous report by Coleman and associates, *Equality of Educational Opportunity*, released in 1966 and widely considered to have been pivotal in the shift away from the equality reforms of the 1960s toward an emphasis on the small effects schools had on student achievement (Coleman et al. 1966). Cohen (2007) asserts that the Coleman report's effect on policy did not follow directly or solely from the quality of the research that went into it (indeed, the scientific legitimacy of the findings was hotly debated within the scholarly community):

> Rather, [the report] helped to focus attention and change ideas in tandem with other developments. Coleman's survey was federally sponsored at a time of unprecedented interest in civil rights, and it was published during the nation's most intense engagement with that issue. That interest and engagement helped to provoke the survey and create an audience for Coleman's ideas; had the study been privately sponsored and done a decade earlier, it likely would have done little to focus attention or to prompt change in understanding. Similarly, Americans' attention to academic outcomes grew during decades in which federal and state policymakers, reformers, and business leaders kept up steady criticism of schools' weakness and devised highly visible policies that aimed to improve academic outcomes.
>
> (p. 368)

In other words, the political "stars" were in perfect alignment for the Coleman report to be heard and to reshape the public's and policymakers' understanding of the key problem with schools and schooling that educational policy needed to address.

Similarly, *A Nation at Risk* (National Commission 1983) synthesized existing research and descriptive survey data to highlight the lagging academic achievement of American students in comparison to students in other countries. The report's huge effect on educational policy took the form of focusing the public's and policymakers' attention on the problem of declining achievement among U.S. students, which in turn led to a number of significant policy reforms. These included "increased course requirements for high school graduation, a longer school day and year, and performance-based compensation for teachers" (McDonnell 1988:94). *A Nation at Risk* was released in the midst of widespread demands that the government take steps to restore American economic competitiveness. Because of this coincidence of timing, the research findings the report publicized helped shape "the terms of the policy debate and the range of acceptable options" (p. 94). Thus it appears that research is most likely to come into play in policy development when major changes in policy direction are already on the political agenda.

Consider as yet a third example Jay Greene's highly influential work on high-school graduation rates. Finn points out in his Spencer essay that Greene "benefited from good timing. He hit upon this idea just as the high school reform movement was getting off the ground (thanks largely to Gates Foundation largess). His numbers fit into the reformers' story line."

There are also important cases that show that "bad" timing can blunt the influence of "good" studies. Take Shirley Brice Heath's *Way with Words*, a study of race and cultural differences in language development published in 1983 and considered an exemplar of good scholarship by the scholarly community. If her study had been published in the 1960s, at the height of the War on Poverty and national concern over racial inequality in education, it might have shaped the terms of the policy discussion in ways similar to the influence exerted by Coleman, Greene, and *A Nation at Risk*. Instead, it was published just as the attention of the public and of policymakers had shifted to an overwhelming concern with problems of school quality and low achievement. In that climate, Heath's careful examination of the importance of cultural differences garnered little attention or interest outside of academia.

Conclusion

Critics who assail education research as generally "shoddy" have often called for change that would render education research rigorous, evidence based, and relevant to policy questions. Indeed, in many debates, critics presume that the goals of being high quality and policy relevant are one and the same.

In this chapter we take issue with this presumption. We have assessed studies and scholars that have been widely viewed as important and influential. The citation counts, award lists, and expert surveys do reveal a group of highly acclaimed educational researchers. There are, as well, many studies that are considered to be high quality, rigorous, and important. There also have been numerous studies that have had an influence on policy, including studies on class size, reading instruction, social promotion, and ability grouping. These studies are more narrowly framed. For the most part, the highly acclaimed studies and the studies with a large impact on policy do not overlap. Generally, they are very different works.

Moreover, political context, rather than the quality of research per se, appears to be crucial in determining if research has an impact. Thousands of empirical studies are completed annually. There are many political factors that bring a particular study to the attention of policymakers and lead that study to have an impact. As we have seen, the tremendous influence of the Coleman report was connected to a fortuitous alignment of political and social factors. Many high-quality studies are ignored; they arrive either too early or too late to be in sync with the political and policy agenda. As we have suggested, the *alignment* of research results with interest groups' goals is a key factor. The political priorities become paramount. Thus there are ample examples of politicians ignoring high-quality research which conflicts with other priorities (e.g., research denouncing one-shot professional development seminars). In addition, in some cases research whose validity was hotly contested within the scientific community (e.g., Peterson's work on vouchers, discussed earlier) has been used widely by policymakers and politicians to lend scientific support to their policy preferences.

We conclude with a reminder that because educational policy takes shape at many different levels (e.g., within federal, state, and local agencies, across a school district, in interactions among educators in a specific school, etc.), there are multiple opportunities for research, including broadly focused and theoretically rich studies, to have an effect—by influencing legislators in drafting legislation, for example, or shaping what principals tell teachers in meetings, or helping to set priorities in the reallocation of federal funding. Most importantly, theoretically rich studies can change the very terms of the debate. For example, the Coleman report changed how researchers conceptualized the relative impact of schools and families on educational outcomes. It also moved the terms of the debate from educational opportunities to educational outcomes.[16] This was a critical shift. It reverberated through many different levels of the system and, in crucial ways, became taken for granted. This was an important policy impact.

Acclaimed researchers often tie a specific case of education research to a broader, more far-reaching, theoretical issue. They tell a story of significance. The best studies, as we have seen, ask important questions. By being attuned to the important role of conceptualization in theory and in policy, as well as being aware of the different characteristics of educational studies, researchers and policymakers have the potential to avoid common mistakes. More importantly, they are also better positioned to bring about genuine advancement in the field of education research in the future.

Notes

1. For details regarding the criticisms directed toward education research, see Chapters 1, 2, and 7.
2. Foremost among the means advocated for repair is greater use of the randomized controlled trial. See Chapter 6 in this volume for a longer discussion of the use of randomized controlled trial methods.
3. This list is not exhaustive. Indeed, reasonable people will disagree over which studies and scholars have most significantly advanced the field. Those cited here, however, emerge consistently as important exemplars, as we show in more detail below. The citations we provide for each of the scholars whose work we mention here are intended to provide examples of their highly influential research for those readers who may be unfamiliar with their work. The citations are illustrative rather than exhaustive. Given the body of work by these scholars, the selection of a short list to cite here is somewhat arbitrary.
4. As described more fully by Walters (in Chapter 1), the most renowned scientists within any scientific field set the standard within that community for what constitutes exemplary research (see, e.g., Collins 1989; Friedkin 1998).
5. See the acknowledgments to this volume for further details about this joint committee and its work.
6. The Research Center is a division of Editorial Projects in Education, Inc., publisher of *Education Week*. For more information about the surveys the Center conducts and the data it collects and analyzes, see the Center's web page (www2.edweek.org/info/about/research.html).
7. The best source for the findings as reported by Peterson is Howell and Peterson (2002). For an influential example of the critique of the scientific validity of the reported finding that vouchers improved the performance of African-American students, see Krueger and Zhu (2004). For examples of the media coverage of the debate over the scientific validity of the key finding reported by Peterson and Howell, see Winerip (2003) and Dillon (2003). What we find noteworthy is that while Peterson's originally-reported finding of a positive effect of vouchers on black students received enormous attention from the media and conservative politicians and policymakers, the critique of the scientific soundness of this finding offered by a number of well-respected scholars did not blunt most policymakers' enthusiasm for vouchers.
8. See http://www.spencer.org/publications/Grant_Analysis/GAMain.htm.
9. They are: Harris M. Cooper, Professor and Director of Education, Duke University; Anne Haas Dyson, Professor, Teacher Education, Michigan State University; Chester E. Finn, Jr., President, Thomas B. Fordham Foundation; James Paul Gee, Tashia Morgridge Professor of Reading, University of Wisconsin-Madison; Patricia Albjerg Graham, Charles Warren Professor of the History of Education Emerita, Graduate School of Education, Harvard University; Amy Gutmann, President, University of Pennsylvania; Maureen Hallinan, William P. and Hazel B. White Professor of Sociology, Department of Sociology, University of Notre Dame; Susan Moore Johnson, Carl H. Pforzheimer, Jr. Professor of Teaching and Learning, Graduate School of Education, Harvard University; James G. March, Professor Emeritus, Stanford University; Charles M. Payne, Sally Dalton Robinson Professor of History, African American Studies and Sociology, Duke University; Andrew Porter, Patricia and Rodes Hart Professor of Educational Leadership and Policy, Vanderbilt University; Mike Rose, Professor, Graduate School of Education and Information Studies, University of California, Los Angeles; Richard Rothstein, Economic Policy Institute, Vanessa Siddle Walker, Winship Distinguished Research Professor, Division of Educational Studies, Emory University; Patricia Wasley, Dean, College of Education, University of Washington. The text of each essay is available on the Spencer Foundation website (http://www.spencer.org/publications/Grant_Analysis/GAMain.htm).
10. Indeed, the Perry Preschool Project is one of the few pieces of education research considered to have been based on a well-designed randomized controlled trial and thus one of the few that has yielded valid information to guide policymakers' decisions, according to the Coalition for Evidence-Based Policy, an organization devoted to identifying for policymakers scientific studies whose findings are reliable. In light of the considerable attention garnered by the Tennessee

class-size experiments, it is notable that that study does not appear on the Coalition's list. See Coalition for Evidence-Based Policy (n.d.).

11   Johnson also writes, "There were so many other potential explanations for the change, the seeming success of this policy did little to advance the cause of smaller classes."

12   A number of the essayists, however, take a different stance, arguing that few studies have had an impact on policy. Harris Cooper points to the decentralized character of policy. He writes, "Often, change in education is a ground up exercises [sic], occurring in classrooms, schools, and school districts, rather than at the state or national level. [But] when most people seek evidence about the impact of research they want to see the big effects, not the small, hard-to-document ones that happen in individual classrooms, schools and communities." Charles Payne notes that "the non-authoritative character of much educational research is an obvious problem. On many questions (Which comprehensive school reform is best? Is progressive pedagogy superior to didactic ones?), research does not allow a confident answer, notwithstanding plenty of research on these issues." Patricia Albjerg Graham stresses the misinterpretation of research and "erroneous conclusion[s]" that were drawn from research. It is important to note, however, that shortcomings in the research itself is not the only problem highlighted; the essayists also identified problems with the policymaking process.

13   It is possible that there has not been sufficient time for the new wave of "evidence-based" and "scientific" studies of education to make their mark. Theoretically, in a decade or two the most influential studies might include more works that use randomized trials. But we think this is an unlikely development. By definition, randomized control trials seek to "hold constant" all of the variables in the equation with the exception of one variable. This means that not only the current wave but also future randomized control trials studies are likely to be very narrowly conceived rather than being the kind of "big picture" studies with a clear theoretical framework that have long tended to be the most widely acclaimed. Thus if past patterns hold, these kinds of studies are unlikely to appear on a future list of acclaimed work in education research.

14   At times the policy-focused studies have been able to demonstrate an outcome but have limited insight into the mechanisms that brought it about. Payne addresses this in his essay for the Spencer Foundation: "Policymakers, including leaders of foundations, bear some culpability for what I think has proven to be an ill-advised emphasis on outcome studies. The question they really want answered is, 'Did it Work?' Questions about context and process get pushed to the side. Thus, even when we know that such-and-such a program has 'worked' somewhere, we may not understand the operations well enough to help it work somewhere else."

15   It is important to note that education is not the only policy domain in which policy development is shaped primarily by political factors. Recent analyses of the development of American health-care policy, for example, similarly highlight the crucial ways in which policy has been shaped by institutional arrangements, the actions of competing interest groups (especially the insurance industry and the medical profession), and broad political values (see, e.g., Hacker 2002; Quadagno 2005).

16   The Coleman report, in many respects, is grandfather to the current emphasis on measuring growth in academic achievement through standardized tests.

References

Bandura, Albert. 1977a. "Self-Efficacy: Toward a Unifying Theory of Behavioral Change." *Psychological Review* 84: 191–215.
——. 1977b. *Social Learning Theory*. Englewood Cliffs, NJ: Prentice-Hall.
——. 1986. *Social Foundations of Thought and Action: A Social Cognitive Theory*. Englewood Cliffs, NJ: Prentice-Hall.
——. 1997. *Self-Efficacy: The Exercise of Control*. New York: W.H. Freeman.
Bandura, Albert, Claudio Barbaranelli, Gian Vittorio Caprara, and Concetta Pastorelli. 2001. "Self-Efficacy Beliefs as Shapers of Children's Aspirations and Career Trajectories." *Child Development* 72:187–206.
Bloom, Benjamin S. (ed.) 1956. *Taxonomy of Educational Objectives; The Classification of Educational Goals, by a Committee of College and University Examiners*. New York: Longmans, Green.
——. 1976. *Human Characteristics and School Learning*. New York: McGraw-Hill.
Bowles, Samuel and Herbert Gintis. 1976. *Schooling in Capitalist America*. New York: Basic.
Campbell, Donald T. and Julian C. Stanley. 1963. *Experimental and Quasi-experimental Designs for Research*. Boston: Houghton Mifflin.

Chubb, John E. and Terry M. Moe. 1990. *Politics, Markets, and America's Schools*. Washington, DC: Brookings Institution Press.
Coalition for Evidence-Based Policy. N.d. "What Works and What Doesn't Work in Social Policy? Findings from Well-Designed Randomized Controlled Trials." Retrieved March 10, 2008 (http://www.evidencebasedprograms.org/).
Cohen, David K. 2007. "Problems in Education Policy and Research." Pp. 349–371 in *The State of Education Policy Research*, edited by Susan H. Fuhrman, David K. Cohen, and Fritz Mosher. Mahwah, NJ: Lawrence Erlbaum Associates.
Coleman, James S. 1964. *Introduction to Mathematical Sociology*. New York: Free Press of Glencoe.
——. 1990. *Foundations of Social Theory*. Cambridge, MA: Belknap Press of Harvard University.
Coleman, James S., Ernest Q. Campbell, Carol J. Hobson, James McPartland, Alexander M. Mood, Frederick D. Weinfeld, and Robert L. York. 1966. *Equality of Educational Opportunity*. Washington, DC: U.S. Government Printing Office.
Collins, Randall. 1989. "Toward a Theory of Intellectual Change: The Social Causes of Philosophies." *Science, Technology, and Human Values* 14:107–140.
Dewey, John. 1916. *Democracy and Education: An Introduction to the Philosophy of Education*. New York: Macmillan.
——. 1938. *Experience and Education*. New York: Macmillan.
——. 1959. *Dewey on Education*. New York: Columbia.
Dillon, Sam. 2003. "Report Defends Vouchers but Fails to Quell Debate." *New York Times*, June 13, page A29.
Friedkin, Noah E. 1998. *A Structural Theory of Social Influence*. Cambridge, U.K.: Cambridge University Press.
Fuhrman, Susan H. 2001. "The Policy Influence of Education Research and R&D Centers." Testimony to the U.S. House Committee on Education and the Workforce, July 17. Retrieved April 12, 2008 (http://www.upenn.edu/pennnews/article.php?id=406).
Gilligan, Carol. 1982. *In a Different Voice: Psychological Theory and Women's Development*. Cambridge, MA: Harvard University Press.
Hacker, Jacob S. 2002. *The Divided Welfare State: The Battle over Private and Social Benefits in the United States*. Cambridge, U.K.: Cambridge University Press.
Heath, Shirley Brice. 1983. *Ways with Words: Language, Life, and Work in Communities and Classrooms*. New York: Cambridge University Press.
Hochschild, Jennifer and Nathan Scovronick. 2003. *The American Dream and the Public Schools*. New York: Oxford University Press.
Howell, William G. and Paul E. Peterson. 2002. *The Education Gap: Vouchers and Urban Schools*. Washington, DC: Brookings Institution Press.
Kelman, Steven. 1988. *Making Public Policy: A Hopeful View of American Government*. New York: Basic.
Kingdon, John W. 2002. *Agendas, Alternatives, and Public Policies*. 2nd edn. New York: Longman.
Krueger, Alan B. and Pei Zhu. 2004. "Another Look at the New York City School Voucher Experiment." *The American Behavioral Scientist* 47:658–698.
McDonnell, Lorraine M. 1988. "Can Education Research Speak to State Policy?" *Theory into Practice* 27:91–97.
McDonnell, Lorraine M. 2007. "The Politics of Education: Influencing Policy and Beyond." Pp. 19–39 in *The State of Education Policy Research*, edited by Susan H. Fuhrman, David K. Cohen, and Fritz Mosher. Mahwah, NJ: Lawrence Erlbaum Associates.
Mintrom, Michael. 1997. "Policy Entrepreneurs and the Diffusion of Innovation." *American Journal of Political Science* 41:738–770.
National Commission on Excellence in Education. 1983. *A Nation at Risk: The Imperative for Educational Reform*. Washington, DC: The Commission.
Palincsar, Annemarie S. and A. L. Brown. 1984. "Reciprocal Teaching of Comprehension-Fostering and Comprehension-Monitoring Activities." *Cognition and Instruction* 1:117–175.
Quadagno, Jill. 2005. *One Nation Uninsured: Why the U.S. Has No National Health Insurance*. New York: Oxford University Press.
Stone, Deborah. 2001. *Policy Paradox: The Art of Political Decision Making*. Revised ed. New York: W. W. Norton.
Swanson, Christopher B. and Janelle Barlage. 2006. *Influence: A Study of the Factors Shaping Education Policy*. Bethesda, MD: Editorial Projects in Education. Retrieved March 20, 2008 (http://www.edweek.org/media/influence_study.pdf).
Weikart, David, James T. Bond, and J. T. McNeil. 1978. *The Ypsilanti Perry Preschool Project: Preschool Years and Longitudinal Results through Fourth Grade*. Ypsilanti, MI: High/Scope Educational Research Foundation.

Weiss, Carol Hirschon. 2007. "Can We Influence Education Reform through Research?" Pp. 281–287 in *The State of Education Policy Research*, edited by Susan H. Fuhrman, David K. Cohen, and Fritz Mosher. Mahwah, NJ: Lawrence Erlbaum Associates.

Winerip, Michael. 2003. "On Education: What Some Much-Noted Data Really Showed about Vouchers." *New York Times*, May 7, page B12.

Word, Elizabeth, John Johnston, Helen Pate Bain, B. DeWayne Fulton, Jayne Boyd-Zaharias, Martha Nannette Lintz, Charles M. Achilles, John Folger, and Carolyn Breda. 1990. *Student/Teacher Achievement Ratio (STAR): Tennessee's K-3 Class-Size Study*. Nashville: Tennessee Department of Education.

APPENDIX A

The Definition of "Scientifically Based Research" in the No Child Left Behind Act of 2001

Editor's notes: The No Child Left Behind Act of 2001 was intended "to close the achievement gap with accountability, flexibility, and choice, so that no child is left behind" (p. 1 of the No Child Left Behind Act of 2001, Public Law 107-110). The law is best known for the strict measures it established to try to close that achievement gap—including making funding for schools contingent on their showing "adequate yearly progress" in growth in average achievement-test results for students. What is less widely appreciated (outside of the education research community) is that it was also a bold attempt to require educators to use services, programs, methods, and instructional practices that "are based on scientifically based research." That is, if schools and school districts wish to receive federal funds available under the terms of the No Child Left Behind Act (which was the name given to the bill that reauthorized the Elementary and Secondary Education Act of 1965—the piece of legislation that provides the vast majority of the federal funding that state and local education agencies receive), they must only choose to adopt educational services, programs, etc. whose effectiveness has been proved through the use of "scientifically based research." Although the restriction applied to educators, not to researchers, it nonetheless was of great significance to the education research community: It limited the kinds of research methods researchers could use if they wished their research to inform certain types of educational policy and practice decisions. Further, it set in motion a series of subsequent efforts to hold the education research community to the standards of "scientifically based research" the No Child Left Behind Act put in place.

The phrase "scientifically based research" (or close variations) appears over 100 times in the No Child Left Behind Act. The authoritative definition of the term *is contained in section 9101 in an alphabetized list of definitions for key terms used in the act (pp. 540–41):*

The term "scientifically based research"—

(A) means research that involves the application of rigorous, systematic, and objective procedures to obtain reliable and valid knowledge relevant to education activities and programs; and
(B) includes research that—
    (i) employs systematic, empirical methods that draw on observation or experiment;
    (ii) involves rigorous data analyses that are adequate to test the stated hypotheses and justify the general conclusions drawn;
    (iii) relies on measurements or observational methods that provide reliable and valid data across evaluators and observers, across multiple measurements and observations, and across studies by the same or different investigators;
    (iv) is evaluated using experimental or quasi-experimental designs in which individuals, entities, programs, or activities are assigned to different conditions and with appropriate controls to evaluate the effects of the condition of interest, with a preference for random-assignment experiments, or other designs to the extent that those designs contain within-condition or across-condition controls;
    (v) ensures that experimental studies are presented in sufficient detail and clarity to allow for replication or, at a minimum, offer the opportunity to build systematically on their findings; and
    (vi) has been accepted by a peer-reviewed journal or approved by a panel of independent experts through a comparably rigorous, objective, and scientific review.

Source: http://www.ed.gov/policy/elsec/leg/esea02/107-110.pdf

APPENDIX B

The Definitions of "Scientifically Based Research" in the Education Sciences Reform Act of 2002

Editor's notes: *The Education Sciences Reform Act of 2002 was intended "to provide for improvement of Federal education research, statistics, evaluation, information, and dissemination, and for other purposes" (p. 1 of the Education Science Reform Act of 2002). It abolished the Office of Educational Research and Improvement in the U.S. Department of Education, and replaced it with a new research unit called the Institute of Education Sciences. Further, it set out a different definition for "scientifically based research" than did the No Child Left Behind Act. Yet another difference with No Child Left Behind is that the Education Sciences Reform Act applied to the research community directly, not to educators: The U.S. Department of Education was required to grant research funds only to those researchers whose proposed studies were based on principles of "scientifically based research." The definition of "scientifically based research" outlined in the Education Sciences Reform Act is broader than the definition in No Child Left Behind, but the act nonetheless indicates a clear preference for "random-assignment experiments." Further, the definition established for "scientifically valid education evaluation" is much closer to the (narrower) definition of "scientifically based research" included in No Child Left Behind.*

In section 102 (p. 4) the terms related to "scientifically based research" are defined as follows:

(18) SCIENTIFICALLY BASED RESEARCH STANDARDS.—
    (A)   The term "scientifically based research standards" means research standards that—
          (i)   apply rigorous, systematic, and objective methodology to obtain reliable and valid knowledge relevant to education activities and programs; and

(ii) present findings and make claims that are appropriate to and supported by the methods that have been employed.
(B) The term includes, appropriate to the research being conducted—
  (i) employing systematic, empirical methods that draw on observation or experiment;
  (ii) involving data analyses that are adequate to support the general findings;
  (iii) relying on measurements or observational methods that provide reliable data;
  (iv) making claims of causal relationships only in random assignment experiments or other designs (to the extent such designs substantially eliminate plausible competing explanations for the obtained results);
  (v) ensuring that studies and methods are presented in sufficient detail and clarity to allow for replication or, at a minimum, to offer the opportunity to build systematically on the findings of the research;
  (vi) obtaining acceptance by a peer-reviewed journal or approval by a panel of independent experts through a comparably rigorous, objective, and scientific review; and
  (vii) using research designs and methods appropriate to the research question posed.

(19) SCIENTIFICALLY VALID EDUCATION EVALUATION.—The term "scientifically valid education evaluation" means an evaluation that—
  (A) adheres to the highest possible standards of quality with respect to research design and statistical analysis;
  (B) provides an adequate description of the programs evaluated and, to the extent possible, examines the relationship between program implementation and program impacts;
  (C) provides an analysis of the results achieved by the program with respect to its projected effects;
  (D) employs experimental designs using random assignment, when feasible, and other research methodologies that allow for the strongest possible causal inferences when random assignment is not feasible; and
  (E) may study program implementation through a combination of scientifically valid and reliable methods.

(20) SCIENTIFICALLY VALID RESEARCH.—The term "scientifically valid research" includes applied research, basic research, and field-initiated research in which the rationale, design, and interpretation are soundly developed in accordance with scientifically based research standards.

Source: http://www.ed.gov/policy/rschstat/leg/PL107-279.pdf

APPENDIX C

Mission and Functions of the Institute of Education Sciences, as Detailed in the Education Sciences Reform Act of 2002

Part A—THE INSTITUTE OF EDUCATION SCIENCES
Sec. 111. ESTABLISHMENT.
- (a) ESTABLISHMENT.—There shall be in the Department the Institute of Education Sciences, to be administered by a Director (as described in section 114) and, to the extent set forth in section 116, a board of directors.
- (b) MISSION.—
  - (1) IN GENERAL.—The mission of the Institute is to provide national leadership in expanding fundamental knowledge and understanding of education from early childhood through post-secondary study, in order to provide parents, educators, students, researchers, policymakers, and the general public with reliable information about—
    - (A) the condition and progress of education in the United States, including early childhood education;
    - (B) educational practices that support learning and improve academic achievement and access to educational opportunities for all students; and
    - (C) the effectiveness of Federal and other education programs.
  - (2) CARRYING OUT MISSION.—In carrying out the mission described in paragraph (1), the Institute shall compile statistics, develop products, and conduct research, evaluations, and wide dissemination activities in areas of demonstrated national need (including in technology areas) that are

supported by Federal funds appropriated to the Institute and ensure that such activities—
- (A) conform to high standards of quality, integrity, and accuracy; and
- (B) are objective, secular, neutral, and nonideological and are free of partisan political influence and racial, cultural, gender, or regional bias.

(c) ORGANIZATION.—The Institute shall consist of the following:
  (1) The Office of the Director (as described in section 114).
  (2) The National Board for Education Sciences (as described in section 116).
  (3) The National Education Centers, which include—
   (A) the National Center for Education Research (as described in part B);
   (B) the National Center for Education Statistics (as described in part C);
   (C) the National Center for Education Evaluation and Regional Assistance (as described in part D).

SEC. 112. FUNCTIONS.

From funds appropriated under section 194, the Institute, directly or through grants, contracts, or cooperative agreements, shall—
  (1) conduct and support scientifically valid research activities, including basic research and applied research, statistics activities, scientifically valid education evaluation, development, and wide dissemination;
  (2) widely disseminate the findings and results of scientifically valid research in education;
  (3) promote the use, development, and application of knowledge gained from scientifically valid research activities;
  (4) strengthen the national capacity to conduct, develop, and widely disseminate scientifically valid research in education;
  (5) promote the coordination, development, and dissemination of scientifically valid research in education within the Department and the Federal Government; and
  (6) promote the use and application of research and development to improve practice in the classroom.

Source: http://www.ed.gov/policy/rschstat/leg/PL107-279.pdf

APPENDIX D

Selection from Request for Proposals for Predoctoral Interdisciplinary Research Training Programs in the Education Sciences, Issued by the Institute of Education Sciences in 2004

2. PURPOSE OF THE TRAINING PROGRAM
The Institute's objectives in creating the Predoctoral Interdisciplinary Research Training Program in the Education Sciences are to support the development of innovative interdisciplinary training programs for doctoral students interested in conducting applied education research, and to establish a network of training programs that collectively produce a cadre of education researchers willing and able to conduct a new generation of methodologically rigorous and educationally relevant scientific research that will provide solutions to pressing problems and challenges facing American education.

3. BACKGROUND
A number of recent reports have described current education practice as not resting on a solid research base (Coalition for Evidence-Based Policy, 2002; NRC, 1999, NRC, 2000, NRC, 2002). Instead, policy decisions are often guided by personal experience, folk wisdom, and ideology. The passage of the No Child Left Behind Act of 2002 signals that the education enterprise of the United States has entered a new era in which policy and practice are expected to be based on evidence. This will require a transformation in the field of education. Practitioners will have to turn routinely to education research when making important decisions, and education researchers will have to produce research that is relevant to those decisions. To achieve this ambitious agenda, there is a need for a cadre of well-trained scientists capable of conducting high quality research that is relevant to practitioners and policy makers.

There are significant capacity issues within the education research community. According to a recent survey conducted by the National Opinion Research Center, only 7% of doctorate recipients in the field of Education cite research and development as their primary postdoctoral activity (Hoffer et.al., 2003). Similarly, a recent membership survey conducted by the American Educational Research Association (AERA) revealed that less than a quarter of its membership cite research as being their major responsibility (AERA, 2002). Perhaps even more worrisome is the fact that the number of Education doctorate recipients in the subfields of Education Statistics/Research Methods and Educational Assessment, Testing and Measures is extremely low compared to other subfields. This imbalance has remained consistent over the course of the past ten years (Hoffer, et.al., 2003; APA Research Office, in press). The situation is no better in closely-related disciplines. For instance, the number of doctoral degrees in educational psychology has declined from 144 in 1978 to 48 in 2001 (Hoffer et al., 2003). Compounding this decline is the fact that of the 48 doctoral degree recipients in 2001, only 16 reported being involved in research within one year of the receipt of their degree (APA Research Office, in press). Transforming education into an evidence-based field is very important work for the nation. It will require training new researchers in sufficient numbers to address the many tasks at hand.

There are also significant issues pertaining to the nature of the training that is currently being provided by graduate programs (Viadero, 2004). Many schools of education are not providing rigorous research training for doctoral students. While research training that is relevant to education is often provided elsewhere in universities, e.g., psychology and economics departments, these disciplines are seldom focused on education topics, and students are pointed towards other careers and research interests. Moreover, there seems to be a mismatch between what education decision makers want from the education research community and what the education research community is providing. Educational practitioners want research to help them make informed decisions in those areas in which they have choices to make, such as curriculum and teacher professional development. They want the research and development enterprise to generate valid and useable assessment instruments. They want information on the relative costs and benefits of different education investments. They want effective management strategies to be developed and validated.

Many of the questions raised by practitioners and policy makers require answers to questions of what works in education for whom under what circumstances. These are causal questions that are best answered by randomized trials of interventions and approaches brought to scale. Yet, these are questions and methods with which relatively few in the education research community have been engaged. While the total number of articles featuring randomized field trials in other areas of social science research has steadily grown over the past 30 years, the number of randomized trials in education has lagged far behind (Boruch, de Moya & Snyder, 2001; Cook, 2001). A recent survey of every empirical article published in the American Educational Research Association's two premier journals over a ten-year span from 1993 to 2002 revealed that only 6% of the research reports utilized a randomized trial. In contrast, over six times as many studies used qualitative methods as the primary research tool (Whitehurst, 2003). Qualitative methods have a valid use in education research, but it is not to answer questions of what works. The dominance of qualitative methods in research reports in leading education research journals and the dominance of what works questions among practitioners is a clear sign of the mismatch between the focus of the practice community and the current research community.

Another category of questions raised by the practice community focuses on assessment. The standards and accountability movement has generated a ballooning demand for people who are trained in the design, implementation, analysis, and use of education tests and measures to assess the results of instruction, to aid in the selection and promotion of staff, and to support the management of schools and districts. Individuals with skills in psychometrics are needed throughout the education sector, from federal statistical agencies to university training programs to state education agencies to test developers, to local school districts. However, no more than 15 Psychology doctoral degrees in psychometrics have been awarded in a given year since 1992, and a ten year low of 2 were awarded in 2001 (APA Research Office, in press). Supply is meager.

Yet another category of problems raised by practitioners and policy makers is the need for a new generation of teaching materials and curricula that take advantage of expanding knowledge of how people learn and that leverage new delivery mechanisms such as the internet and personal computers (NRC, 2000). The design, testing, and implementation of new teaching methods will require scientists who are well trained in cognition, learning, and motivation, and who also are prepared to grapple with the challenges of extending laboratory-derived knowledge of these topics to teaching and learning in complex, real-world environments. Researchers who can straddle the worlds of cognitive science and education practice are very badly needed.

The needs of education policy and practice are served not only by research that directly addresses problem solution but also by research that raises questions and generates hypotheses that can eventually lead to new applications or refinements of existing approaches (NRC, 2002). Frequently hypothesis-generating research relies on complex statistical methods that can tease out potential causal influences in large, correlational datasets. Statistical training is also needed in the design and analysis of experimental and quasi-experimental studies, as well as survey and observational data. While there are many doctoral training programs that focus on applied mathematics and statistics, the application of this expertise to problems in education requires that students be grounded in education content. That, in turn, requires a concentration of students and faculty who are focused on education topics.

In order to increase the supply of scientists and researchers in education who are prepared to conduct rigorous evaluation studies, develop new products and approaches that are grounded in a science of learning, design valid tests and measures, and explore data with sophisticated statistical methods, this initiative will fund the creation of innovative interdisciplinary research training programs in the education sciences. Grants will be awarded to institutions that can put together a program across disciplines such as psychology, political science, economics, statistics, sociology, education, and epidemiology that will provide intensive training in education research and statistics. Predoctoral students will graduate within a traditional discipline, e.g., economics, but will receive a certificate in education sciences, and will be expected to conduct dissertations on education topics.

Source: Pp. 3–5 of archived document titled "Predoctoral Interdisciplinary Research Training Program in the Education Sciences," issued by the Institute of Education Sciences on February 4, 2004. Request for Applications NCER-04-06. Retrieved December 10, 2007 (http://www.ed.gov/programs/predoc/predoctoralrfa2004.pdf)

Notes on Contributors

Jennifer Hanis-Martin is a Ph.D. candidate in the Department of Sociology at the University of Chicago. Her dissertation examines the narratives of women who are both mothers and also serious runners and triathletes. It investigates the intersections between the ideologies and the lived experiences of sport, gender, and the family.

Larry V. Hedges is the Board of Trustees Professor of Statistics and Social Policy at Northwestern University. Although his scholarship spans many fields, he is best known for his work to develop statistical methods for meta-analysis (a statistical analysis of the results of multiple studies that combines their findings) in the social, medical, and biological sciences. He is convener of the Campbell Collaboration's statistics group, which is part of a larger effort to produce an online database of "best practices" in the social sciences and education. He chairs the Technical Advisory Group of the U.S. Department of Education's What Works Clearinghouse, an initiative to give educators and researchers a library of systematic reviews to aid in the development of evidence-based educational policy.

Annette Lareau is the Stanley I. Sheerr Term Professor in the Department of Sociology at the University of Pennsylvania. Her most recent book, *Unequal Childhoods: Class, Race, and Family Life*, uses ethnographic methods to examine the impact of social class on children's daily lives. *Unequal Childhoods* won the best book award from three different sections of the American Sociological Association. With Jeff Schultz, she is editor of *Journeys through Ethnography:*

Realistic Accounts of Fieldwork. She spent 2005–06 as a fellow at the Center for Advanced Study in the Behavioral Sciences.

Denis C. Phillips is Professor Emeritus of Education, and by courtesy of Philosophy, at Stanford University. He is a philosopher whose work focuses on the epistemology of the social sciences and educational research; in his writings and workshops he stimulates educational researchers to be reflective about the methods they are using, the assumptions they make that underlie their research, and the implications for policy and practice that they draw from their work. Phillips' writings place him at the center of the vigorous debates among scholars in education around the world over the nature of knowledge and its claim to be objective. He served as a member of the National Research Council's Committee on Scientific Principles for Educational Research that produced the 2002 volume *Scientific Research in Education*.

Sheri H. Ranis is Senior Research Officer in the U.S. Programs/Education Division of the Bill & Melinda Gates Foundation. Prior to joining the foundation in 2005, Ranis was Program Director for Education at the Social Science Research Council (SSRC). Her research has centered on under-represented youth and their transitions to college. She has served as co-editor of several publications on this topic, including the SSRC report "Questions That Matter" and a special issue of *Teachers College Record* that reviews research on transition in the social science disciplines. She also was a guest co-editor for the Winter 2006 edition of the *Review of Research in Education* focused on the No Child Left Behind Act.

Barbara Schneider is the John A. Hannah University Distinguished Professor in the College of Education and the Department of Sociology at Michigan State University. Her research interests focus on how the social contexts of schools and families influence the academic and social well-being of adolescents as they move into adulthood. Relying on multiple research methods, she has examined how schools can become more effective in reducing persisting academic achievement gaps among children of different racial, ethnic, and socioeconomic backgrounds. She is the current editor of *Sociology of Education*.

Maris A. Vinovskis is the Bentley Professor of History, Professor of Public Policy, and a Senior Research Scientist at the Center for Political Studies in the Institute for Social Research. He has authored or co-authored ten books, the most recent being *From A Nation at Risk to No Child Left Behind: National Education Goals and the Creation of Federal Education Policies* (2009). Vinovskis was the Deputy Staff Director to the U.S. House Select Committee on Population in 1978 and the Research Advisor to the Assistant Secretary of the Office of Educational Research and Improvement (OERI) in both the Bush and the Clinton administrations in 1992 and 1993. He is currently a member of the Independent Review Panel for the U.S. Department of Education as well as a former member of the federal Even Start evaluation board.

Pamela Barnhouse Walters is the James H. Rudy Professor of Sociology and Director of the Center for Education and Society at Indiana University. Her research is on social inequality, with a particular emphasis on American education. She is a former editor of *Sociology of Education*, former co-chair of the Study Committee on Education Research co-sponsored by the Social Science Research Council and the National Academy of Education, and a Guggenheim fellowship recipient. She spent 2005–06 as a fellow at the Center for Advanced Study in the Behavioral Sciences and 2007–08 in Chicago as a resident fellow at the Spencer Foundation.

Index

Note: "n" following a page number refers to a note.

Advancing Scientific Research in Education 99
agriculture 17, 21, 32, 107–8
Alberts, B. 34
Alexander, K. 148
Altman, L. 89
American Educational Research Association (AERA) 6, 7, 23, 26, 37, 40, 42, 64, 70, 75, 100, 129, 164–5, 229; awards 199, 202–5; journal publications 89–90, 91, 93, 96, 98; membership survey 228
Angrist, J. 39, 109
applied research 22, 32, 44, 57, 106–7, 128, 164, 224
Armstrong, J. 85, 90, 92
Atkinson, R. 57, 58
Awful Reputation of Education Research, The 4; *see also* Kaestle

Bailey, S. 53
Bakanic, V. 90, 91
Ball, D. 123
Bandura, A. 198, 201, 205
Barlage, J. 206, 209
Barnes, C. 130
Bayer, A. 115

Becker, H. 158
Bell, T. 56
Bennett, W. 56
Berenholtz, S. 155, 156
Berk, R. 29, 30
Berliner, D. 7, 63, 65, 166
Berry, B. 96
Best Evidence Encyclopedia (BEE) 130, 132–3, 134, 135
Big Brother/Big Sister program 147
Blank, R. 84, 93
Bloch, M. 100
Bloom, B. 198
Bond, J. 198
Booth, W. 177
Boruch, R. 28, 29, 30, 39, 42, 146, 192n
Bowles, S. 200, 201
Boyd-Zacharias, J. 30
Brademas, J. 55
Brainard, J. 36–7
Braskamp, L. 115
Braxton, J. 115
Brewer, D. 96, 130
Broad, W.J. 89
Brookings Panel on Social Experimentation 54, 71
Brown, A.L. 201

Brown, K. 135, 139
Burbules, N. 176, 192n, 193n
Burns, S. 96, 209
Bush administration (G.H.W. Bush) 57–9
Bush administration (G.W. Bush) 36–7, 64–74, 76

Calhoun, C. 128
Camic, C. 19
Campanario, J. 85, 91, 94, 96
Campbell Collaboration 34–5, 39, 41, 98, 131, 133, 134, 135, 136
Campbell, D. 28, 29, 30, 106, 107, 110, 111, 183, 185, 203
Cannella, G. 25
career success, measuring 115–16, 119–21
Carriker, D. 52
Cartter, A. 115
Castle, M. 35, 38, 61, 62, 64, 66, 68, 73
causal effects in non-randomized designs 105–24; a case study using regression discontinuity design 110–21
causation and purposes of education research 180–4
Cawkell, T. 85
Centra, J. 116
Child Development 89–90
Chubb, J. 212
Chubin, D. 84, 91, 96
Cicchetti, D. 90, 92, 99
citation count 84–5, 86, 87, 88, 89; of education articles in social science journals 97; in identifying influential research 199–202; and measuring scholar career success 116, 120, 121, 122
citation indexing 85–6, 116
Clampet-Lundquist, S. 148
Clark, D. 52
Clemens, E. 94
Clifford, G. 22, 23
Clinton administration 33–4, 59–64, 69, 72–3
Coalition for Evidence-Based Policy 37–8, 41, 46n, 227
Cochrane Collaboration 35
Cohen, D. 123, 130, 165, 167, 212, 214
Cohen, J. 115
Cole, J. 19

Cole, S. 19
Coleman, J. 53, 198, 203, 205, 214, 216
Collins, R. 19, 217n
Comer's School Development Program 30, 151–2, 154
Committee on Scientific Principles for Educational Research 62–3, 75
compatibilism 184–5
Comprehensive School Reform Demonstration program 61
Confrey, J. 140n
Constas, M. 27
Cook, T.D. 45, 48, 107, 100; evaluation of Comer program 151, 152–3, 154; lack of random assignment 229; support for random assignment 29, 30, 31, 39–40, 42, 147
Council on Educational Development and Research (CEDaR) 55, 56
Cowan, K. 65
Crader, B. 94
Craft of Research, The 177
Crane, D. 19, 115
Cronbach, L. 52, 57, 164, 169, 170, 181, 183
Cross, C. 57
Curran, E. 56

Darling-Hammond, L. 96
data sharing 98
de Loya, D. 29, 30
Dershimer, R.A. 52, 53, 55
Dewey, J. 126, 174–5, 176, 179, 198
Diamond, A. 83
Diamond, J. 150
doctorates in education 94, 228
Dreeben, R. 97
Duncan, G. 147
Dyson, A.H. 210, 213

Editorial Projects in Education (EPE) Research Center 206
education researchers 27, 43, 88, 129, 134, 166–7; controversy over "scientific" research 6, 11, 18, 39–41, 43; effort to gain legitimacy 20, 22–7, 43–4; insider concerns over quality of research 18, 26–7, 163–5; paradigm wars 24, 25, 26, 168, 184
education sciences movement 2, 3–8, 19, 20, 27, 31, 39, 43, 44, 125; setting standards for an 34–43

Education Sciences Reform Act (ESRA) 2002 6, 38, 66, 68, 72, 223–6
Educational Opportunity Survey 53
educational psychology 19–20, 24–6, 28, 29, 30–1, 45, 201
Educational Resources Information Center (ERIC) 53, 56, 57, 89, 101n
Ehlers, V.J. 64
Ehrenberg, R. 98
Eisenhart, M. 5, 6, 35, 38, 39
Elementary and Secondary Education Act 1965 (ESEA) 35, 52
Elliott, E. 56, 57
Elmore, R. 53, 209
Entwisle, D. 148
Epstein, J. 149, 158
Epstein, S. 18
Equality of Educational Opportunity 214
Ericksen, K. 149
Erickson, F. 7
evaluation research 20–1, 28–31, 34, 44–5, 107, 170
Evans, A. 92
evidence-based field, education as an 11, 21, 34; Coalition for Evidence-Based Policy 37–8, 41, 46n, 227; constraints on 212–15; initiatives for 4, 17, 34–5, 43, 45, 69, 130, 228
Experimental and Quasi-experimental Designs for Research 28, 203
experimental methods 22, 23, 25, 28, 30–1, 127, 138, 222; and lack of suitability for much of education research 108–9; for teaching reading 207

Featherman, D. 52, 140n
federal education research 51–79; under Clinton 33–4, 59–64, 69, 72–3; under G.H.W. Bush 57–9; under G.W. Bush 36–43, 64–74; under Johnson 51–3; under Nixon 53–5; under Reagan 32–3, 55–7, 74
fellowship programs, evaluating postdoctorate 105–21
Feuer, M. 63, 67
Feyerabend, P. 174
Finn, C. 32, 53, 56, 57, 68, 214
Fisher, R.A. 107
Fiske, E. 32
Fletcher, R. 84, 93, 99
Fletcher, S. 84, 93, 99

Flyvbjerg, B. 171
Follow Through 53–4, 55
Frickel, S. 17, 19, 97
Friedkin, N. 19, 217n
Fuchs, S. 17, 18
Fuhrman, S. 71, 209
Furman, J. 149

Gage, N.L. 25
Gardner Task Force on Education 1964 52, 54
Garfield, E. 85, 88, 89
Garfinkel, J. 92
Garg, A. 149
Gawande, A. 155, 156, 157
Getzels, J. 164
Gilligan, C. 198, 201
Gintis, H. 200, 201
Glenn, N. 115
Goals 2000: Educate America Act 32, 59, 60
Goldhaber, D. 96, 130
Goldman, R. 63, 65
Goldstein, L. 68
Gomez, K. 150
Goodling, B. 61
Goodman, S. 92
Greene, J. 215
Griffin, P. 96, 209
Griffith, B.C. 19
Groen, J. 94
Gross, N. 17, 19, 97
Grossman, J. 147
Gueron, J. 30
Guetzkow, J. 94
Guthrie, J. 22, 23
Gutierrez, K. 7
Gutmann, A. 210

Hacker, J. 218n
Hackett, J. 84, 91, 96
Hakuta, K. 42, 66
Hallinan, M. 97, 148, 210
Hammersley, M. 192n
Harding, S. 18
Haro, A. 23
Harvey, William 177, 178, 179, 182
Haynes, R. 149
Head Start program 53, 54
Heath, S.B. 198, 201, 215
Heckman, J. 107, 109
Hedges, L. 114

hermeneutical methods 185, 187, 191
Hertling, J. 56
Hess, F.M. 72, 126, 128
Hines, P. 57
History News Network 94
history, teaching of American 73
Hochschild, J. 213
Hoff, J. 69
Hoffer, T. 25, 94
Hood, K. 7
Horne, J. 67–8
Howe, K. 7, 184
Hubbard, L. 148, 153
Huberman, M. 192n
Hunt, D. 152–3, 154
Huston, A. 147

Imbens, W. 109
influential research 199–205; AERA awards for 202–5; citation analysis to identify 199–202; impacting on policymaking 170–1, 205–11, 212–13, 214–15; links between relevance and quality 169–72; and making education an evidence-based field 212–15; *see also* utility of education research
Ingersoll, R. 96
Institute for Scientific Information (ISI) 84, 85–6, 88, 89–91, 96, 99
Institute of Education Sciences (IES) 40, 75, 225–30; creation of 4, 38, 68, 130; national research centers 70, 71, 132; promoting new standards of scientific research 38, 39, 40, 41, 68–74
interest groups 17–44, 212–13, 216
interpretive methods 185, 187, 191; *see also* qualitative methods
Issues in Education Research 4, 34

Jackson, G. 57, 58
Jackson, P. 25, 26, 169
Johnson administration 51–3
Johnson, S.M. 210, 213
Jones, L. 53, 55
Journal of Research on Educational Effectiveness 100
journals 9, 83–104; abstracts 98; acceptance and rejection rates 90; article selection process 93–5; blinding process 93; citation indexing 85–6, 116; distinguishing quality 86–8; education in the hierarchy of science 95–6, 97; education research in the top 105–6; of education within the ISI database 89–91, 99; improving the quality of education articles 96–101; measuring career success through publication in 115–16, 119–21; outlets for RCT studies 100; peer review process 90–1, 91–3, 94–5, 95–6, 97, 98–9; plagiarism 94, 97; ranking scientific 84–5; RCTs in medical 150–1; special issues on scientific research debate 6, 7; styles of research 95

Kaestle, C. 4, 45, 163, 170
Kaplan, A. 172–5, 176
Katz, L. 147
Katz, M. 23
Kelman, S. 212, 213
Kennedy, D. 37, 94
Kerlinger, F. 164, 169
Kessler, R. 64
Kieslar, S. 169
Kim, J. 148
Kingdon, J. 212
Klinenberg, E. 149
Kling, J. 147
Knudsen, D. 115
Kohlmoos, J. 68
Konstantopoulos, S. 114
Kozol, J. 180
Kuhn, T. 96, 173, 201

Labaree, D. 23, 24, 140n, 165, 166, 170–1
Laboratory Life 188
LaFollette, M. 92
Lagemann, E.C. 4, 23, 24, 25, 26, 27, 31, 34, 51, 63, 70, 84, 165
Lamont, M. 84, 90, 91, 94, 95, 96
Lareau, A. 148, 150
Larrabee, H. 172
Lather, P. 25
Latour, B. 17, 188
Lazarsfeld, P. 52
legitimacy: quest for scientific 18, 20, 21–2, 23–4, 43–4; of research findings 27, 135–6, 214; role of research in advancing agendas of interest groups 213
Levine, D. 56
Liebeman, J. 147

Light, R. 114
Lightfield, E.T. 115
Lincoln, Y. 25, 192n, 200
Lindblom, C. 165, 166, 167
Lindsey, D. 115, 116
Lock, S. 92
Logic: The Theory of Inquiry 176
Long, S. 19
Louie, V. 129
Lyotard, J-F. 188

Mallard, G. 84, 90, 91, 94, 95, 96
Manis, J. 115
Manski, C. 107
Manzo, K. 61, 74
Matthews, J.R. 108
Maxwell, J. 7
McDonald, H. 149
McDonald, S-K. 100
McDonnell, L. 212, 213, 215
McGinnis, R. 19
McLaughlin, M. 153–4
McNeil, T. 198
McNutt, R. 93
McPhail, C. 90
McSweeney 29
McVeigh, M. 88
medicine 32, 108, 145, 153; double-blind 3, 152; journals 150–1; patient non-compliance 149; problems of policy implementation 155–7
Mehan, H. 148, 153
Merton, R. 83
Michaels, D. 37
Miller, A.J. 19
Miller, G. 74
Miller, R. 115
Milwaukee voucher study 30
Mintrom, M. 214
Mitchell, T. 23
mixed methods research 184–5
modus operandi (MO) 182
Moe, T. 212
Montori, V. 150, 151
Mooney, C. 36
Morgan, R. 38
Mosher, E. 53
Mosteller, F. 53, 114, 146, 192n
Motterlini, M. 174
Moving to Opportunity (MTO) 138, 147
Moynihan, D.P. 53, 55

Murphy, F. 152–3, 154

Nagel, T. 173
Nation at Risk, A 31, 56, 200, 201, 215
National Academy of Education (NAE) 4–5, 6, 26, 63, 75, 110, 122, 130, 164
National Academy of Sciences (NAS) 34, 56, 57, 59, 63, 66, 75
National Assessment of Educational Progress (NAEP) 53, 56, 206
National Board for Education Sciences 41–2
National Center for Education Statistics (NCES) 53, 57, 66, 68, 72
National Commission on Excellence in Education 31, 56
National Educational Research Policy and Priorities Board (NERPPB) 5, 34
National Institute of Education (NIE) 31, 32, 55, 56, 71, 75
National Institute of Health (NIH) 32, 61, 72
National Reading Panel 61, 207, 208
National Research Council (NRC) 4, 5, 35–6, 38, 62, 66, 67, 83, 96, 99, 127, 128, 130, 164, 189–91, 229
National Science Foundation (NSF) 54, 72, 76, 110, 116
Nature 36–7
New York Times 32, 89
Newman, F. 67
Nixon administration 53–5
No Child Left Behind (NCLB) Act 2002 64–5, 73, 74, 76, 131; definition of "scientifically based research" 6, 38, 65, 147, 221–2; RCTs become the "gold standard" 6, 39, 65, 95, 150
Noddings, N. 65
Nye, B. 114, 122

Obey, D.R. 61
observation 182, 183
O'Day, J. 70
Office of Education 51–2, 53
Office of Educational Research and Improvement (OERI) 4, 5, 32, 37, 39, 56, 71, 75; 2000 reauthorization of 35, 61, 67, 68, 72; under Clinton 59–64, 72–3; under G.H.W. Bush 57–9; replacement of 38

Office of Innovative Improvements 68, 73, 76
Olkin, I. 53, 55
Olson, L. 5, 34, 61, 65, 148
Orfield, G. 148
Ory, J. 115
Owens, A. 89

PACE 154, 155
Paige, R. 37, 69
Palinscar, A. 201
paradigm wars 24, 25, 26, 168, 184
parent involvement in education 149–50
"Pasteur's Quadrant" 128, 139, 170
Payne, C. 210, 218n
Payne, M. 29, 30, 147, 148
peer review process 90–1, 91–3, 94–5, 95–6, 97, 98–9, 168
Peirce, C.E. 175
Pellegrino, J. 63, 65
Perry Preschool Project 198, 210
Peterson, P. 207, 216, 217n
Phillips, D. 170, 176, 179, 187, 189
philosophy of education 167–8
policy: influence of research on 205–11, 212–13, 214–15; politicization of 170–1; problems with implementation 153–7
Popkewitz, T. 100
Popper, K. 179
Porter, J.E. 61
Portner, J. 35, 46n
Postmodern Condition: A Report on Knowledge 188
postmodernism 18, 27, 167, 168, 187–9
Predoctoral Interdisciplinary Research Training Program 40, 227–30
Pressman, S. 94
Price, D. 128
Provonost, P. 155, 156
psychology 20, 22, 23, 24, 26, 28, 39, 201
psychometrics 229
Pudovkin, A. 88
purposes of education research 180–4

qualitative methods 25, 27, 35, 43, 75, 191, 201, 229; and compatibility with quantitive methods 7, 146, 148, 184–7; overlooking of 65, 71
quality of education research 163–95; compatibility of quantitative and qualitative methods 184–7; and debate on utility of research 10, 126–30; debate within the community 18, 26–7, 163–5; diagnosing the problem with 163–9; and establishing causation 180–4; and identifying effective interventions 130–5; and making education an evidence-based field 212–15; methodology and links to 172–5; NRC report views on scientific rigor 189–91; postmodern debate 187–9; relevance and links to 169–72; and scientific methods 175–80
quantitive methods 25, 35, 43, 65, 75, 91; and compatibility with qualitative methods 7, 146, 148, 184–7
quasi-experimental designs 131, 133, 134, 178, 185, 207, 222; funding for 6, 38

R&D centers: demise of the larger 70, 71; funding 54, 55, 57, 70, 71; NAS panel report on 57–9; review of work 60, 72, 73
randomized controlled trials: advantages of 100; in agricultural research 107–8; barriers to 150–3; critique of 40, 131, 145, 150, 157, 164, 178, 179, 183; difficulties of using in schools 0–2, 146, 151, 154–5; education research community on the defensive 43; education researchers opposition to 39–41; for evaluation of social programs 28–9, 44, 151–3; "gold standard" for education research 1, 4, 6, 18, 21, 22, 43, 131; and lack of AERA awards for research using 203; and lack of suitability for much of education research 108–9, 122–3, 148, 157–8, 178–9, 183; in medicine 108, 151–2; and No Child Left Behind Act 6, 39, 65, 95, 150; numbers of trials in education research 228–9; omission of the discovery phase 178–9, 183; policymakers and lawmakers call for 3, 17, 19, 20, 28–30, 35, 38, 41–2, 45, 212; preferential funding for 39, 69, 131; problems of implementing the results 146, 153–7; publication outlets for studies using 100; reported in AERA

journals 229; suitable for a narrow range of research questions 145–6, 146–50, 157; *see also* US Department of Education
Ranis, S. 129
Raudenbush, S. 123
Ravitch, D. 57, 58, 59
reading 5, 32–3, 61, 64, 65, 71, 207, 208, 213
Reading Excellence Act 1998 5, 61
Reading First programs 74, 109
Reagan administration 32–3, 55–7, 74
reform assistance laboratories (RALs) 58
regional education laboratories 56, 57–9, 60, 66, 72, 75, 76
regression discontinuity design 110–21, 131
Reid Lyon, G. 62, 64, 132
Reliable Knowledge 172
replication of studies 98
Resch, N. 147
Reuben, J. 23
Riecken, H. 28, 29, 30
Riesman. D. 173
Rivlin, A. 54
Rizzo, M. 94
Robarts, J. 23
Robelen, E. 72
Rosenbaum, P. 107, 109
Rossi, P. 29, 30
Rothman, R. 59
Rubin, D. 107, 109, 112
Rubin, R. 149
Ryan, K. 7

Sachs, J. 114
Sack, J. 68
Samuels, C. 72
Schnaiberg, L. 59
Schneider, B. 7, 89, 97, 98, 100
Schneider, M. 72
schools 53, 61, 71, 149–50, 221; attack on education in 21, 31–2, 44; and priorities for promoting student learning 137–8; problems of implementing policy 154–5; unsuitability of randomized control trials for 146, 151–2, 154–5
Schwandt, T. 39
Science 37, 94, 106
science: natural vs. social sciences 185–6; policy under the Bush administration 36–7, 41, 74; and scientism 175–80
Scientific American 37
scientific fields 18–19
scientific method 174, 175–80, 190
Scientific Research in Education 6, 36, 38, 67, 96, 127, 164
"scientific rigor" 38, 146, 150, 189–91, 198; calls for broader approaches to 133, 146; calls for standards of 2, 3, 5, 8, 9; questioning the rigor of education research 10, 17, 25, 26, 44, 74, 126, 164, 167; WWC assessment of 68, 131
"scientifically based research" 5, 6, 34, 35–6, 38, 223–4; funding for 6, 34, 35, 39, 167, 189, 220, 221; in No Child Left Behind (NCLB) Act 6, 38, 65, 147, 221–2; political struggle to establish 19–22; and rise of evaluation research 28–31
Scovronick, N. 213
Scriven, M. 182
Seglen, P. 88
Seldin, P. 115
self-regulation 168–9
Shadish, W. 107, 110
Shapin, S. 17
Shaughnessy, M. 132
Shavelson, R. 6, 36, 38, 62, 63, 67, 83, 127, 129, 164
Shulman, L. 4, 25, 26, 27, 34, 63, 165, 198, 204
Shulman, S. 74
Sieber, D. 52
Siegel, H. 188
Simon, R. 90
Slavin, R. 132–3
Smith, J. 92
Smith, M. 70
Snow, C. 66, 96
Snyder, B. 29, 30
social programs 28–9, 44
Society for Research on Educational Effectiveness 69–70
Soderstrom, J. 29
Sorenson, A. 97
Spencer Foundation essays 209–11, 213
Sproull, L. 55
Sroufe, G.R. 70
St. Pierre, E.A. 65, 189
Stamp, A. 94

standards for research, setting 35–43
Stanley, J. 28, 29, 111, 183, 185, 203
Stein, K. 148
Steinmetz, J. 127, 153
Stokes, D. 128, 170
Stone, D. 212, 213
Strategic Education Research Partnership (SERP) 130, 139
styles of research, social 95
Sunderman, G. 148
Suppes, P. 52, 164, 169
Swanson, C. 206, 209
Szigeti, H. 85

Teaching Children to Read 207
Tennessee class-size experiment 30, 113–14, 122, 138; influence on policy 198, 207, 210, 212
Testa, J. 84, 86, 87, 88
Thistlethwaite, D. 111
Thomson Scientific 85, 199
Thoreson, A. 96
Tierney, J. 147
timing 214, 216
Timpane, M. 54
Toombs, W. 115
Towne, L. 5, 6, 35, 36, 38, 39, 62, 63, 67, 83, 127, 129, 164
training programs 40, 42, 52, 69, 126, 228; Predoctoral Interdisciplinary Research Training Program 40, 227–30
Trends in International Mathematics and Science Study (TIMSS) 206, 208
Trochim, W. 111, 112
Tyler, R. 163, 164

universities 23, 83; education research training 40, 42, 52, 69, 126, 228; schools of education 20, 22–7, 228
US Department of Education 4, 18, 55, 56, 60–1, 62, 65, 66, 69, 72, 135; identifying trustworthy research findings 130–5; support for randomized trials 1, 18, 32–42, 131, 134, 157, 158, 221–30; *see also* Whitehurst
US House 37, 62, 64, 66, 67, 71, 73
USA Today 94
utility of education research 125–41; identifying effective interventions 130–5; new approaches to 135–9; quality and links to 10, 126–30, 169–72; *see also* influential research

Vaughn, T. 115
Verstegen, D. 55
Viadero, D. 4, 5, 25, 27, 32, 34, 35, 37, 38, 39, 41, 42, 62, 65, 66, 68, 69, 70, 71, 72, 73
Villemez, W. 115
Vinovskis, M. 51, 52, 53, 54, 55, 56, 57, 58, 59, 60, 62, 64, 70
Vygotskii, L.S. 201

Walters, P.B. 129, 157
Way with Words 200, 215
Weikart, D. 198
Weiner, S. 55
Weisner, T. 147
Weiss, C. 134, 213, 214
Weiss, R. 36
Werner, L. 32
What Works Clearinghouse (WWC) 32, 39, 41, 68–9, 98, 126, 130, 131–4, 135, 136, 149
Whitehurst, G. 37, 38, 39, 65–6, 68, 69, 70, 150
Wilson, L. 115
Wolf, D. 55
Woolgar, S. 188
Word, E. 198
Wright 29, 30

Xie, Y. 19

Yankauer, A. 92

Zodhiates, P. 56

eBooks – at www.eBookstore.tandf.co.uk

A library at your fingertips!

eBooks are electronic versions of printed books. You can store them on your PC/laptop or browse them online.

They have advantages for anyone needing rapid access to a wide variety of published, copyright information.

eBooks can help your research by enabling you to bookmark chapters, annotate text and use instant searches to find specific words or phrases. Several eBook files would fit on even a small laptop or PDA.

NEW: Save money by eSubscribing: cheap, online access to any eBook for as long as you need it.

Annual subscription packages

We now offer special low-cost bulk subscriptions to packages of eBooks in certain subject areas. These are available to libraries or to individuals.

For more information please contact webmaster.ebooks@tandf.co.uk

We're continually developing the eBook concept, so keep up to date by visiting the website.

www.eBookstore.tandf.co.uk